Beyond the Lean Revolution

Achieving Successful and Sustainable
Enterprise Transformation

Deborah J. Nightingale
and Jayakanth Srinivasan

AMACOM
American Management Association
New York • Atlanta • Brussels • Chicago • Mexico City • San Francisco
Shanghai • Tokyo • Toronto • Washington, D.C.

Special discounts on bulk quantities of AMACOM books are
available to corporations, professional associations, and other
organizations. For details, contact Special Sales Department,
AMACOM, a division of American Management Association, 1601
Broadway, New York, NY 10019.
Tel.: 212-903-8316. Fax: 212-903-8083.
Web site: www.amacombooks.org

This publication is designed to provide accurate and authoritative
information in regard to the subject matter covered. It is sold with the
understanding that the publisher is not engaged in rendering legal,
accounting, or other professional service. If legal advice or other expert
assistance is required, the services of a competent professional person should
be sought.

Library of Congress Cataloging-in-Publication Data

Nightingale, Deborah J.
    Beyond the lean revolution : achieving successful and sustainable enterprise transformation /
Deborah J. Nightingale and Jayakanth Srinivasan.
        p.   cm.
    Includes bibliographical references and index.
    ISBN-13: 978-0-8144-1709-6
    ISBN-10: 0-8144-1709-4
    1. Organizational change.   2. Leadership.   3. Strategic planning.
I. Srinivasan, Jayakanth.   II. Title.
HD58.8.N544   2011
658.4'06—dc22
                                                    2010046673

About AMA

American Management Association (www.amanet.org) is a world leader in talent development,
advancing the skills of individuals to drive business success. Our mission is to support the goals of
individuals and organizations through a complete range of products and services, including
classroom and virtual seminars, webcasts, webinars, podcasts, conferences, corporate and
government solutions, business books and research. AMA's approach to improving performance
combines experiential learning—learning through doing—with opportunities for ongoing professional
growth at every step of one's career journey.

Printing number

10   9   8   7   6   5   4   3   2   1

Debbie:

To my parents, who inspired me to be the person I am; and to my children, Jessica and Jordan, who continually inspire me to transform.

JK:

To my parents, for their love, patience, and sacrifice.

Contents

List of Figures and Tables

FIGURES

TABLES

Acknowledgments

THE IDEAS IN BOOKS such as this one do not emerge fully formed and ready for publication. Rather, they are developed over a long period, based on real-life experiences, and nurtured in an environment that allows for research and reflection and that provides opportunities for collegial discussion and debate. We are deeply appreciative to the Massachusetts Institute of Technology for creating just such an environment and for the resources that allow us to do interdisciplinary research. At MIT, the Lean Advancement Initiative (LAI) has provided a particularly important home in which we have been able to cultivate and test our ideas. We thank our many MIT and LAI colleagues with whom we have worked over the years: Earll Murman, who provided invaluable coaching, mentoring, and guidance, as well as Dan Roos, John Carroll, Joe Sussman, Dick Lewis, Warren Seering, Alexis Stanke, Terry Bryan, Kirk Bozdogan, Eric Rebentisch, George Roth, Donna Rhodes, Tom Shields, Ricardo Valerdi, Nicolene Hengen, and Juliet Perdichizzi.

Working at a university also creates opportunities to engage with the fresh minds of students, many of whom unknowingly contributed to this book. We thank in particular Cory Hallam, Dave Tonaszuck, Ignacio Grossi, Jorge Oliveira, Ted Piepenbrock, Vikram Mahidhar, Doug Matty, Craig Blackburn, Jordan Peck, Erisa Hines, and all the students in the Integrating the Lean Enterprise and Enterprise Architecting graduate classes, from whose work we have drawn to illustrate many of our ideas.

We have also drawn a great deal of our material from our transformation research work carried out in partnership with our Lean Advancement Initiative consortium members. We are extremely grateful for their continued support of our research and of our students.

We would not have been able to complete this book without the last-minute reviews by several colleagues who offered unique perspectives and new insights, suggestions for changes that strengthened our writing, and caught the stray error here and there that we had missed: John Carroll, Dick Lewis, and Wiljeana Glover. We would also like to express our sincere appreciation to Mark Prendergast, who has provided us with wonderful graphics creativity and support, not only for the book, but in the development of the Roadmap and related materials over the past several years. His ongoing support has made our lives much easier.

A special note of gratitude is due our editor, and now friend, Scott Cooper. Over the last year, he has helped moderate and meld two distinct voices into a coherent book. He has provided us with encouragement, "flexible" deadlines, needed clarity, and frequent levity that enabled us to actually finish the book.

Finally, we wish to thank our mentors and our families. Debbie would like to thank Joe Mize, who has served as a mentor and friend, embarking on the path of enterprise thinking and transformation several decades before this book was written. Debbie's thanks also go to her parents, Jack and Velma Roeckner, for teaching her to think holistically, and her children, Jessica, Danielle, and Jordan Seifert, who supported her in transformations of many kinds.

JK would like to thank his mentors Kirk Bozdogan, Debbie Nightingale, John Carroll, Kristina Lundqvist, and Christer Norström, for being fantastic sounding boards and constantly challenging him to be a reflective scholar; his parents, Bhuvaneswari Srinivasan and Kandaswamy Srinivasan, for teaching him to reach for the stars and believing that he could actually get there; his wife, Neira Teicu-Srinivasan, for putting up with him, reading drafts, and pulling him through the writing and reviewing sessions; and friends and family, including Srikalyani Srinivasan, Narayanan Sitaraman, Fabio Dalan, Samantha Grandi, Vijay Subramonian, and Deepti Pookat, for always being there.

We should point out that all statements, opinions, and conclusions expressed herein are solely those of the authors.

Beyond the Lean Revolution

—1—

Why Enterprise Transformation?

The whole is greater than the sum of its parts.

Aristotle[1]

PERHAPS YOU and your company are standing at the edge of the proverbial cliff. Challenges beset you from within and without. The competitive environment is changing. Your R&D organization has an idea that has great promise, but you just can't find a way to capture the opportunity. Employees are finding it difficult to be heard when they have ideas for making the business run more efficiently. A supplier has advised you about a problem with providing your manufacturing organization what you need, and you can't figure out where in the business that problem originates. How do you fix something you can't find?

Or perhaps you and your company are *not* standing at the edge of the cliff. Maybe everything is humming along, but the general sense is that the organization is not coming close to meeting its potential. Even though you've been trying to improve your business processes, things aren't making it to the next level. All those Six Sigma black belts are helping run projects, but the incremental changes don't seem to amount to very much. You're not achieving the kind of total benefit you thought you would.

We encounter businesses and organizations all the time that are facing one or all of these challenges. Many of them have been working hard to change. Again and again, though, they tell us they are failing to *sustain* change. They feel as if they are taking two steps forward and one step back. Their improvement projects suffer from false starts. Or they get only so far, and then whatever they were changing plateaus and cannot reach a higher level of efficiency or effectiveness. The bottom-line effects are just not happening.

Why do improvement efforts so often fail to provide all the benefits expected? Typically, it's because businesses are trying to do things in a piecemeal fashion—in silos. They spend a lot of time on things that do not affect the bottom line or that are not linked to the company's most important strategic objectives. They may not even know that their efforts are disconnected.

To be sure, you can make some improvements through these sorts of efforts, and your company might even realize some big benefits. However, the best opportunities to *transform* an organization are usually found somewhere other than in the silos. Often, they are found in the interfaces. They become clear only when you look at the entire **enterprise**—a complex, integrated, and interdependent system of people, processes, and technology that creates value as determined by its key stakeholders.* A **stakeholder** is any group or individual that can affect or that is affected by the achievement of the enterprise's objectives. **Value** is the particular worth, utility, benefit, or reward that stakeholders expect in exchange for their respective contributions to the enterprise.

Enterprise transformation is the taking of an enterprise from its current state to an envisioned future state, a process that requires a significant change in mindset, the adoption of a holistic view, and execution to achieve the intended transformational goals and objectives. Transformation requires that you know the enterprise. You have to take a step back and look at the big picture. You need to gain a deep understanding of where things stand. What are your strategic objectives? How are you currently performing against those objectives? How should you be performing? How will you close the gap? What is the current state of the different key components and levers that comprise your enterprise?

We have seen many organizations undertake improvement projects with a lot of fanfare but with little or no sense of the big picture.

---

* This is the first of our key terms. Throughout this book, key words appear in **bold italics** when first used and are defined when they first appear. These definitions may also be found in the Key Terms section at the end of the book.

We have seen them adopt *lean*—a term describing the philosophy centered on minimizing resources and eliminating waste to create value. We've seen improvement projects on the shop floor aimed at reducing overall company costs by, say, a stated goal of 20 percent. Only after later analysis did the businesses discover that less than 5 percent of company costs could be attributed to direct labor. Talk about failing to see the forest for the trees!

Why does this happen? It has to do with how the business world has embraced concepts from lean manufacturing. All too often, we hear senior business leaders talking as though all they have to do is figure out a way to adopt the Toyota Production System (TPS, to which lean traces its origins), and Toyota-like results will fall into place. This perspective is very narrow and tends to miss the strategic element. Many organizations embrace TPS but apply its concepts only to certain operations in the organization, such as manufacturing, but not to others, such as the leadership and enabling operations: Together, these constitute the *whole* organization. Still others apply lean principles and TPS to their manufacturing operations quite well, but they never look beyond their internal organizations to embrace a broader perspective that might include, for example, suppliers or other stakeholders. People in business also tend to think that TPS is a bottom-up miracle worker, missing the fact that it is driven strategically from the highest level of the Toyota enterprise. It is only a means to enact the enterprise's strategy, not the strategy itself.

When we visit companies, we often see telltale signs that the focus of change efforts is askew. One day, when we were invited to visit Mega-Corp (a pseudonym for a company that makes aerostructure parts and components and that employs some ten thousand people), a group of managers presented the firm's improvement plan. It sounded plausible enough, but there wasn't a senior leader of the company in the room. That was the first clue that something was amiss. Then we were given a tour that began in the manufacturing area (a typical starting place, we've found). On bulletin boards, we found performance measures posted, but they were either not very current or partially obscured by other postings. In the office areas and elsewhere, we saw the same thing. It was obvious that these *metrics*—the objective, quantified data or information that an enterprise collects to support decision making—were not at the heart of people's daily work lives. No one was paying much attention to them.

The types of metrics were telling too. Mega-Corp was measuring machine and operator utilization on its manufacturing line, as well as the quality of parts coming in from its suppliers. But where were the metrics about Mega-Corp's performance with respect to its suppliers? When we visited the engineering department, we found nothing about how well the company was supplying specifications to its suppliers.

On top of all that, no one in manufacturing or engineering could explain how what he or she did on the job worked toward achieving any vision or strategic objective. Yet Mega-Corp had a full-blown set of improvement projects underway.

Build-Create Corp. (a pseudonym for a five-thousand-employee firm in southern California that makes space system components) told a different story. A worker on the manufacturing line described how his work was part of the larger process and how people in his organization had redesigned some of the process flow. He cited some specific reductions in costs and cycle times that had been achieved and explained where the company stood with respect to work-in-process. The worker put everything he told us in a context that sounded like a strategic objective that the enterprise expected to achieve four or five years down the road. A production manager introduced us to someone on his team who turned out to be a supplier. An engineer in Build-Create's R&D group explained how they had reduced their cycle time for new product development.

The differences between Mega-Corp and Build-Create were palpable. At Build-Create, everyone was enthusiastic about transforming the enterprise. The employees used a similar vocabulary to talk about change and improvement, suggesting to us that they were all on the same page. They could share insights into processes, metrics, stakeholders, resources, and other aspects of their enterprise, implying that they had been part of figuring out analytically where things stand. With ease, they put what they were doing into a larger context and explained how it fit with a vision of the future.

At Mega-Corp, the senior leaders could go on and on about how they are transforming their enterprise. But we saw no evidence beyond some disconnected change initiatives related to lean.

Paradigms of Change

How do enterprises change? The classical model of *organizational change* comes from Lewin:[2] a three-stage process of unfreezing the organization, introducing the desired change, and then refreezing the organization. Unfreezing prior to introducing a change provides the organization with a period to reflect on how it got to its current state and enables it to involve stakeholders in determining the right needed change or set of changes. The refreezing stage enables the organization to institutionalize the change.

There are two broad categories, or paradigms, of change in organizations: episodic change and continuous change. The first, *episodic change*, tends to focus on the organization as a whole and is aimed at changing the entire organization. It is deliberate, triggered at distinct moments by technological change or increased competition or by other major changes in the external or internal environment. These sorts of major change efforts are typically decided on by senior leadership, which opts to alter key processes or even restructure the organization as a whole. The underlying assumption is that senior leadership is able to perceive a divergence between what the triggers demand and what the enterprise can deliver and then make corrections with structural and behavioral changes that allow the enterprise to remain sustainable. This sort of episodic change is driven top-down, using a select few change agents.

The second paradigm, sometimes referred to as *continuous* change, may also be organization-wide, but specific changes are more focused on particular local work practices within the larger organization. Though the intent may be to change the organization as a whole as the specific efforts disperse within the organization, the specific efforts may not have organization-wide ramifications. In this paradigm, change efforts such as Six Sigma[3] and Total Quality Management[4] are often targeted at creating the capability to introduce change that is not necessarily intended to have organization-wide effects, often resulting in pockets of change that may even be suboptimal to the total enterprise. In this paradigm everyone is a change agent responsible for and empowered to make the changes needed. Underlying this paradigm is the view that cumulative change will eventually translate into enterprise-level change.

These two paradigms are sometimes not enough to effect the wider change, based on a holistic view of the enterprise, that is needed to meet the challenges an enterprise faces. Enterprise transformation combines both paradigms and takes them further. Two excellent "philosophies" underlie enterprise transformation as a change paradigm:

➤   One is classical lean thinking, which has limitations: It is focused primarily on eliminating waste at the shop-floor level. There is little acknowledgment that the enterprise from which lean thinking derived its foundations—Toyota—was and remains predominantly a top-down organization.

➤ The second is lean enterprise value,[5] which highlights the need to recognize stakeholder value.

However, both philosophies fall short, even though they certainly speak to enterprise transformation. Neither provides specific methods and analytic approaches that enable you to actuate what the philosophies teach at a holistic, enterprise-wide level to make things actionable and drive genuine enterprise transformation.

Further, when transformation is framed as an adaptation of the enterprise as a whole to meet the needs of its stakeholders, we see that transformation requires both episodic change and continuous change that are aligned. It needs the top-down directive intervention of the senior leadership team, and at the same time it must empower stakeholders to make the required adaptations at the work-practice level. Enterprise transformation begins with the commitment of the senior leadership team, which must invest the resources needed to change the way the enterprise works on the large scale. At the same time, leadership must require the personal dedication of all stakeholders to make local changes on an ongoing basis.

In this book, we present an enterprise transformation paradigm that incorporates these ideas, overcomes the limitations described, and employs a Roadmap for ensuring that transformation is successful.

Going Beyond Lean

To be sure, we recognize the value of lean and lean principles. In fact, as you'll read in more detail in Chapter 2, the principles of lean are part of the foundation of thinking in the enterprise context. Traditional lean, though, has many limitations. The classical lean "tool kit" doesn't lead to success when it is applied at a broader, enterprise level.

Traditional lean tools—be it root cause analysis, or 5S, or value stream maps alone—tend to be applied in a rather prescriptive, cookie-cutter manner. They are effective in their own ways and at what they measure, but their scope is limited. People get hung up with their tool kits. They try to apply them everywhere. That is what Rockwell Collins learned.

Rockwell Collins is an aerospace and defense company based in

Iowa that was using the classical lean tool kit to attack six hundred or more improvement projects. Senior leadership, though, was finding it difficult to see how all that activity was helping. Yes, they saw improvements, but the enterprise as a whole wasn't really changing for the better. So Rockwell Collins tried broadening the application of the tool kit throughout the enterprise. The canvas was expanded, but the same brush was used. Only when the company adopted a holistic view, did an end-to-end analysis of all its processes, and mapped its value stream did it see the possibilities not for incremental change alone, but for *enterprise transformation.*

At Capital One, senior leadership tried to implement change projects but soon came to recognize that the projects were a lot of potshot efforts that did not approach the larger transformation that was needed.[6] To achieve *enterprise transformation*, everything had to be connected to the enterprise's strategic objectives. The entire enterprise—from the senior leaders on down—needed to adopt a holistic perspective. That, the leaders realized, was the only way out of a cycle of local improvements that may or may not aggregate into having overall enterprise impact.

These enterprises learned the difference between improvement and transformation. Improvement can be done locally, and you can realize worthwhile, but limited, successes. Transformation takes place at the enterprise level. It is the whole of improvements, specifically chosen to serve the wider enterprise objectives, and it is greater than the sum of its parts.

Thinking in the enterprise context begins with seeing the forest for the trees and having a strategic approach. From there, it embraces an understanding of the current state of the enterprise. If an appropriate strategic objective for you is to reduce your time to market, for instance, don't you need to know everything that goes into how you currently get to market—the players, the processes, and so on—and how these are performing? How else can you create an actionable plan for achieving your objective?

Enterprise thinking also looks at the players—your stakeholders—differently than in most traditional lean thinking. In lean, the customer is almost the sole focus, and creating value for the customer rules the day. Our approach is about total stakeholder value creation. Once you start thinking that way, you look at all your stakeholders and at how your enterprise engages those stakeholders in a very different light.

What Is an Enterprise?

As we wrote earlier, an enterprise is a complex, integrated, and interdependent system of people, processes, and technology that creates value as determined by its key stakeholders. An enterprise typically comprises multiple organizations (e.g., suppliers, partners, regulators), rather than a single corporation, division, or government entity. An enterprise has distributed leadership and diverse stakeholders who have some interests in common.

An enterprise is not a program, although a program may be an enterprise. An enterprise is not an organization *per se*, although an organization may be an enterprise. A single firm may have multiple enterprises. No enterprise is totally self-contained. For example, although Boeing Helicopter may be an enterprise, elements of the Boeing Helicopter enterprise are elsewhere in Boeing, such as corporate finance.

Enterprises are contextual. They really have little to do with size. An engineering department is not an enterprise, nor is your manufacturing function, because they are not stand-alone entities (although, of course, rare exceptions prove the rule). Rather, engineering departments and manufacturing operations, as complex as they may be as entities, almost always exist to serve a larger purpose—the mission and value proposition of the enterprise of which they are parts. Typically, they are components among other components: other value-creating organizations or functions such as design, R&D, and so on; enabling organizations or functions such as information technology; and the enterprise's leadership and management.

The correct definition of an enterprise matters. If you don't know what you're dealing with, you cannot transform it. If you can't draw the boundaries and scope, you'll work on the wrong things.

The Value Proposition

Your enterprise exchanges value, and it has a value proposition—even if it has never been articulated clearly. A value proposition defines your enterprise's reason for being. The concept of the value proposition comes, in its traditional use, from the customer perspective:

> The core of any business strategy is the value proposition, which describes the unique mix of product and service attributes, customer relations, and corporate image that a company offers. It defines how the

organization will differentiate itself from competitors to attract, retain, and deepen relationships with targeted customers. The value proposition is crucial because it helps an organization connect its internal processes to improved outcomes with customers.[7]

Whether it is operational excellence, customer intimacy, or product leadership[8]—the three generic types of customer value propositions that have entered the business vernacular—your enterprise probably has one. These are the areas in which companies usually strive to excel.

➤ *Operational excellence* is all about efficiency, streamlined operations, managing the supply chain, and so on; customers see limited variation on products, but reasonable quality at a low price.

➤ *Customer intimacy* is just what it sounds like: The company gets close to the customer, with a focus on customer service and with products and services tailored to individual or almost individual customers.

➤ *Product leadership* is about strength in innovation and branding.

Typically, businesses pick one of these value propositions as its main focus and seek to reach a minimal level with the other two.

Customer value propositions are coming at you all the time. If you watch television or read magazines, you've certainly seen the value proposition from the German automaker BMW. It is encapsulated in the company's slogan: "the ultimate driving machine." BMW is a luxury car company; it doesn't compete on price but on the quality of its products and the experience of the user. It is all about product leadership. The slogan expresses this focus.

What's missing from customer value propositions is that they ignore the fact that enterprises have many stakeholders who are not customers. An ***enterprise value proposition*** is a description of the unique mix of products and service attributes, stakeholder relationships, and other intangibles that an enterprise offers to its key stakeholders. Thus, it builds on the traditional concept of a customer value proposition and extends it to encompass all of the key stakeholders of the enterprise and the key values that are exchanged with those stakeholders. When you have an enterprise value proposition, you have truly defined the core reason for your enterprise's existence. Thus, extending the value proposition to the enterprise level, rather than leaving it at the customer level, corrects for the traditional value proposition's failure to capture all the dynamics of the enterprise.

It also expresses something that may come as a surprise if you've never thought beyond the customer value proposition. If your enterprise chooses, it can go beyond operational excellence, customer intimacy, and product leadership to *shape* its own market. In other words, creating an enterprise value proposition—that is, a value proposition for *all* your stakeholders—means identifying what your stakeholders will want and value in the future. It provides a starting point for transforming your enterprise so that you can create the very capabilities your enterprise will require to meet the needs that you have defined.

Do you have a sense for why your enterprise really exists? Can you articulate it? Can everyone else in the enterprise articulate it?

Seeing Things Holistically

We find that most businesses can articulate their products or services but that they fall short when it comes to expressing the enduring reason for the enterprise to exist. With an enterprise value proposition, you've already begun to see the big picture, which is a critical part of setting off on a journey of enterprise transformation. Without an enterprise value proposition to which everything you do can be linked, you will forever be engaging in piecemeal improvement rather than in enterprise transformation.

If your enterprise can change fundamentally the way it thinks and operates, though, it can achieve something greater and more enduring than any traditional change management program could even hope to provide. That fundamental change in thinking is to see things holistically. Once you take the wide, broadened view, you can see what to work on that matters strategically and that has benefits for the entire enterprise and for the enterprise value proposition.

This book is addressed to anyone interested in transforming an enterprise, whether you are a senior leader or a middle manager. We explain to you the principles of enterprise transformation. We take you on a journey, with an Enterprise Transformation Roadmap, that engages you and the senior leadership of your enterprise in assessing the current state of your enterprise, articulating what needs to change to benefit the enterprise as a whole, and planning for how to do it—all in the context of your strategic objectives and your enterprise value proposition. Along the way, we share analytic tools and methods that have worked and that have been refined in the course of more than seventy-five enterprise transformations.

Throughout, we also show you real-life examples of transformation efforts. In Chapter 2, you'll read how our seven Enterprise Transformation Principles are illustrated by the example of Rockwell Collins. Along the Roadmap, you will encounter InfraProv, a global information technology infrastructure provider, and see how an enterprise stakeholder assessment unfolds. You will meet High Power Engines (HPE) and learn how an assessment of the processes that an enterprise uses feeds into an enterprise transformation plan. Raytheon provides an example of how to measure the enterprise's performance in a formally defined way.

The software developer ZED used one of our tools to determine whether its strategic objectives were aligned with how it measures its enterprise performance. We show you how the results inform the next steps along the Transformation Roadmap. In Chapter 12, after you have learned about all the parts of the Roadmap, we take you through a complete current-state assessment and development of a transformation plan for StayCool Engineering. Other examples from other companies are peppered throughout the text.

When you finish this book, you will know how to reframe how you work, how you deliver and acquire value, and how you can create an enduring transformational enterprise that achieves the kind of results that will enable you to fulfill your value proposition.

CHAPTER

$-2-$

The Seven Principles of Enterprise Transformation

To become caught up in immediate realities,
and to fail to live and act on the basis of a more
holistic view of things, is a myopic way of life.

Tsunesaburo Makiguchi[1]

TO TRANSFORM AN ENTERPRISE, you must have a new mental model that is based on principles that are immutable but also flexible enough to be adapted as required. A written set of principles, though, is not sufficient. You must know how to apply the principles.[2] Enterprise transformation is a challenging "art" that requires holistic thinking. Throughout this chapter, we will show you real-world examples of how these principles have been applied and the outcomes that they helped achieve.

The seven enterprise transformation principles we detail in this chapter evolved from what scholars and practitioners have written about the Toyota Production System (TPS), lean thinking, and lean enterprises, as well as from our own experiences with transformation efforts. The elevation of classical lean principles and practices to the enterprise level can be traced back more than three decades, to the mid-1970s.[3] While lean principles and practices were then taking hold in Japan, however, there was little evidence that they could be applied in other countries or even in sectors other than manufacturing. More than a decade later, along came a groundbreaking study that produced the widely read book *The Machine That Changed the World*.[4] Soon, an explanation for Toyota's success in steadily increasing market share while lowering costs and improving quality was entering the broader consciousness. Two of that book's authors then provided one of the first attempts to generalize the understanding of the Toyota Production System, presenting five principles of lean thinking.[5]

While the first set of principles were drawn from a study of the automotive industry, it wasn't long before other researchers were testing their applicability in other domains. A long-term effort to apply lean principles to the aerospace industry resulted in five lean enterprise principles that broadened the focus to value creation rather than waste elimination exclusively.[6] Enterprise transformation research and experience continued through the Lean Advancement Initiative at MIT, resulting in our seven Enterprise Transformation Principles. Table 2-1 shows how these principles evolved.

To illustrate the real-world application of the seven Enterprise Transformation Principles, we draw from a variety of cases. One case in particular runs like a thread throughout this chapter—that of Rockwell Collins, a spinoff from Rockwell International that became an independent company in March 2001. Its evolution as one of the best managed aerospace and defense companies is a testament to the ability to instill a culture of continuous improvement that complements and supports the company's strategic focus on stakeholder-centric value delivery.[7]

The seven enterprise transformation principles provide a lens for understanding Rockwell Collins' evolution. The company's key messages (often with aviation-related themes) from annual reports show how the transformation unfolded (see Table 2-2). The emphasis over the years has grown from managing the current value proposition (2001–2004) to designing the future value proposition and its underlying enablers (2005–2008). The focus of the transformation expanded from the core value creation processes of the enterprise to include Enabling Processes such as shared services and Leadership Processes—growing leaders, defining identity, and strategy.

Principle: Adopt a Holistic Approach to Enterprise Transformation

In the context of enterprise transformation, the term *holistic* emphasizes the need to understand the impact of transformation on the enterprise

(text continues on page 16)

Table 2-1

The Evolution of Principles

Lean Principles (1996)

- Specify value from the standpoint of the end customer by product family.
- Identify all the steps in the value stream for each product family, eliminating whenever possible steps that do not create value.
- Make the value-creating steps occur in tight sequence so that the product will flow smoothly toward the customer.
- As flow is introduced, let customers pull value from the next upstream activity.
- As value is specified, value streams are identified, wasted steps are removed, and flow and pull are introduced, begin the process again and continue it until a state of perfection is reached in which perfect value is created with no waste.

Lean Enterprise Principles (2004)

- Create lean value by doing the job right and by doing the right job.
- Deliver value only after identifying stakeholder value and constructing robust value propositions.
- Fully realize lean value only by adopting an enterprise perspective.
- Address the interdependencies across enterprise levels to increase lean value.
- People, not just processes, effectuate lean value.

Enterprise Transformation Principles (2009)

- Adopt a holistic approach to enterprise transformation.
- Secure leadership commitment to drive and institutionalize enterprise behaviors.
- Identify relevant stakeholders and determine their value propositions.
- Focus on enterprise effectiveness before efficiency.
- Address internal and external enterprise interdependencies.
- Ensure stability and flow within and across the enterprise.
- Emphasize organizational learning.

Table 2-2

Key Messages in Rockwell Collins' Annual Reports

Year	*Theme*	*Notes*
2001	Takeoff	First report issued as an independent company
2002	Balance	Emphasis on balanced portfolio of government and commercial business—an almost even split that enables Rockwell Collins to ride out cyclical, short-term challenges in either market
2003	Ideas that fly	Emphasis on the organization's innovation capabilities and recognition that every cutting-edge product and service is rooted in the ideas of *people*
2004	Performance and accomplishment	Focus on building on the successes of the previous year, for which Rockwell Collins was named the best managed aerospace company
2005	Above and beyond	Emphasis on the personal leadership demonstrated by employees in delivering increased value both to customers and shareholders
2006	Building trust every day	Unveiling of a new brand identity and this theme as a new slogan, highlighting the underlying philosophy that trust is the primary driver of value creation, capture, and enhancement; also, an increased emphasis on innovation and building a powerful workforce
2007	Accelerating success	Circling back to 2002's "balance," plus (a) an integrated business model focused on efficient operation of a shared-services infrastructure, (b) centers of excellence

		that maximize technology reuse, and (c) innovative programs that incent employees to promote cross-business opportunities
2008	Focus/Innovate/ Deliver/Expand	Emphasis on the need to focus on customers, innovate solutions that provide enhanced value, deliver solutions that meet customer needs on time and on budget, and expand to meet the needs of current and future customers.

as a whole. Strategically, a holistic enterprise view is the articulation of who the relevant stakeholders of the enterprise are and what they value. It calls for a deep understanding of the core capabilities and competencies of the enterprise and an assessment of whether the enterprise, as currently constructed, can deliver the value required from it. From an operational perspective, it is having the required resources to deliver on the enterprise value proposition: having the right leaders, capturing the right knowledge, and having the right people and processes to create the required value.

This systems approach to transformation builds on an understanding of the interactions and interdependencies within and across the enterprise. It highlights the ability to analyze enterprise interconnections, identify enterprise *waste* (an action, process, or activity that does not directly add value for a stakeholder but that still consumes resources), and create strategies to translate those wastes into opportunities for value creation.

A school of thought on organizations—called Strategic Choice[8]—argues that the behavior of an organization is driven by both the constraints imposed on it by its external environment as well as by the choices that its senior leadership makes in responding to the constraints imposed by the external environment. Taking a holistic approach, we believe, constitutes just such a strategic choice. It is about finding the right mix of short-term gains while building up the capabilities and culture needed to support a more fundamental shift in how stakeholders think and act within the enterprise.

Adopting a holistic approach makes the impacts of various components of the enterprise as a whole more visible and thus more manageable. For example, taking a holistic view may reveal that the root cause of why the enterprise cannot meet its cost, quality, and delivery objectives is not something that lies exclusively in any one of the functional areas of material acquisition, manufacturing, or logistics, but rather in the integration across all three functions.

Let's look at this approach at Rockwell Collins, where lean thinking has consistently been elevated beyond traditional improvement efforts to focus on enterprise-wide transformation challenges. The company's lean journey began in 1998 with a mandate to reduce costs by 30 percent over the following three years. But even an increase in the number of improvement events (of the sort typical in lean efforts) from 28 in 1998 to more than 600 in 2000 did not result in the kind of transformation senior leadership was seeking. The increased number of events, combined with a wide variety of approaches to implementing the improvements, led the organization as a whole to grow rather weary of so much change.

So the branded Lean Electronics program—an umbrella for all of the company's continuous improvement approaches—was created to establish a common set of problem-solving tools and to build a shared vocabulary for implementing change efforts. Furthermore, a more focused approach to selecting improvement projects was put into place that provided greater alignment with strategic objectives. The branding enabled senior leaders to present additional change initiatives as a natural progression of their transformation efforts, as opposed to the "flavors of the month" that were being replaced before enterprise-level benefits could be seen. In other words, "the branding connected the notes of separate initiatives into a transformational score."[9]

Over time, Rockwell Collins took other steps: A 2001 assessment of the company's core process optimization effort uncovered a need to accelerate transformation efforts, to increase the efficiency with which the company applied the tools at its disposal, and to emphasize leadership involvement in transformation. The discovery highlighted the importance of tracing benefits to a given stakeholder. A transformation roadmap created in 2002 has allowed Rockwell Collins to create a holistic approach that aligns local improvement efforts with its long-term strategic objectives. It partitioned transformation efforts into two distinct streams: one stream of activity flows that specified what it took to win and a second stream that increased emphasis on leadership. Since then, the company has succeeded in building a transformation system that addresses challenges at multiple levels through a mix of lean events, core process optimization, and life cycle value stream management.

Taking a holistic approach mandates a transformation strategy consistent with the principles detailed in this chapter. This transformation strategy is made actionable through the tools and techniques presented throughout our book.

Principle: Secure Leadership Commitment to Drive and Institutionalize Enterprise Behaviors

It is absolutely critical that enterprise transformation be driven, at the outset, from the highest levels of the enterprise. A transformation effort must have the full commitment of the senior leadership team. A process must then unfold to distribute that leadership commitment throughout the enterprise. The institutionalization of enterprise behaviors that follows—that is, the adoption of a holistic approach to top-to-bottom transformation in the enterprise—makes success achievable.

At Rockwell Collins, the consistent, vocal support of senior leadership has driven the lean enterprise transformation effort. As CEO Clay Jones noted in his keynote address to the LAI Annual Conference in 2007, "Do not even start your transformation journey if you do not have alignment and commitment right at the top. It is like teaching a pig to talk; you are wasting your time and annoying the pig."[10]

The awareness at the highest levels of the challenges that Rockwell Collins faces in this effort has led to a major emphasis on distributing leadership across the entire enterprise. It has also led to a recognition of the need for a leadership development program—since established—that identified the common challenges faced by emerging leaders and that defined leadership roles for everyone in the enterprise, ranging from personal leaders to executive leaders. The emphasis is on the nature of the change initiated by the leader. A *personal leader* identifies local opportunities for enhancing value provided to key stakeholders and personally initiates an effort to exploit that opportunity. An *executive leader* identifies opportunities at the enterprise level, and ensures that those opportunities are leveraged.

In an enterprise with institutionalized enterprise behaviors, the top leadership team communicates the strategic objectives of the enterprise clearly and provides the rationale that their subordinates need to execute the transformation efforts. Cultivating distributed leadership across all levels of an enterprise helps support the alignment of the enterprise with its strategic objectives by distributing awareness of and authority to meet those objectives throughout the organization. It also drives decision making to the lowest appropriate level, which means that the person making the decision either generates the decision or is close to the information needed to support it.

Principle: Identify Relevant Stakeholders and Determine Their Value Propositions

Our concept of an enterprise is a network of stakeholders that contribute to and receive value from the enterprise. The common stakeholders of an enterprise are its shareholders, customers, suppliers, employees, and managers. Enterprise thinking treats stakeholder centricity as a fundamental tenet: All relevant stakeholders must be sufficiently satisfied so that they continue to engage with the enterprise. Our approach makes this actionable. (Chapter 5 explores stakeholder analysis in detail.)

A basic requirement for successful transformation is having an understanding of the enterprise value proposition and ensuring that the constructed value proposition is a true reflection of the values of its stakeholders. The stakeholder analysis—that is, identifying and prioritizing stakeholders as well as eliciting and interpreting stakeholder values—is neither linear nor simple, but it is essential. Applying this principle requires going beyond the techniques (employee surveys, market analyses, etc.) typically used to capture information about the needs of specific stakeholder groups to analyze who the stakeholders are and what they value. The value exchange can be decomposed into the value expected from the enterprise and the value delivered by the enterprise. When the enterprise leaders understand stakeholder value, they can then assess how to deliver the value that stakeholders expect.

Over time, the amount of value distributed to stakeholders varies, and some receive more than others. What is critical is that value is distributed in a way that keeps the relevant stakeholders engaging as active participants in the enterprise. Constructing the value proposition of the enterprise as a function of the value exchange between the enterprise and all of its relevant stakeholders allows the enterprise to determine whether that value is distributed fairly. In the long run, the goal is to create greater value for all stakeholders—an aim that is impossible without a valid stakeholder analysis (detailed in Chapter 5).

It is not enough for the enterprise to identify its stakeholders. The enterprise must also determine why a given stakeholder is important. This knowledge allows the enterprise to make informed decisions about whether the value proposition is correct and viable over the long term. And while the enterprise's senior leadership team can usually identify key stakeholders and stakeholder groups, other stakeholders emerge as the enterprise continues its day-to-day operations. For example, corporate social responsibility and environmental sustainability movements have led to the creation of new stakeholder groups that the enterprise leadership may not have accounted for explicitly even a decade ago.

Because the enterprise value proposition is constantly evolving, the senior leadership team must actively engage in a dialogue with the enterprise's stakeholders. Doing so signals that the enterprise cares and generates goodwill that can be parlayed into more tangible assets.

For its part, Rockwell Collins has always been explicit about the importance of managing the value expectations of its key stakeholders. This goal has been made clear through the company's focus on building trusted relationships with customers, employees, and shareowners. Rockwell also works actively to satisfy other stakeholders, including its community, its suppliers, and its employees' families. Let's look at three stakeholder groups—employees, shareholders, and the community—and how Rockwell Collins works to satisfy their expectations of value.

Rockwell Collins has always recognized that the strength of the enterprise lies in its employees. The importance of this focus on employees is visible through an explicitly articulated value proposition for people[11] that comprises four initiatives: diversity, talent management, leadership development, and flexible benefit choices.

For shareowners, the focus is on delivering increased value, but not at the cost of the company. As part of this focus, Rockwell Collins began a stock repurchase program in 2003. Although such a program would typically result in increased distrust on the part of the capital markets, Rockwell Collins' emphasis on continually relaying the rationale behind the share repurchase program, using investor calls and other communication channels, enabled the company to mitigate the markets' negative reaction. In the end, the program contributed to the increase in overall shareholder value.

Finally, Rockwell Collins invests in the community through employee volunteering, education efforts, and charitable giving. For instance, when floods in Iowa reached 500-year levels in 2008, Rockwell Collins came to the rescue—even though the company's main plants were not affected by the disaster. The company immediately donated $2 million to help in the recovery and established the Rockwell Collins Flood Recovery Fund to provide longer-term help.

Principle: Focus on Enterprise Effectiveness Before Efficiency

Doing the right job and doing the job right: These dicta capture the notions of *effectiveness* and *efficiency*. An *effective* enterprise requires a value proposition that meets the current needs of stakeholders and is perceived to be able to meet their future needs. If you are able to execute at a lower cost (where cost is some function of resource utilization), yours is an *efficient* enterprise.

For example, consider an enterprise that recognizes it is losing market share due to a lack of new products and that sees the need to innovate to retain its customer base. If the enterprise chooses to compete on cost differentials by streamlining production processes, rather than to invest in new product development, the enterprise is focusing on efficiency rather than effectiveness.

By definition, an effective enterprise is, to some degree, efficient; it meets the value expectations of its stakeholders. The converse, though, is not always true. An enterprise can be extremely efficient and yet completely ineffective; consider the (perhaps apocryphal) story of the nail manufacturing plant in the former Soviet Union that met its production target, which was based on tons. It simply created completely useless 500-pound nails with tremendous efficiency. That is why a focus on effectiveness should come first: An efficient but ineffective enterprise will rapidly become extinct, but an effective enterprise—because of the value it provides—gains some time to become efficient.[12] The level of analysis strongly influences effectiveness and efficiency: What is efficiency in terms of corporate strategy may be effectiveness from an operational perspective.

With this principle, we do not advocate ignoring efficiency to pursue effectiveness exclusively. On the contrary, both are needed; what matters is which comes first. A successful transformation effort is, in fact, a mix of effectiveness-oriented and efficiency-oriented initiatives. Generally, efficiency-focused initiatives are easier to measure and yield results faster than effectiveness-focused efforts because they are targeted at some combination of well-established and well-understood structures, policies, or processes. These efforts also provide immediate impact, and hence they can demonstrate success and increase buy-in from the various stakeholders involved in the transformation efforts. But their very quick and tangible results can become a capability trap (that is, doing only what you already know how to do)[13] if they crowd out effectiveness-oriented actions.

Our Rockwell Collins example illustrates the point. The company sees innovation as its lifeblood, which translates into a focus on effectiveness before efficiency. Despite the hit-or-miss nature of innovation, Rockwell Collins has consistently invested between 18 and 20 percent of gross sales in R&D—an amount far exceeding that invested by its industry peers. Recognizing early on that conducting all R&D in-house was not a sustainable strategy, Rockwell Collins adopted an alternative approach to build long-term effectiveness in bringing new products and services faster to the market than its competitors—namely, to leverage the strengths of its own talent base while exploiting the so-called global brain. Today, Rockwell Scientific focuses on basic research (traditional R&D) and Rockwell Collins uses Advanced Technology Centers to focus on next-generation products and services and domain-specific centers of excellence. These are augmented by the 10X Program,[14] which is aimed at evoking breakthrough, out-of-the-box thinking from Rockwell Collins employees and open innovation to find and incorporate usable technologies into the company's portfolio.

Principle: Address Internal and External Enterprise Interdependencies

Every enterprise is a highly integrated system whose performance is determined by the degree of alignment among the major elements,[15] including its key structures, policies, processes, and stakeholders. One of the most difficult challenges in enterprise transformation is to specify the boundaries of the enterprise, because what is internal to the enterprise at one time may not necessarily remain within the boundaries as the enterprise evolves and transforms. With the boundaries identified, the structures, policies, and processes need to be mapped so that interdependencies can be determined. A successful transformation effort must account for both the internal and the external interdependencies.

The importance of this principle becomes clear when you consider, as an example, the relationships that enterprises typically have with suppliers. For one enterprise we examined, many of its requirements were dictated by a larger organization (of which it was part), and its suppliers were primarily sister operations (themselves enterprises) that were essentially parallel in the organizational structure. Each of these sister firms both supplied and was supplied by the others, and so each was highly interdependent. However, supplies did not always flow smoothly, and sometimes the understanding of the requirements differed from one operation to another. It became obvious, after an analysis, that enterprise performance could be improved considerably if these problems could be resolved at the interface points. Almost every large enterprise that interacts with other units, divisions, or entities faces these types of challenges with its internal interdependencies.

At another enterprise we examined, technical requirements came from an external source, and implementation happened with key external suppliers. Many of the opportunities for improvement were found at these interfaces, or points of external dependency.

Successful management of internal and external interdependencies is critical to maintaining transformation momentum. Rockwell Collins demonstrated this capability in the way it dealt with a 2008 strike at Boeing, its largest customer. Understanding Boeing—a key external dependency for Rockwell Collins—means being prepared for anything. So, having assessed in advance the potential impact of a strike on its manufacturing and engineering organizations, Rockwell Collins determined that, should the looming strike happen, no value was added by maintaining its current work pace and throughput. The company decided to account for the change in demand due to the strike by asking some Iowa production workers to take voluntary layoffs and delaying about 200 engineering hires. In addition, production staff was realigned, and overtime was cut. Earnings projections were also lowered. Although these cuts presented a temporary challenge for the enterprise and its employees, the identification of the strong interdependency between Boeing and Rockwell Collins, these actions made it possible for the enterprise to remain viable during this difficult period. Rockwell Collins succeeded in maintaining its margins at 20 percent for commercial systems sales—despite a 14-percent decline in sales from the strike and airline capacity reductions.

Principle: Ensure Stability and Flow Within and Across the Enterprise

Stability provides the foundation for creating a baseline against which enterprise performance can be assessed. In the presence of stability, flow within the enterprise enables you to see the presence of bottlenecks and identify root causes to problems. Both are central to any transformation effort.

When the enterprise environment is turbulent, only the tip of the iceberg is visible, and attempts to navigate around the iceberg may be disastrous if the underlying problems are not understood. In an environment of stability and flow, the enterprise can see more of the iceberg; it can lower the water level through problem solving that focuses on revealing the root causes of problems.

Examples of stability and flow abound. When an organization implements an enterprise information system, for instance, it does so to establish the flow of information across the enterprise to enhance the decision making of the key senior leadership—and good decision making builds stability.

The focus at Rockwell Collins on ensuring information flows across the enterprise can be traced back to 1997, when the company implemented its first Enterprise Resource Planning system to span the entire enterprise. As the comfort level grew, cost estimation tools and, later, the sourcing and procurement process were integrated into the system, winning the company the 2005 Medal of Excellence from *Purchasing* magazine.[16] Establishing a seamless flow of information across the enterprise has given Rockwell Collins the ability to understand its use of information and to leverage newer business models to improve enterprise performance, beginning with storage area networks in 2003 and transitioning to a pay-per-use strategy for harnessing computing power.

The case of Southwest Airlines illustrates stability.[17] As the carrier has grown in the 1990s and the first decade of the twentieth-first century, expansion has been kept at a slow, steady pace to ensure that everything continues to work in as stable a manner as possible. The company wants to make sure the right people are in the right places and that the airline will not be stressed in a way that will make it difficult to maintain its level of service. In the aftermath of the 9/11 terrorist attacks, Southwest Airlines was one of the few carriers that did not lay off employees, keeping employment stable. When things turned around and the public began to fly again in large numbers,

Southwest's stability—which includes having some of the most loyal employees of any company in any industry—served it very well.

Principle: Emphasize Organizational Learning

Learning in an enterprise occurs at three levels: individual, group, and organizational. Individuals have insight and intuition, often from having seen something similar at an earlier experience point (*expert intuition*). Sometimes, expert intuition comes in the form of being able to project into the future (*entrepreneurial intuition*). Individuals interpret these insights and elevate them to the group level, which happens more easily when the enterprise has a common language and all its members share an understanding of the metaphors that are often used to communicate insights and learning. The process of integration at the group level results in the creation of new knowledge, approaches, and concepts that the enterprise can institutionalize in the form of organizational routines and contexts. This organizational learning is a key to successful enterprise transformation efforts.

Emphasizing organizational learning is as much about creating the context and culture to support a learning organization as it is about establishing the formal structures and policies that govern the learning process. In the transformation context, organizational learning can happen in two ways:

➤ Through *exploration*, as stakeholders at various levels across the enterprise determine potential areas of improvement

➤ Through *exploitation*, as well-understood, well-governed transformation tools and techniques are deployed

Exploration enables the enterprise to determine, as new information emerges, whether the strategic decisions that placed the enterprise on its transformation path are still correct. Piloting new tools and techniques can help with selecting the ones best for exploitation on a broader scale.

Some enterprises find—or believe—that they are so busy executing that they cannot learn. This may actually mean that they lack the infrastructure to capture the wealth of learning actually occurring every day, as part of the execution, or that no mechanisms are in place for the enterprise to make sense of the vast amount of data and knowledge generated and collected. In either case, it indicates that the enterprise leadership team needs a better understanding of the role of learning in sustaining enterprise transformation efforts.

Rockwell Collins embarked on a deliberate journey to change how employees thought about learning and how they accessed information. The objective was to change what was perceived to be a "conservative, change-averse company, with a cynicism towards new ideas, and a highly cautious approach to transformation"[18] and thus establish a learning organization.

The "first step," in the words of CEO Clay Jones, was to create "a general expectation across the company that lifelong learning is a priority."[19] In the Rockwell Collins context, this is about the importance of keeping up with ever-changing technology and process environments. The view is that, when people learn enough to become adaptable, the organization as a whole becomes adaptable. The true strength of the company's effort in this regard lies in its ability to translate that learning into competitive advantage and bottom-line results. It has been augmented with pioneering e-learning approaches and a system of mentoring and coaching that calls on the so-called graybeards—the more experienced employees with whom a large portion of this knowledge-intensive company's knowledge resides. A more formal knowledge management system has also been rolled out enterprise-wide; in addition to traditional search capabilities, it provides access and security controls to protect classified information and intellectual property.

These enterprise transformation principles inform everything else you will read in this book, which builds on the classical principles of lean thinking and lean enterprises to address the unique challenges of transformation at the enterprise level. The principles of lean thinking have been shown to have a significant impact on how work is done, and lean enterprise principles have allowed us to redefine where lean principles and tools can be applied. However, neither effectively articulate how transformation can and should be carried out.

Again, here are the seven enterprise transformation principles:

➤ Adopt a holistic approach to enterprise transformation.
➤ Secure leadership commitment to drive and institutionalize enterprise behaviors.
➤ Identify relevant stakeholders and determine their value propositions.

➤ Focus on enterprise effectiveness before efficiency.

➤ Address internal and external enterprise interdependencies.

➤ Ensure stability and flow within and across the enterprise.

➤ Emphasize organizational learning.

The enterprise transformation principles represent the distillation of lessons learned from transformation efforts, lessons that an enterprise can tailor to its unique requirements. The principles we have just discussed recognize that transformation requires a holistic approach that effectively integrates the specification and analysis of the current state, the articulation of a desired future state, and the actual process of transforming to achieve that specified future-state vision. A vision is not achievable without a leadership team that remains committed to the transformation effort, understands the need to create a baseline of performance, ensures a flow of information and resources to surface challenges, and can establish a system of organizational learning that enables the enterprise to avoid repeating the mistakes of the past. At the heart of a transformation effort is the stakeholder value proposition that reflects not only what the stakeholders of the enterprise want, but also what the enterprise wants from its stakeholders. Enabling a successful transformation also requires that the enterprise emphasize doing the right thing before trying to do it right, and understanding both internal and external enterprise interdependencies.

These seven enterprise transformation principles do not operate in isolation. Rather, they are deeply connected, and their application creates a system of transformation. Your enterprise can become, like Rockwell Collins, an exemplar of how to create change constructively and proactively rather than simply responding to change. An enterprise transformation shapes your environment to create the change that will lead to greater success. The principles are the foundation for our approach to enterprise transformation, as illustrated in the Enterprise Transformation Roadmap—an analytic framework that comprises the next chapters, in which you will learn to assess the current state of the enterprise through seven lenses, envision the future state of the enterprise, create a transformation plan, and execute that plan for successful enterprise transformation.

CHAPTER 2 TAKEAWAYS

▲ Transformation requires a holistic approach that effectively integrates the specification and analysis of the current state, the articulation of a desired future state, and the actual process of transforming to achieve that vision.

▲ Enterprise transformation requires leadership commitment to embrace enterprise thinking, commit the resources necessary for transformation, and personally lead the transformation effort.

▲ At the heart of any transformation effort is the ability to understand, articulate, and deliver on the enterprise value proposition.

▲ Effectiveness—doing the right job—comes before the efficiency of doing the job right.

▲ The enterprise must manage dependencies within and across its boundaries as part of the transformation journey.

▲ The combination of stability and an effective flow of resources and information enables an enterprise to achieve dramatic gains in performance.

▲ Enterprise transformation is a journey on which time must be taken to reflect on lessons learned and take corrective action when necessary.

—3—

A Roadmap to Successful Enterprise Transformation

Men never plan to be failures;
they simply fail to plan to be successful.

William Arthur Ward[1]

L ET'S BE BLUNT: Most transformation efforts fail. That's what we see from our experience working with many organizations. By "fail," we mean either the efforts are not sustainable or they do not achieve the desired strategic objectives. But why do they fail? Our experience shows that almost always, in the end, failure results from the absence of a holistic view of the enterprise at the beginning of the process (in other words, the failure to abide by the first principle of enterprise transformation). Lacking such a view, the effort ends up omitting key elements of a system of transformation that is necessary for success. Of course, the initial path to failure (so to speak) often begins with something quite specific.

Why Enterprise Transformation Fails

The reasons behind the failure of transformation efforts seem to fall into one or more of a number of categories. Table 3-1 summarizes them.

Table 3-1

Types of Enterprise Transformation Failure

Failure Type	Results from . . .
Only in my backyard	Undertaking only local projects, with no consideration for their impact across the enterprise
Activity	Feeling the need to "do something" and measuring/valuing activity rather than progress
Low-hanging fruit	Focusing efforts on the easiest problems to address
Pet project	Working on whatever a leader or leaders want, whether it is the right thing to do or addresses root issues
New leadership	Heading down the path set by a new leader with no regard for where the organization is or has been going
Leaders who don't lead	Delegating all transformation work to underlings, with leaders taking no part in the efforts
Hire the transformers	Bringing in outsiders to develop and implement transformation, who leave behind no plan
Flavor-of-the-month	Undertaking transformation efforts that shift from one methodology to another . . . again and again

The one most obviously related to the absence of a holistic view of the enterprise is when organizations undertake only local projects, with no consideration for their impact across the enterprise. This type of failure tends to be a function of a lack of awareness. We saw this at a major defense manufacturer, where the engineering function had decided to downsize significantly the number of its engineers working with the process engineers in manufacturing. Why? The engineering leaders saw no value-added from an engineering perspective. Only after the decision had been translated into action did anyone recognize the critical downstream implications in terms of delays in production and associated cost overruns. The transformation effort turned into what we call an *only in my backyard failure*.

Sometimes organizations just feel the need to do something, anything, to gain traction for what they (incorrectly) characterize as transformation, but they never really make any progress. These organizations, whose transformation efforts suffer what we call *activity failure*, tend to measure activity rather than progress, and they may even value activity more than progress. A major government organization we know focused on measuring the number of improvement events it undertook and how many people it trained to do what it called improvement. Yet it never reflected strategically on whether those events were actually moving the organization forward on its transformation journey.

At a large aerospace company, we found an emphasis on reducing direct labor costs on the shop floor, even though it represented less than 5 percent of the company's total costs. The reason for this effort was that addressing direct labor was easy to do, and the company's transformation suffered from *low-hanging fruit failure*.

Several types of transformation effort flow directly from senior leadership behaviors and decisions taken only because they are leaders (i.e., they can), often for little or no strategic reason. Sometimes, power and politics intervene to cause *pet project failure*—working on the wrong things and not getting at root issues. A hospital recently avoided pet project failure by conducting a deeper enterprise analysis of the root causes of delays in the emergency department. The executive in charge had been pushing to introduce a self-check-in kiosk to improve the flow of patients, but the analysis showed that the delays in the system were being introduced not because of long check-in times, but the lack of in-patient beds.[2]

Similarly, failure often results from a new leader insisting that the organization set out on his or her path, regardless of where the organization has been and is going. As an example of this *new leadership failure*, when Christian Streiff took over as the CEO of Airbus in July 2006, he initiated a review of all programs currently underway. Presenting the results three months later to the Airbus senior leadership team, he proposed sweeping restructuring plans, including moving A380 production solely to France. The proposal was met with significant resistance because it did not meet the needs of key stakeholders, including those of the corporate parent EADS.[3] Although he had been brought in for his previous successes as a turnaround specialist elsewhere, Streiff could not relate to the Airbus enterprise as a whole and ultimately was forced to resign.

Conversely, some leaders simply refuse to lead. They aren't engaged and delegate all the transformation work to others. We're sure nearly every reader has seen this in action at some point in her or his career. We call what results *leaders-who-don't-lead failure*. When Larry Bossidy was CEO of AlliedSignal, he became well known throughout the business world for his approach to making sure that this type of failure didn't happen, holding leaders accountable for personally leading change efforts. He shares some of his experiences in leading transformation in his best-selling book *Execution*.[4]

Some leaders manifest their unwillingness to be involved by bringing in consultants or anyone else they think can transform their organizations for them. One of the U.S. defense services hired a major consultancy firm to develop and implement transformation. When the consultant left, there was no actionable transformation plan to follow, nor any commitment or drive within the service to move the effort forward. The organization suffered a *hire the transformers* failure.

Linked to the problem of bringing in outsiders to do what the enterprise itself needs to do is the tendency to undertake transformation efforts that shift from one methodology to another in a continual quest for a "silver bullet"—with constant rebranding of the transformation effort. We found change fatigue had set in at one organization. A tired employee told us, "When I started here, we did Quality Circles, then we called it TQM, and then they had a new program, and finally now we have Lean Six Sigma. Nothing works!" That organization ultimately suffered *flavor-of-the-month failure*.

With our Enterprise Transformation Roadmap (Figure 3-1), we set out to fix the problem of transformation efforts that fail to see the entire enterprise. In doing so, we developed ways to avoid each of the types of failures just described.

Avoid Failure with the Roadmap

The Enterprise Transformation Roadmap was developed based on more than ten years of enterprise research. It provides a way to see, think about, and enact both radical and incremental change simultaneously. Because these types of change happen at the same time, leadership must account for both types. The Roadmap provides a framework for effective and efficient transformation strategy, planning, and execu-

Figure 3-1

Enterprise Transformation Roadmap

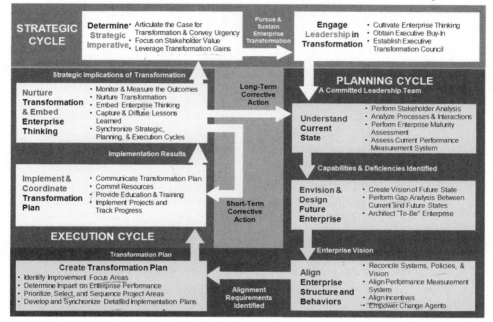

tion. It also serves as a guide for enterprise leaders as they consider the critical strategic, cultural, and operational changes of both types that are required to transform an enterprise.

The Roadmap comprises three cycles.

> ➤ The first is a **Strategic Cycle** in which the business case for transformation is made as the organization's leadership becomes engaged (as we discussed in Chapter 1, and on which we elaborate in Chapter 4).

> ➤ The second is a **Planning Cycle** that involves analyzing and defining both the current and future states of the enterprise, and then articulating a transformation plan to achieve the future vision.

> ➤ The third is an **Execution Cycle**, during which the plan is put into practice.

Throughout this book, we provide examples of how enterprise leaders have employed the Roadmap to enhance the quality of their thinking about enterprise transformation issues, as well as how the Roadmap has guided them to develop transformation plans for increasing value delivery that provides maximum benefit for the entire enterprise.

➤ You'll see organizations that have avoided the *leaders-who-don't-lead failure* because the Roadmap process forces the leaders to lead from the very beginning of a transformation effort and keeps them engaged throughout.

➤ The Roadmap helps you avoid *flavor-of-the-month failure* because it provides an integrated and cohesive approach to transformation that is not governed by any specific tools you might choose to employ.

➤ By forcing internal ownership and understanding of the transformation that permeates the entire enterprise, the Roadmap helps avoid *hire the transformers failure*.

➤ Transformation effort projects are chosen because they are the right thing to do and drive explicitly toward achieving long-term objectives, thus avoiding *low-hanging fruit failure*.

➤ *Pet project failure* is avoided because projects get done *only* if they make sense for the enterprise. The enterprise follows a structured approach in the Planning Cycle, ensures that decisions are based on data that uncover root causes and issues, and builds consensus throughout the transformation effort.

➤ *Only in my backyard failure* is similarly avoided because the Roadmap makes you look at the interactions across processes and organizations. Any "local" projects get done only with consideration of their impact across functional boundaries, that is, how they serve the entire enterprise by improving the delivery of value.

➤ Finally, the Roadmap process creates the conditions for avoiding *new leadership failure*. If the entire executive team of your organization has followed the Roadmap, the new leader has to choose to ignore a very compelling consensus among other senior leaders, a rationale for transformation, and a shared understanding and mental model, all backed up by data.

The Roadmap draws from comprehensive discussions with industry executives, from the experience of a team of industry, government, and academic representatives working to create the framework, and from research in change management and organizational dynamics over many decades by many scholars. As a guide for enterprise leaders, it seeks to answer a number of key questions: Is there a way to transform an enterprise that continually builds on successes? How can an enterprise ensure that its strategic objectives are tightly aligned with any transformation effort? What steps must be taken to ensure that a transformation plan has an impact at the enterprise level and is not simply a set of activities? These questions flow from the observation that most enterprise change programs tend to focus far too much on activity at the nonenterprise level and do not focus enough on the enterprise as a whole and on the results that cut across the entire enterprise.

Enterprise Transformation and Strategic Planning

The underlying assumption in the Enterprise Transformation Roadmap is that you are not simply tweaking your organization, but that you are setting out to do something fundamentally different: transform the enterprise. Enterprise transformation involves changing how the enterprise thinks, its processes, its relationships with employees, how the enterprise shares information, its relationships with suppliers, the kinds of people the enterprise hires, the organizational development steps it takes, and so on. It can be all or some of these elements—and many more. Part of the Roadmap serves to help enterprise leaders determine which of these changes, and in which areas of the enterprise's activities, they need to effect in order to reach their strategic objectives.

Enterprise transformation, however, is not strategic planning, even though from the preceding paragraph you may get that impression. Rather, the enterprise transformation process assumes that strategic planning has already been done and that strategic objectives have been articulated. To be sure, following the Roadmap will, by the very nature of the process, refine the articulation of strategic objectives that may already exist.

Table 3-2 summarizes the differences between strategic planning and enterprise transformation.

Even when an enterprise has not articulated strategic objectives but has only a clear sense that something must be undertaken, follow-

Table 3-2

Comparison of Strategic Planning and Enterprise Transformation

Strategic Planning	*Enterprise Transformation*
Strategic planners develop a set of options for the enterprise leader	The senior leadership team collaboratively develops transformation options.
Dominantly customer- and competitor-focused	Stakeholder-centric analysis addresses both internal and external stakeholder needs.
The planners analyze product/market	Analyzes the enterprise value proposition as a whole.
Focus on budget allocation and strategic options	The focus is on enabling structural and behavioral enterprise changes.

ing the Roadmap can help define a *strategic* something. So, although it is not a substitute for strategic planning, the Roadmap can clearly indicate what is needed for an enterprise to be effective, especially from a capabilities perspective. In organizations whose clock speed of change is extremely high and that need to be highly responsive to fluctuations in their environment, the Roadmap's transformation process specifies the bounds within which the enterprise can operate effectively. Thus it supports making the strategic decisions you need to steer your enterprise.

Consider the example of an entrepreneur we know from MIT who started his own small technology-oriented company that specializes in engineering environmental equipment. When the company suddenly became very successful, he found himself needing to shift very quickly to high-volume manufacturing. This step-up raised a number of challenges for the company, including a need for different personnel. The entrepreneur had no idea how to handle the sudden shift, and he began to make changes that, in retrospect, appear to be *activity failures*. The absence of a company strategic plan only made things worse. Our team took him and his leadership through the Roadmap. As a result, the company was able to articulate at a strategic level what it needed to do to meet its new and unanticipated manufacturing and human resource challenges.

A Europe-based global software developer with which our team worked[5] illustrates the more typical case, where the strategic objectives are articulated and the Roadmap allows the enterprise to refine those objectives. The company—we'll call it ZED—had been experiencing exponential growth, in terms of both revenue and full-time employees. When our team began its work, that growth had been 40 percent in the past year. The company's great success was accompanied by many challenges, though, and the general feeling among the senior leadership was that something needed to change. ZED was thinking in terms of "lean" as a way to stay on its growth path. Our team was invited to use the Enterprise Strategic Analysis for Transformation (ESAT) tool and to help create a transformation plan. (ESAT is explained in greater detail at the end of this chapter.)

The enterprise had five strategic objectives that any transformation plan would have to serve. The first was to *grow in size*. This meant moving to new markets and retaining existing customers, hiring new people and inculcating them with the corporate identity, and opening new offices where talent was available. The objective to remain on its growth trajectory, though, had to be met in the context of maintaining and improving ZED's quality of service and products.

The second strategic objective was to *improve revenue*. This objective was linked directly to the growth objective. Taking what ZED called a "venture capital–like approach," the company had become good at keeping an eye out for research projects and ideas from its employees or new hires and providing seed capital and funding to enable those ideas to flourish. Then the board would decide each quarter whether to spin off any of these projects. ZED was regularly developing new projects internally in this way, as well as by hiring new staff from the universities where it had offices.

The third strategic objective was to *achieve higher margins*. Even before enterprise transformation planning, the senior leadership at ZED had planned to move up in the value chain of their products and services. They felt that this shift could be achieved by investing in employees, research and development, and training and by enhancing value delivery by subcontracting some day-to-day, repetitive non-value-added activity in its operations. Reducing some of the overhead associated with the services business would be key to ensuring long-term success.

To *improve brand recognition*, the fourth strategic objective, ZED aimed to support its first two strategic objectives and to achieve greater flexibility in pricing and its ability to hire and retain the best talent.

The capacity to *attract and focus on larger projects*, the fifth strategic objective, was something ZED also expected to gain through better brand recognition.

These objectives encapsulated ZED's strategic planning. They were not something to discard but formed the very basis for embarking on a journey along the Enterprise Transformation Roadmap. We will return to ZED in later chapters and show you some of what the company's enterprise transformation effort looked like.

With all of these points in mind about the Roadmap, let's get an overview of each of the three cycles and the activities that take place within each cycle. In subsequent chapters, we go into detail for each one.

Strategic Cycle: Determine the Strategic Objectives and Engage the Leadership

The Roadmap begins in the Strategic Cycle with determining the strategic imperative of the enterprise. As discussed in Chapter 1, the first step in this process is to articulate the business case for transformation, keeping a focus on stakeholder value.

In this first step in the Strategic Cycle, you create the leadership conditions under which it is possible to pursue and sustain enterprise transformation. One executive we worked with told us, "Now that we think there's an actual imperative for change, here's what we're going to do."

At this point, the leadership of the enterprise must become fully engaged. A CEO would engage all of his direct reports; a division president would engage all of hers. The entire executive leadership must be brought fully on board, and the urgency of transformation must be conveyed without equivocation. All of this must unfold while ensuring that the entire leadership team is thinking not about their individual silos but in terms of the interrelationships among their different organizations within the larger enterprise, how what they do affects things downstream, how what others do affects them, and so on.

We cannot overemphasize how important it is to foster enterprise thinking. For example, we once went into a company to help it begin the path to enterprise transformation. As part of the initial analysis, we asked a number of the executives to describe, from their individual perspectives, what was going on. The vice president of engineering told us, rather matter-of-factly, that the major issue was that manufacturing never delivered on time and our help was needed to fix that problem. The head of manufacturing operations told us that his people felt fully capable of delivering on time, but that suppliers never got them the materials they needed in time to meet deadlines. When we asked suppliers about this, we were told that engineering was always six months late getting them the drawings they needed to provide materials. When we went back to engineering, the executive acknowledged that what should take six months usually took twelve. He confessed to having no idea of how the delays affected the entire stream in the enterprise. Believe it or not, he had never really given any serious thought to whether others could make up the extra time his people were taking.

Later that year, we returned to the company and spoke again to the vice president of engineering. He told us that people in other parts of the enterprise now come to him for help and that he understands how what his organization does affects their work.

The simple fact is that, in hierarchical organizations operating in a silo-thinking mode, these kinds of issues very often fail to percolate to the top. The power of putting everyone in a room together to discuss the enterprise can be stunning. Executives discover things they didn't know or hadn't thought about. More significantly, they develop a shared mental model of the enterprise.

At this early stage in enterprise transformation, obtaining executive buy-in is an important part of the process of engaging the leadership. In fact, a consensus that things need to be done differently is crucial. You cannot simply tell executives that something new is afoot and that they need to get onboard. The agreement must be fully embraced, and the leadership needs to take their direct reports through the evidence and demonstrate the urgency of transformation.

Once senior leaders are onboard, steps must be taken to solidify their commitment. Part of this process is the establishment of an Executive Transformation Council. This council serves an oversight function, and its membership comprises people who are tasked with making sure the transformation takes place. If the structure doesn't exist to establish such a council, it needs to be created.

It is critical that line organizations take responsibility for driving the transformation. However, at the same time there is often so much going on that a staff position or staff team needs to be established and given the responsibility of championing transformation in specific areas. For instance, in one enterprise with which we worked, the manufacturing and engineering vice presidents were made cochairs of a special team to champion the enterprise's specific goal of reducing its time to market. Those two vice presidents led organizations that would be key in any effort to achieve such an objective.

Efforts to engage the leadership in transformation culminate in establishing a kind of governance system for the transformation. This is an effective way to ensure that responsibility, authority, and accountability rest squarely in the same place. Having it all in one place is itself a precondition for success.

Planning Cycle: Understand, Envision, Design, Align

The second cycle in the Enterprise Transformation Roadmap is the Planning Cycle. With a committed leadership team in place, it encompasses:

➤ Understanding the current state of the enterprise.
➤ Envisioning and designing the future enterprise.
➤ Aligning the enterprise infrastructure.
➤ Creating the transformation plan needed to achieve that future vision.

People undertaking an enterprise transformation often want to jump ahead to dealing with the future, but understanding the current state of the enterprise cannot be skipped. All too often, we find that enterprise executives lack a holistic understanding of the current enterprise state; they see their individual pieces almost to the complete exclusion of the whole. We also find that executives commonly lack a shared understanding of the current state of the enterprise. Absent a holistic view and shared understanding, any cohesion among the leadership team built in the Strategic Cycle is likely to be unsustainable.

Analyzing and improving overall enterprise performance is a process that requires systems methods and tools. We use our Enterprise Strategic Analysis for Transformation (ESAT), which is designed to support and enact the Planning Cycle; Figure 3-2 shows the steps we take to actuate the Roadmap, derived from ESAT. No matter what method you choose, the process allows you to analyze the enterprise holistically as you make the Roadmap actionable.

Each step in the process is linked to the activities of the Planning Cycle, represented by the bullet points in the Roadmap in Figure 3-1. Let's go through the Planning Cycle step by step and get an overview of how the process is employed. The details will be found in subsequent chapters.

Figure 3-2

Actuating the Roadmap

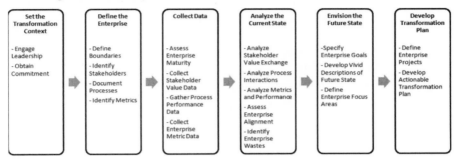

The first specific activities in the Planning Cycle give you an understanding of the enterprise's current state: a stakeholder analysis, an analysis of current processes and interactions, an assessment of how well the enterprise employs a variety of practices that are key to enterprise transformation, and an assessment of how performance is measured.

In the stakeholder analysis, you first identify stakeholders and then specify how each stakeholder or stakeholder group provides value to and receives value from the enterprise. Value, in this case, is partially defined by the stakeholder.

Analyzing the enterprise's processes and interactions is, in essence, analyzing the value stream. Most readers are familiar with the concept of the *product value stream*, defined as "the set of end-to-end and linked actions, processes and functions necessary to transform raw materials into a finished product delivered to the customer."[6] This is a starting point for defining the enterprise value stream, which is at a higher level and more general than a product value stream. The enterprise value stream encompasses support and leadership/executive processes in addition to product lifecycle processes. It illustrates how the enterprise relates to its external environment and to the general ordering of its own high-level internal processes. In short, the enterprise value stream forms the business case for describing why the enterprise exists.

Our approach adapts a method many organizations have used in their transformation efforts but incorporates some significant differences. Value Stream Mapping (VSM) exposes sources of waste and so helps give direction for increasing value to the customers of the enterprise's products and services. The traditional VSM approach is a bottom-up analysis and was originally used mostly to analyze manufacturing and production operations. Although it is used much more broadly today, it is not the kind of top-down analysis of the total enterprise that is needed. The necessary analysis is one that focuses on delivering value to all stakeholders and that addresses Lifecycle, Enabling, and Leadership Processes, and multiple programs or lines of business.

Uncovering sources of waste, which is so central to Value Stream Mapping, is thus elevated to the enterprise level in our approach. Enterprise-level waste may be less tangible and is more difficult to identify than waste in the product value stream, but the tools you will read about in coming chapters make this step in the transformation effort a challenge that can be met.

Another tool we use is the Lean Enterprise Self-Assessment Tool (LESAT),[7] developed in conjunction with industry, government, and academic colleagues in the United Kingdom. It supports the as-is analysis by providing a way for an enterprise to self-assess its current state of leanness and its readiness to change, based on a capability maturity model for both enterprise leadership and on both Lifecycle and Enabling Processes. The data collected through LESAT inform the construction of current-state perspectives and identification of future-state opportunities that feed into the to-be vision expressed in the transformation plan. (Appendix A provides more detail about LESAT in the form of two case studies.)

Thus, this first part of the Planning Cycle provides the enterprise leadership with, in essence, a diagnosis of the current state of the enterprise. This is the baseline for creating any realistic, achievable vision for the future and identifying what it will take to get there, which is the transformation plan: a set of high-level projects aimed at achieving enterprise-wide performance that speaks to the future vision. This document shows how the gap will be closed between the present and intended states of the enterprise. The intended impact of the projects on enterprise performance is determined, priorities are set, a sequence is established for the work to come, and a communication plan is developed to ensure that the entire enterprise is kept abreast of the progress along the transformation journey. To keep everyone informed and engaged, communication activities of successful transformation efforts typically include using a variety of media and venues, from newsletters to town hall meetings.

The seven principles discussed in Chapter 2 provide the philosophical foundations for enterprise transformation; the Roadmap provides the framework within which the principles can be effectively applied. The overall transformation approach is shown in Figure 3-3.

Figure 3-3

Enterprise Transformation Framework

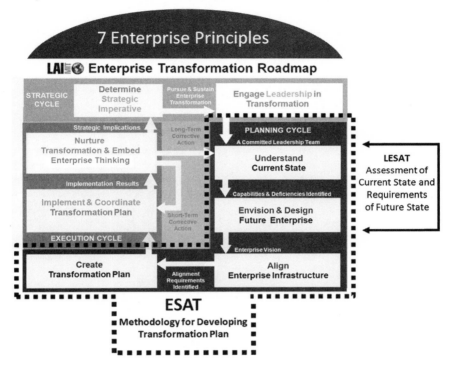

Execution Cycle: Nurture, Embed, Implement, Coordinate

The third part of the Roadmap is the Execution Cycle. We call it the third part, not the final part, because it feeds back into the Strategic Cycle, and the enterprise continues (ideally) on a never-ending path of improvement.

The Execution Cycle, which is detailed in the last part of this book, is where the transformation plan is implemented and coordinated. Success requires detailed project implementation plans linked to and synchronized with each other and with the overall plan. Progress is tracked carefully as implementation unfolds. Resources are committed, and education and training are provided where needed.

Also in the Execution Cycle, enterprise thinking is nurtured and embedded into the entire enterprise. This happens through several activities on an enterprise-wide scale. Outcomes of the projects estab-

(text continues on page 46)

Table 3-3

Examples of Transformation Efforts

Industry	Organization	Reason to Transform	Insights from Enterprise Analysis
Aerospace	Air cargo carrier program	Reduce costs and cycle times	Multiple stakeholder (industry, government regulatory) essential for enterprise success
	Space center	Long development and procurement times at high cost	Criticality of including extended enterprise, including key suppliers and requirements generators
Health care	Mental health hospital	Breaking cultural norms to drive needed change, improve service, and reduce costs	Despite expertise in patient care, inadequate traditional behaviors were for enterprise optimization and operation across boundaries
	Hospital	Emergency department overcrowding	Traditional lean approaches prone to sub-optimization; strong interdependencies with other hospital units (inpatient, operating rooms, etc.) and external entities (insurance companies, primary care, etc.); ensuing transformation efforts based on holistic principles

	Medical device manufacturer	High growth rate; improve quality and profitability	Governance structure required to oversee enterprise transformation; critical to span cross-organizational boundaries
Services	Commodity provider	Misalignment of customer service with development and delivery platform	Leveraged front-end enterprise interface while supplying holistic stakeholder value propositions; adoption of both effectiveness as well as efficiency measures
Automotive	Auto manufacturer	Reduced time-to-market in global product development	Required more than just traditional R&D; streamlining of cross-functional information exchange across organizational boundaries as key to transformation
Government	Air logistics center	Increase aircraft availability; commercial competition for logistics support	Focus for prioritizing projects to achieve increased mission effectiveness provided by shared enterprise strategic vision
	Acquisition, technology, and matériel support	Higher levels of support to the field at reduced costs and cycle time; organizational integration	Extensive involvement of leadership, inclusion of supply base, and integration of processes with IT systems required for integrated enterprise model

lished in the transformation plan are monitored, measured, and communicated. Lessons are captured and diffused throughout the enterprise. Long- and short-term efforts are synchronized.

We've taken a large number of organizations through the Roadmap, using ESAT and LESAT to help analyze, design, and transform their enterprises. Table 3-3 offers representative examples of where this overall enterprise transformation framework has been applied. The examples run the gamut from aerospace to health care and defense acquisition to the service sector. In each case, significant insights were gleaned from taking an enterprise perspective. The organizations learned and transformed, to greater or lesser degrees, and we learned about how our tools work.

In the chapters that follow, we draw on many of these examples to illustrate the details of how the tools and methods work, what self-assessments look like, and so on. To begin, in Chapter 4, we explore in detail the first part of the Roadmap and how to engage the enterprise's leadership in transformation.

CHAPTER 3 TAKEAWAYS

⚠ Most transformation efforts fail, and the reason can almost always be traced to the absence of a holistic view of the enterprise at the beginning of the process. This limited view leads to the omission of key elements of a system of transformation necessary for success.

⚠ Enterprise transformation unfolds in three cycles: strategic, planning, and execution. Having a framework or roadmap that shows the steps within these cycles helps guide the process and ensure success.

⚠ Enterprise transformation is not strategic planning, but builds on the strategic objectives that come from strategic planning. Absent such objectives, the Roadmap can guide an enterprise to setting some strategic goals.

CHAPTER

—4—

Transformation Leadership

A leader without a vision is a stamped letter without address;
it can never reach its destination.

Mehmet Ildan[1]

A MONG THOSE WHO STUDY and work on enterprise transformation, there's a healthy debate about the direction from which change ought to come. Some argue that the bottom-up model is best, and others prefer a hybrid of bottom-up and top-down. Our experience has demonstrated that, although transformation must evolve to be a hybrid, it absolutely must start at the top.

Hence, ours is a leadership-driven view of transformation. Although every stakeholder participating in the enterprise must understand, implement, assess, and enhance the transformation effort, our experience shows that those things occur—and result in success—only when the senior leadership team leads by example. The rubber hits the road when the enterprise leadership team is committed to, and accountable for, the success of enterprise transformation. Only then can the idea of making transformation everyone's responsibility become a practical reality. Only with an active leadership that makes a full commitment of significant time, energy, and dedication is it possible to go further and engage every stakeholder of the enterprise.

We believe a transformation effort must engage the hearts and minds of people at all levels of the enterprise, but it must start with an *engaged leadership team* that understands the context in which enterprise transformation must take place and that is committed to making it happen. Every enterprise has an associated culture, to which a leader must be well attuned. Part of the role of a leader is to be able to understand the culture and shape it to support continuous enterprise transformation. With an engaged leadership team, the transformation can emanate outward in concentric circles to reach every part of the enterprise. Then it becomes both top-down and bottom-up, with continual iteration.

Figure 4-1 shows the *Strategic Cycle* of the Roadmap we introduced in Chapter 3, where leadership engagement is put front and center as a prerequisite to planning and execution. But what really needs to happen in those first few boxes of the Enterprise Transformation Roadmap? The answer involves what an engaged leader must *be* and the mindset of an engaged leader, as well as what an engaged leader must *do*.

Figure 4-1

Leadership's Role in the Roadmap's Strategic Cycle

Strategic Perspectives

In Lewis Carroll's *Alice in Wonderland*, Alice comes upon the Cheshire Cat and asks, "Would you tell me, please, which way I ought to go from here?" When the Cheshire Cat answers that it depends on where Alice wants to get to, she explains that she doesn't much care where as long as she gets somewhere. Alice, had she been engaged in a transformation effort, would have been a prime candidate for *activity failure*, as we explained in Chapter 3.

The Cheshire Cat tells Alice that, given her objective, "Then it doesn't matter which way you go."

This exchange is often mistakenly misquoted as: "If you don't know where you're going, any road will get you there." In fact, both are true—and both are relevant to our discussion. Unlike for Alice, transformation begins with a strategic perspective that identifies the imperative for change, a problem or problems to solve, and a "place" at which the organization intends to be. That place could be, among many other possibilities, increased market share, or reduced time to market, or lower costs, or streamlined cycle times, or improved customer satisfaction. Senior leaders must articulate a vision of getting from one place (the present) to a better place (the future), which prepares them and the broader enterprise to take the entire journey embodied in the Enterprise Transformation Roadmap.

It takes a particular kind of leader to step up and play the required leadership role. Such a leader must be able to see across boundaries both inside and outside the enterprise. Such a leader must be able to see the sum of the parts, which means seeing the enterprise as a whole. Such a leader then has to be able to articulate that holistic view to the rest of the enterprise. It doesn't matter whether the leader starts out as a *transactional leader*—the type who tends to get things done—or a *transformational leader*—the type skilled at motivating and directing.[2] Both types need to become engaged enterprise leaders. *Enterprise leaders* are those who see across boundaries, have a holistic view, and can articulate the transformation vision.

Every organization that wants to set out on an enterprise transformation must build a cadre of engaged enterprise leaders. The cadre is a critical factor for future success. Mechanisms within the enterprise need to be created to develop leaders who sense the changes that are always taking place in the business environment, who understand that the world doesn't allow the enterprise ever to remain static, and who can maintain an enterprise perspective about change in real time.

If senior leadership fails to articulate the case for transformation from the outset of the transformation effort, the enterprise might as well be Alice in Wonderland. At the end, the enterprise might wake up and realize the effort was only a dream (in other words, no fundamental change was successfully implemented). Or perhaps the transformation effort itself will suffer a fate similar to what almost happened to Alice just before she woke up—a (metaphorical) beheading.

Transformation, then, begins with a vision of what's possible. That vision emerges because senior leaders believe that something fundamentally different needs to be done to change the enterprise, and they believe the change possible.

To be sure, the strategic vision doesn't have to emerge full-blown from the most senior leader's mind. It can come from different sources. It may be an amalgam of what all the senior leaders envision. It could reflect what senior leaders witnessed somewhere else or were engaged in when they were part of other enterprises. The vision could flow from something that was read, something that opened up a senior leader's mind to the possibilities in the organization. There is no set recipe from a single cookbook for whipping up a strategic vision.

Urgency

Engaging the leadership in a transformation effort and keeping them engaged require believing in the urgency of taking action. The sense of urgency usually emerges from a potential change in the enterprise value proposition driven by changes in the external environment, stakeholder needs, the way the enterprise creates and delivers value, or some combination of influences.

When leaders recognize the need for change, they have a responsibility to take action. If the action they take, though, is nothing more than a statement that "We have to do something," their efforts will not lead to transformation. Leadership may not always know instantly what action to take. Nor will they always have the time for an exhaustive analysis of all alternatives (which typically takes place during conventional strategic and operational planning efforts). They must, though, analyze the need for change sufficiently to ensure that the enterprise's strategic objectives remain valid and that any action taken is aligned with achieving those objectives. A sense of urgency played out in this way avoids so-called analysis paralysis.

In essence, a sense of urgency, coupled with the real need to achieve a genuine strategic vision, is a key motivational factor in bringing along the entire executive management of the entire enterprise. Complacency is the enemy of transformation, whereas establishing a sense of urgency is one of the most important things required of a transformation leader. A lot of companies fail before they even get started with enterprise transformation precisely because they fail to establish a sense of urgency. They are sunk by their complacency, which is why a successful leader will do almost anything to create that sense of urgency.

In his book *A Sense of Urgency*, John Kotter even suggests that in the absence of an externally imposed crisis—what has come to be known in business parlance as a "burning platform"—leaders and organizations ought to torch their own platforms.[3] Kotter goes so far as to suggest doing things that take a tremendously confident leader, such as allowing a financial loss that creates a crisis, thereby exposing weaknesses vis-à-vis competitors.[4]

The link between urgency and genuine strategic vision cannot be overstated in the context of enterprise transformation. Consider the speech to the U.S. Congress by President John F. Kennedy, on May 25, 1961, when he urged the nation to "commit itself to achieving the goal . . . of landing a man on the Moon and returning him safely to Earth" before the end of the decade. Kennedy articulated a vision and conveyed urgency not simply because it would be a tremendous achievement to go to the Moon and not simply because of the gloomy mood of Americans in the wake of the failed Bay of Pigs invasion of Cuba a month earlier. Rather, as chief executive officer of the enterprise called the United States, he recognized the need for the enterprise to make technological advances that would give it a competitive advantage over its chief rival, the Soviet Union. Then he set out to rally the nation around that vision, to get Americans to believe that it should and could be achieved.

You don't have to be as charismatic as JFK to be motivational. Contrast Kennedy's style with that of John Wooden, the legendary UCLA basketball coach, who died in 2010. Wooden was known for his modesty and his character, and, although he gave many speeches, he was never famous as an orator. He was once described as "quiet as an April snow and square as a game of checkers . . . walking around in his sensible shoes and Jimmy Stewart morals."[5] Yet his former players speak with reverence about his motivational skills, not only in playing basketball but in living life. He placed enthusiasm as one of the cornerstones of his philosophy of success, as well as getting cooperation by giving it, not being afraid to fail, exhibiting confidence without arrogance, and being loyal to one's self and one's organization. He taught that success was not defined by victories. Wooden, as Hall-of-Famers Bill Walton and Kareem Abdul-Jabbar said so eloquently in paying tribute to him after his death, changed their lives.

Whether its leader has the charisma of a Kennedy or the quietude of a Wooden, what matters in a transformation effort is that the leader has to convey a sense of urgency for the need to effect change. If you lay out a genuine vision for the enterprise and convey urgency for something real, you can engage the stakeholders in action. You maintain the sense of urgency as short-term goals are set and achieved by keeping the long-term vision at the forefront of everyone's mind.

In the first block of the Roadmap's *Strategic Cycle*, you determine that you are going to undertake a transformation effort. What follows is the beginning of translating that decision into action.

Enterprise Thinking

As we wrote in Chapter 2, transforming an enterprise requires a new mental model that is based on immutable—but flexibly adaptable—principles and on the knowledge of how to apply those principles. Enterprise transformation in this book is based on a set of seven principles that evolved from lean thinking in the automotive and aerospace industries, from decades of testing of lean principles and their applicability in other domains, and from a subsequent set of enterprise principles that broadened the focus to include value creation rather than just waste elimination.[6]

Lean is the underlying concept, and hence the word appears in the title of our book. Traditionally, though, lean has been relegated to one or another silo within the broader enterprise, usually manufacturing or operations. From our perspective, this silo-based perspective is a major factor in the failure of so many transformation efforts. It is certainly a major cause of *only in my backyard failure*, as discussed in Chapter 3.

Enterprise transformation means that nothing should be seen in terms of silos. The entire enterprise must be part of the transformation effort. Every specific change objective must be viewed and measured in the context of what it means for, and how it will affect, the enterprise as a whole.

Again and again, we see organizations plateauing when they set out to achieve lean objectives because they don't have leadership support and because they are working within their silos without ever looking over the boundary. For instance, an aerospace company had been working for some time on making its manufacturing operations lean. The manufacturing team, though, just could not get the support required from either the engineering or supply chain management teams. Yet they need that support to work collaboratively on standardizing designs, including manufacturing considerations in the design, reducing the part count, and so on. The manufacturing organization could do only so much on its own and, as a result, the enterprise plateaued in its progress toward becoming a lean organization.

Only after an enterprise analysis was manufacturing able to break through to the next level. One of the steps taken was to reassign a senior engineer to lead final assembly operations, and a customer support executive was asked to manage supplier interfaces. Working together, the three functional organizations were able to make significant improvements in on-time delivery and customer satisfaction. As we've seen so many times elsewhere, a single silo may be able to make changes, but rarely can genuinely transformational change be accomplished without going across silo boundaries.

Hence, an early step in building the enterprise leadership cadre so critical to a successful transformation effort is for all senior leaders to become fully knowledgeable about the *enterprise thinking* paradigm. This means building an understanding that the enterprise will undergo a paradigm shift, one that will change fundamentally how the enterprise acts, learns, focuses on delivering value to all its stakeholders, and adapts to its environment. Senior leaders will need to spend time together, regularly and frequently, as they cultivate enterprise thinking among their team.

Enterprise thinking must be *learned,* and the old ways of thinking must be *unlearned.* This learning and unlearning process happens through experience and iteration—doing new things again and again. Observing and interacting with executives who have been engaged in enterprise transformation, reading case studies, and facilitated leadership sessions are all ways to inculcate enterprise thinking. The process of building executive buy-in fosters enterprise learning and thinking. Working to achieve buy-in is the first of several things a transformation leader must *do.*

Executive Buy-In

Typically, among an executive leadership team, some individuals will embrace the idea of enterprise transformation almost immediately. They will be excited, they will believe, and they will be ready to go. Others won't be so excited, and they will resist big changes. Maybe they don't see the need, or they don't want to undertake the work, or they're just averse to change. Still others will have a difficult time grasping the role they will need to play in change, and that lack of understanding is discomforting.

Yet an essential key is creating a shared understanding of the current situation in the enterprise and a shared vision of what is possible. We have said a bit about motivation, but what are the nuts and bolts of getting the entire executive leadership team onboard with a transformation effort? Sometimes all the internal discussion in the world does not accomplish the intended buy-in. People need to see a different way of operating, and they need to see examples of roles like the ones they will need to play, in action. This goes beyond benchmarking. You can consider a number of actions.

One approach we've found useful is to *go and see* what other companies have accomplished. You're not likely to get an invitation from your competitors. But you can bring your executive team to visit other companies in other industries that are successfully engaged in enterprise transformation. Such visits can provide a powerful boost to building executive buy-in.

Another approach is to *bring the successful transformers to you.* Some years ago, a firm that was going through its own transformation effort reached out to a large equipment manufacturing company that was then a leader in enterprise transformation and that had an incredible story to tell. As the firm's leader set out to take her executive team through the early part of the Roadmap, she had someone from the transformation leader come in and tell its story. The manufacturing company's transformation leader made the effort vivid and understandable, and the people on her team were wowed. They began to talk about how they might be able to do something similar. She also brought in a colleague from a company that had previously employed her; the colleague discussed things that had worked in enterprise transformation there and helped her team to see what was possible.

You can also talk to, and have your team talk to, other executives at *conferences and meetings.* Seek out people from companies that you've heard are engaged in enterprise transformation, and ask them what they're doing.

Finally, *bringing in knowledgeable outsiders* can help an executive team understand and embrace what needs to happen in an organization. Recently the CEO of a local company asked us to talk about enterprise transformation to his executives. He was looking for a way to inspire them, and our visit helped lay the groundwork for what was to follow. We talked about transformation at the conceptual level and shared some of our experiences and observations, making the process real for the team and helping the CEO build the buy-in he needed to move forward.

Executive Transformation Council

Before the enterprise embarks fully on its transformation path and heads into the Planning Cycle on the Roadmap, an Executive Transformation Council should be established to lead, oversee, and nurture the transformation. Typically, such a council comprises the top executives from each of the major organizations that together make up the overall enterprise. It is the enterprise-level governance of the total transformation effort.

For example, one enterprise we worked with was a multinational manufacturer of integrated guidance systems for a wide variety of vehicles. The Transformation Council comprised the vice presidents of engineering, operations, finance, human resources, and strategy. The line leaders were especially key. Often, Transformation Councils are chaired by a senior person who reports directly to the head of the enterprise. At this multinational, that person was the vice president of continuous improvement, who was a direct report of the CEO/president. His role was to make sure transformation projects were being implemented appropriately, to ensure their alignment with the enterprise's strategic objectives so goals were being achieved, to break down barriers, and to manage the process of measuring progress.

The council serves several functions. It is the body that approves the initial set of projects that will turn the transformation vision into an actual effort. (This is discussed in greater detail in coming chapters). A single decision body at this level is an important element of success. The council also participates visibly in monitoring performance. The council makes available the resources that are needed to succeed, and it creates a composite picture of where the enterprise is on its path to transformation. An equally important role of the council is to see to it that the appropriate education and training are provided across the enterprise. This ensures that the project teams have the requisite capability to progress smoothly and that everyone in the enterprise uses the same transformation-related vocabulary.

The council is also a place for those who may be responsible for discrete transactional aspects of the enterprise to come together and get the big picture of overall transformation progress. The council should be heralding and reinforcing successes.

Further, the council will play a key role in capturing the lessons learned along the transformation path and in diffusing those lessons throughout the enterprise. These latter two roles are critical in imbuing enterprise thinking within and across all the boundaries of the enterprise.

In short, an Executive Transformation Council leads, oversees, and nurtures the transformation.

How It All Comes Together

Debbie's own experience leading a transformation effort is illustrative of the role of leadership and how leadership is engaged. She had taken over an enterprise that had recently experienced massive cutbacks and layoffs, going from 700 to 400 people. These blows were just part of the changes buffeting the organization. Debbie saw that the firm needed to do things differently.

She set a vision of what the enterprise could become and began the process of bringing a key set of ten of her direct reports onboard with that vision. In some cases, she tapped executives who had been retained despite the layoffs. In some other cases, she recruited people from outside the organization. This group of enterprise leaders, motivated because they understood the need for change, began to refine the vision into what was possible. They created a story of what the enterprise would look like as the vision became reality. The story was about how the enterprise would operate: how it would work internally, how it would work with suppliers, the kinds of processes it would employ going forward, the information that would need to be accessible, the results that could be achieved, and so on. From there, the leadership team articulated the story in the form of a presentation that could be given throughout the enterprise, to create buy-in and to build the transformation outward so that it could become a bottom-up as well as a top-down effort.

The presentation—the articulation of the vision—set so-called stretch goals that showed what the enterprise should look like a year later, three years later, and five years later. It explained the key strategic thrusts for the enterprise to achieve those goals. The presentation was rolled out to groups of employees over the next few weeks, at sessions attended by Debbie's entire enterprise leadership. The message was clear: Here's our direction; we need your help; share your ideas.

As Debbie's enterprise segued into the Planning Cycle of the Roadmap, specific projects were rolled out and tasks were assigned. Measurements were set for improvement projects, and weekly reviews became the norm. Once each week, a different project team reported to the Executive Transformation Council on what the team was doing, what was needed, and how the leadership could help.

All of the projects were linked to the enterprise vision. Through these meetings and other larger meetings, the transformation effort broadened and widened as it captured the hearts and minds of more and more of the enterprise's stakeholders. The implementation of ideas generated feedback on the process itself, as well as lessons learned, which in turn were sent back out into the organization.

How did leadership know it had succeeded in imbuing the transformation effort into every nook and cranny of the enterprise? Debbie says that people at every level of the enterprise would come to her with ideas. Someone would say, "I know we just lost 40 percent of our people, and we're all working like crazy, but I have this idea that I feel strongly about." Colleagues would cover the regular work of other colleagues as ideas were tested in the context of the overall enterprise transformation.

As a result, the enterprise accomplished things way beyond its stretch goals. The supplier base was rationalized to reduce the number of suppliers by about 40 percent, and long-term agreements were struck with the most critical suppliers. Manufacturing lead time was cut by roughly 25 percent, and on-time deliveries rose to nearly 100 percent. In addition, product development lead time was reduced by 20 percent, thanks in large part to the creation of integrated product teams that involved the engineering and manufacturing organizations along with key suppliers. Quality numbers also went way up. Together, as surveys revealed, these accomplishments improved customer satisfaction. It all was made possible because of leadership in articulating a vision, gaining the buy-in of the leadership team, and taking that vision to the "masses."

A key message from Debbie's experience is that, if everyone doesn't understand what the enterprise transformation effort is all about, embarking on the transformation path is useless. It will be one step forward and two steps back, again and again. But with the leadership requirements achieved before entering the Planning Cycle, the results going forward can be nearly miraculous, beyond anything you ever thought possible. That's what was achieved in the preceding example: extraordinary results in a short time, with employees performing in ways that they could not have imagined and with dramatically improved and more valuable relationships with suppliers, customers, and partners.

If you are a senior leader and don't have the intestinal fortitude to undertake this journey, the rest of our book will be a waste of your time. Jim Hackett of Steelcase shows the kind of intestinal fortitude we mean.

As president and CEO of Steelcase, Hackett has led the company through major transformation. He began with Steelcase in 1994, when the company was still family owned. He oversaw the initial public offering in 1998. The transition from family-owned to publicly traded company is a huge undertaking for any major corporation, and for a leader who rose from the ranks but not a member of the founding family, the challenges can be daunting, to say the least. Hackett showed the skill and tenacity to see this transition through successfully. This included evolving Steelcase from a "work effectiveness company" in the early 2000s, focused on office furniture, to a company in 2010 that "creates great experiences." Through everything, Hackett has kept Steelcase true to its values.

Just how much intestinal fortitude has Hackett shown? Ten years after taking the helm at Steelcase, Hackett made a decision that cost the company a $40 million write-off and caused his team to lose their annual performance bonuses. Steelcase had discovered that some of the panels in its cubicle walls might not be up to the higher fire standards for floor-to-ceiling walls. Hackett overruled managers who wanted to ignore the problem—and even the customers who told the company not to worry about it. Hackett rejected all the rationales his managers gave for sweeping the problem under the rug. He had established a standard for Steelcase of unyielding integrity. If that standard were to be meaningful, Hackett reasoned, panels already out there had to be recalled and replaced with ones that met stricter fire code. Hence the big financial losses.

Jim Hackett's intestinal fortitude and his unflinching willingness as a leader to do what was right for Steelcase in the face of strong opposition were vindicated when the Department of Defense reviewed building materials at the Pentagon after the 9/11 terrorist attacks. The fire-retardant Steelcase panels had helped keep the resulting fire from spreading in a way that would have been even more disastrous.[7]

The most successful enterprises have senior leaders with intestinal fortitude like that of Jim Hackett. Absent senior leadership with courage, determination, and the stamina to see it through, there is no point in embarking on a transformation effort—assuming, of course, that *success* is the ultimate goal.

As Leonardo da Vinci once wrote, "I have been impressed with the urgency of doing. Knowing is not enough; we must apply. Being willing is not enough; we must do."

With a committed leadership in place, in Chapter 5 we set off into the Planning Cycle and explore the lenses through which you will assess the current state of your enterprise. The first lens is stakeholder analysis.

CHAPTER 4 TAKEAWAYS

⚠ Although enterprise transformation is both a bottom-up and top-down process, it absolutely must be driven by the top enterprise leadership and from the leadership's strategic vision.

⚠ To succeed, enterprise transformation requires a sense of urgency shared by the senior leadership team and communicated across the enterprise.

⚠ Transforming an enterprise requires a new mental model based on holistic thinking about the creation of value, not on the traditional silo-based view.

CHAPTER

—5—

The Stakeholder Lens

*He who wishes to secure the good of others
has already secured his own.*

Confucius[1]

WHEN IT COMES TO STAKEHOLDERS, most business school programs emphasize shareholders. The so-called quality move-
ment prioritizes the customer. Stakeholder centricity is a
fundamental tenet of enterprise thinking, but it should never mean
the primacy of a single stakeholder group. Every enterprise, in fact, has
multiple stakeholder groups whose needs must be met.

Who are stakeholders? Chances are that you have at least some
idea; the term *stakeholder* has been a part of the common management
vocabulary for a quarter century. One of the earliest definitions was
supplied by R. Edward Freeman, and it still rings true today: "The
stakeholder approach is about groups and individuals who can affect
the organization, and is about managerial behavior taken in response
to those groups and individuals."[2] Freeman also highlighted the need
for corporations to take their stakeholder needs and expectations into
account as they formulated strategy and to do so actively. This umbrella definition of stakeholder spawned considerable debate about
who really is a stakeholder and what role stakeholders play in determining a corporation's success. Answering those questions is a central
component of stakeholder analysis.

From an enterprise perspective, the concept of stakeholders
takes on even greater meaning. In our view, the enterprise is actually a
network of stakeholders configured by the flow of value, which moves

between the enterprise—which is also a node in its own network—and its stakeholders. Within that value exchange network, the enterprise must *satisfice*[3] those stakeholder groups, that is, it must provide sufficient value so that the groups are able to participate in the network. Implicit is the assumption that these stakeholder relationships are dynamic, evolve over time, and are deeply connected to the overall value proposition of the enterprise. The process of stakeholder analysis is the means by which that connection is made and is key to shaping and driving enterprise transformation.

At its core, stakeholder analysis is a process for aligning the enterprise with its stakeholders. The analysis not only brings to the forefront the disconnects and misalignments in the enterprise value proposition, but it also provides an opportunity for the enterprise to reflect on whether its value proposition is correct. This concept of finding an effective alignment of the enterprise's values to that of its stakeholders applies to every type of enterprise, be it a for-profit company, a nonprofit, or a government agency.

As Figure 5-1 shows, our approach to stakeholder analysis unfolds in four linear steps: identifying the stakeholders, prioritizing stakeholder groups, eliciting stakeholder values, and assessing the value exchange. The process is driven by the enterprise's senior leadership team, thus tapping into the deep knowledge of stakeholders they presumably have, but also building a shared mental model of the enterprise's stakeholder network.

Figure 5-1

Stakeholder Analysis Process

The first step is to determine the stakeholder groups and the key individual stakeholders within those groups. Since the objective is to gather data for analyzing the current state of the enterprise and its value proposition with respect to stakeholders, the number of stakeholder groups identified may prove too large. The enterprise then needs to make explicit the stakeholder prioritization that most organizations engage in implicitly and thus reduce the sample to a manageable size. An explicit prioritization process fosters enhanced transparency and better decision making.

When the enterprise has determined a manageable set of stakeholders representative of the current state, the value exchange between them and the enterprise is identified and assessed. *Value exchange* refers both to the value delivered by the enterprise to its stakeholders and to the value that stakeholders deliver to the enterprise. The data gathered from the stakeholders provide a perspective of the value they expect from the enterprise, as well as an assessment of the enterprise's performance in delivering that value. Furthermore, the gathered data make explicit the value the stakeholders believe they are delivering to the enterprise.

The performance of stakeholders in delivering value to the enterprise is usually assessed by integrating information from the formal mechanisms that many enterprises already have in place. In following a structured approach to identifying and prioritizing stakeholders and to gathering the requisite data, the leadership team can then assess the value exchange in a holistic manner. Needed transformation actions related to stakeholder value exchange will thus be grounded in data rather than in opinion. Having a structured stakeholder analysis process ensures that the enterprise can identify gaps in its value proposition and reconfigure the value exchange to ensure sustainable value delivery.

Let's look at stakeholder analysis in more detail.

Stakeholder Identification

Our process for identifying an enterprise's stakeholders begins with the senior leadership team. The objective is to answer this question: "Who matters to the enterprise?" The task is to generate a first-order list of the stakeholder groups relevant to the enterprise, to articulate who within those groups (be they individuals, organizations, or even, in some cases, entire markets) are essential and, in doing so, to build a shared mental model. In our own work with senior leadership teams, we've found that expert facilitation can help a team stay focused on the task at hand and provide an unbiased stimulus for discussions. Whether senior leaders do this with facilitators or on their own, the effort ought to produce a simple stakeholder map like the one in Figure 5-2, which depicts the high-level stakeholder groups identified by the top leadership team of one enterprise. This high-level categorization provides the broad sampling areas from which value data are gathered for later analysis. The map in Figure 5-2 is simple; the differences in roles and relationships among various stakeholder groups will become clearer as you read this chapter.

Figure 5-2

Stakeholder Map

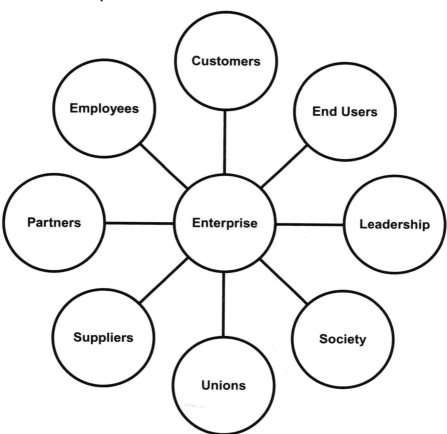

Table 5-1 defines the common stakeholder groups in Figure 5-2 (along with an additional category). The groups in Table 5-1 are typical of enterprises in general, but they may not all be relevant to your particular enterprise. To illustrate this point, consider Sierra Club, the oldest, largest, and possibly the most influential grassroots environmental organization in the United States. Although it is definitely an enterprise, it relies on donations from individuals and foundations; so an entire stakeholder group—shareholders—is irrelevant. The stakeholder identification process for Sierra Club would therefore substitute donors for shareholders.

Table 5-1

Common Stakeholder Groups

Stakeholder Group	Definition
Customers	Customers specify requirements and pay money in return for products and services delivered.
End users	End users specify requirements based on actual use or consumption of products and services delivered. They may or may not be customers. For instance, an airline is the customer, whereas the passenger is the end user.
Suppliers	Suppliers deliver products and services based on requirements specified by the enterprise in exchange for money.
Partners	Partners are suppliers with whom the enterprise has a close relationship, often involving risk and reward sharing, long-term interaction, and codependency.
Employees	Employees are all people who work for the enterprise, either directly or on site as contract employees. This category includes employees represented by unions.
Unions	Unions are formal organizations of employees who have banded together to achieve common goals, which could be better wages, improved working conditions, and so on. In organizations that do not have formal unions, this stakeholder group would include employee associations and other informal employee groups.
Leadership	Leadership internal and external to the enterprise provides strategic direction and allocates resources to be used by the enterprise. In some cases, leadership may include other organizational units.

Stakeholder Group	Definition
Society	Society includes the local communities where the enterprise exists and in which the enterprise does business (or operates). This often includes government representatives working at various levels (tax authorities or environmental compliance agencies).
Shareholders	Shareholders provide the enterprise with capital in anticipation of a return on investment.

For any given enterprise, stakeholder groups can be combined or expanded. Sierra Club might combine end users, customers, and society into a single group. Equal Exchange, a fair trade cooperative that distributes coffee and other products from farmer cooperatives throughout the developing world, could combine employees and share-owners into a single stakeholder group because it is worker owned. A second- or third-tier supplier, such as Aerovac Systems Ltd., which provides vacuum bagging systems to the advanced composites industry, may not see an end user stakeholder group as at all relevant.

The stakeholders identified as part of the stakeholder lens used by InfraProv,[4] a global information technology infrastructure provider, illustrates how broad stakeholder groups can be. InfraProv categorized its stakeholders in seven groups.

➤ *Customers* are found in many of the industries InfraProv serves.

➤ *End users* are those who use Web sites supported by InfraProv technologies (and they are a stakeholder group InfraProv believes one day will include everyone in its other stakeholder groups).

➤ *Leadership* comprises InfraProv's own executive team.

➤ *Employees* are those who work for InfraProv.

➤ The *partners* stakeholder group reflects that partnerships are an important part of the InfraProv stakeholder constellation; the enterprise partners with various companies to establish standards and develop innovative technologies.

➤ As a service company, InfraProv has a *supplier* stakeholder group, comprising suppliers that provide both hardware and human resources.

➤ Finally, InfraProv considers *society* to be a stakeholder group and interacts with this group both generally and specifically through its scholarship-granting foundation and the free services it provides to certain customers with socially conscious organizational missions.

Note that, depending on the size of the team undertaking stakeholder identification and on the size and complexity of the enterprise being analyzed, the number of stakeholders identified may need to be reduced to some manageable number.[5]

Stakeholder Prioritization

Although stakeholders are important to the enterprise, the enterprise must understand that it does not have a responsibility to deliver value to all of its stakeholders equally. Take Campbell Soup Company, which began an enterprise transformation effort in 2001. The goal then was to revitalize a company that had long been a leader in the food industry but that was facing stagnant sales in its core product category—soup. In Campbell's case, revitalization meant making long-term funding investments in marketing, innovation, infrastructure, and a competitive compensation structure. In the shorter term, one key stakeholder group, shareholders, found itself lower on Campbell's priority list. There was a 20 percent reduction in earnings per share in 2002, and the annual dividend went down 63 cents per share (which put Campbell on par with the returns of its peer companies).

Over several years, Campbell Soup Company evolved its transformation strategy from being primarily focused on revitalizing the U.S. soup market and finding new avenues of growth to a focus on the company's brands and on customers transitioning to products presumed to offer greater levels of satisfaction. Underlying these transformation efforts has been a consistent focus on the organizational enablers, whether enhancing quality while driving productivity or building organizational excellence, vitality, and diversity. Campbell's current strategic emphasis goes beyond the core elements of the enterprise's value proposition to include sustainability and corporate social responsibility.

The effort paid off for all the enterprise's stakeholders, and shareholders once again realized significant monetary benefits. In fiscal year 2008, sales increased to $7.988 billion from $7.388 billion in the previous year, and adjusted net earnings per share rose 7 percent. The company's three-year average of value returned to shareowners in 2008 was 7.7 percent; its peer group in the industry was 6.1 percent. Campbell Soup Company succeeded in constructing a value proposition that both appeals and delivers *to* its stakeholders.

Enterprises that undertake transformation efforts like Campbell Soup Company can prioritize stakeholders using either of two approaches: stakeholder salience or stakeholder relationships.

Stakeholder Salience

One challenge in putting stakeholders at the center of enterprise thinking is that it can be difficult for senior leadership to measure accurately the trade-offs among various stakeholders. Enter the notion of **stakeholder salience**—the degree to which the enterprise gives priority to different stakeholder needs. The creators of this idea contend that each stakeholder possesses one or more of three key attributes that are of interest to the enterprise:[6]

> ➤ *Power*: Stakeholders possess power in their relationship to the enterprise when they can gain access to coercive, utilitarian, or symbolic means by which they impose their will in the relationship.

> ➤ *Legitimacy*: Defined as "a generalized perception or assumption that the actions of an entity are desirable, proper, or appropriate within some socially constructed system of norms, values, beliefs, and definitions," legitimacy can exist in the absence of power. When combined with power, it creates authority.

> ➤ *Urgency*: Exists when the relationship or stake is either time-sensitive or of importance to the stakeholder's strategy and operation; its inclusion is the key attribute that provides a dynamic characteristic to stakeholder analysis.

Definitive stakeholders are those possessing all three attributes; *expectant stakeholders* possess any two; and *latent stakeholders* possess one attribute.[7] When prioritizing, salient stakeholders must be accounted for; after all, they can significantly influence enterprise transformation for better or worse. The definitive and expectant groups are key, but latent stakeholders cannot be ignored. Table 5-2 illustrates the attributes of each stakeholder type.[8]

Although there are limitations to computing salience quantitatively in order to compare individual stakeholders or stakeholder groups (especially gaining consensus among the senior leadership team regarding power, legitimacy, and criticality), visual maps can help. Figure 5-3 provides a high-level understanding of the stakeholder salience in the experimental certification for unmanned aerial systems (UAS) enterprise. In this enterprise, which is defined as the certification system, the applicant who is trying to get a system certified must work collaboratively with various elements of the Federal Aviation Administration (FAA) to determine whether the developed system is certifiable.

➤   The *definitive* stakeholders—those whose values must be met—are the applicant who has developed a product that needs to be

Table 5-2

Stakeholder Typology Based on Salience*

Type of Stakeholder (Grossi)	Type of Stakeholder (MAW)	Power	Legitimacy	Urgency
Definitive	Definitive	X	X	X
	Dominant	X	X	
Expectant	Dependent		X	X
	Dangerous	X		X
	Dormant	X		
Latent	Discretionary		X	
	Demanding			X
Nonstakeholder	Nonstakeholder			

* In the table, the first column of stakeholder types is based on a typology by Grossi, cited in Grossi, op. cit., whereas the types in the second column are based on a typology in Mitchell, Agle, and Wood, op. cit. The terms from the latter are subsumed by the more general terms of the Grossi typology.

Figure 5-3

Example of Stakeholder Salience Represented in a Map

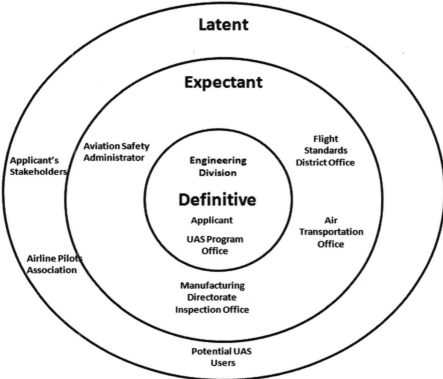

certified, the FAA engineering division charged with assessing the flying properties of the UAS, and the UAS program office that makes policy to guide the use of UAS in the national airspace.

➤ The *expectant* stakeholders—those whose values should be met— are all groups within the FAA, from the safety office to manufacturing and standards, that influence whether certification is given.

➤ The *latent* stakeholders—those whose values could potentially be met—are the applicant's stakeholders (including employees and shareholders), potential users of the system, and the Airline Pilots Association.

Stakeholder Relationships

The waterdrop model[9] (see Figure 5-4) was developed to represent the relationships between the stakeholders and the enterprise. This model is built on a concept called the *ladder of stakeholder loyalty*,[10] in which organizations build up their relationship with their stakeholders, growing them from potential stakeholders to advocating stakeholders. In other words, the goal is to evolve the stakeholder relationship from one that is adversarial and requiring constant monitoring and management to a collaborative relationship that is win-win for both the enterprise and the stakeholder. In the waterdrop model, the enterprise acts as the concentrator of all stakeholder activities. Using this model, the senior leadership team can visualize a wide range of stakeholder relationships, including (but not limited to) highly collaborative relationships, those with some collaboration, and those limited to formal transactions.

In the visualization, each stakeholder is shown in an ellipse. Connections between and across stakeholders are indicated in several different ways. Overlapping ellipses depict highly collaborative relationships with high trust and cooperation. A so-called water neck connects stakeholders that have some collaboration and coordination, with the length of the neck indicative of the degree of formality in the relationship. The transactional relationships are shown using a simple

Figure 5-4

Waterdrop Model of Stakeholder Relationships

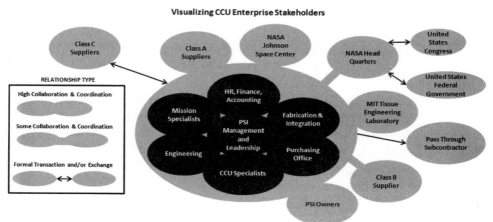

arrow, with the direction indicating whether the value flow is unidirectional or bidirectional.

This waterdrop model provides a single-shot representation of the current relationships between stakeholders and the enterprise, and it is a very useful tool for prioritizing. It can also be a powerful tool in identifying where stakeholders are disconnected from the enterprise in some way and in modeling the extended enterprise. These two concepts are discussed in coming chapters.

Consider the case of the Cell Culture Unit (CCU) Enterprise, one of the key programs at Payload Systems Inc. (which was acquired by Aurora Flight Sciences in 2007). The program was focused on developing one of the first habitats for long-duration life science experiments onboard the International Space Station. The habitat would allow scientists previously impossible opportunities to determine the role of gravity in the lifecycle of living organisms and to understand how cellular organisms and cultures adapt to microgravity over multiple generations. At the time of the enterprise analysis in 2003, CCU had successfully completed its preliminary design review and was entering the critical design phase.

The partial waterdrop model of the CCU enterprise (Figure 5-4) enabled the senior leadership team to visualize key stakeholder relationships effectively. In the model, Payload Systems Inc. (the prime contractor for the program) forms the core of the model, with key internal stakeholders represented in terms of the various functional organizations. Around that core are all of the primary stakeholder groups of the CCU enterprise. The enterprise maintains highly collaborative relationships with its key partner laboratories at NASA and the MIT Tissue Engineering Laboratory. The absence of these close relationships would have been an indicator to the CCU enterprise leaders of a serious gap, because space research requires significant communication, coordination, and collaboration.

In addition to these close-knit relationships, the CCU enterprise also has three kinds of relationships with its suppliers:

➤ A highly collaborative relationship with Class A suppliers providing critical program components that cannot be found elsewhere.

➤ A less collaborative relationship with Class B suppliers providing less critical components that can be substituted if necessary.

➤ A transactional relationship with Class C suppliers that provide commodity components.

Much less visible to the enterprise are stakeholders such as the U.S. Congress and the U.S. federal government, because their impact is felt through their funding of NASA headquarters, which in turn funds CCU. That is not to say that the CCU enterprise leadership team is not cognizant of these stakeholders. The waterdrop model enables the enterprise leadership team to identify the relationships with key stakeholders and then focus on the relationships that need greater analysis.

Stakeholder Value Elicitation

Most enterprises measure, in one way or another, how effective stakeholders are at delivering value to the enterprise. The stakeholder value elicitation process turns this around to focus on the flow of value in the reverse direction. Specifically, the process measures how the enterprise is doing in delivering *value* to stakeholders and how important that value is to stakeholders.

Again, value is the worth, utility, benefit, or reward that stakeholders expect in exchange for their respective contributions to the enterprise.[11] Once stakeholders have been identified and prioritized, what they value can be elicited. Table 5-3 provides an example of the values elicited from a parts and raw materials supplier of a given enterprise. The supplier, TrueMetal, identified the elements of the value ex-

Table 5-3

Value Elicitation Template

Value Expected from the Enterprise	Stakeholders	Value Contributed to the Enterprise
	Group Name: Suppliers	
↗ Fair and equitable treatment ↗ Timely payment ↗ Long-term relationships ↗ Joint forecasting ↗ Early and accurate requirements identification	TrueMetal	↗ Products (parts and raw materials) ↗ Design input ↗ Ideas and innovation ↗ On-time delivery ↗ High quality

change with the enterprise at both the strategic and execution levels. From the strategic standpoint, TrueMetal believed that a long-term relationship built on fair and equitable treatment by the enterprise would enable it to gain market share and to contribute ideas back to the enterprise. The supplier highlighted the need for early and accurate requirements identification, along with joint forecasting and timely payments, as key to enabling it to execute more effectively. This value, the supplier felt, would make it possible to create higher-quality products and increase on-time delivery rates.

The story of TrueMetal is not new to most enterprises, whether they are traditional manufacturers or in services. What makes this value elicitation step important is that it brings to the surface the current expectations of stakeholders. When these values are examined by the enterprise leaders, they can immediately identify disconnects. For example, consider the case of an employee who highlights the lack of meaningful nonmonetary rewards: Senior leadership can see that a key part of the enterprise's incentive system is not functioning.

We find that stakeholder value is best elicited by talking to stakeholders in an interview-like setting. Stakeholders can be asked to articulate what they value in their participation in the enterprise and what they expect in return for their participation. Their answers help create a first pass of the value flow between stakeholders and the enterprise. Asking stakeholders to rank the importance of their values and to rate the enterprise's performance in meeting those values provides important data for the next step: value exchange assessment. And asking stakeholders to articulate what they believe they contribute to the enterprise is a very effective way to assess whether there is a match between the mental model of what the enterprise expects from its stakeholders and the value being delivered to them. Table 5-4 is a template for the type of interview we find works well.

Stakeholder Value Exchange Analysis

The value exchange between each stakeholder and the enterprise can be analyzed using a simple matrix that depicts the stakeholder value and its importance, along with how well the enterprise currently delivers that value. The data that come from the value elicitation and value assessment templates can be visualized using a simple 2·2 matrix like the one in Figure 5-5, which shows how an enterprise stacks up in delivering what one of its suppliers values. You can see that, although the supplier feels that it is being treated fairly and equitably, it is not satisfied with how well the enterprise is delivering two of its values: establishing a long-term relationship and joint forecasting.

Table 5-4

Value Assessment Template

Stakeholder Group: *Supplier*

Stakeholder Name: *XYZ Company*

Questions to guide stakeholder conversation: What does the stakeholder value? What does the stakeholder expect from its involvement with the enterprise? What are the things that would make the enterprise be highly thought of by the stakeholder?	How important is this value for the stakeholder? 1 = low 5 = high	How well is the enterprise delivering this value? 1 = low 5 = high
Fair and equitable treatment	5	5
Reasonable ROI	5	4
Long-term relationship	5	2
Timely payment	4	4
Joint forecasting	4	1
Early and accurate requirements	3	1

A similar value assessment can be carried out for the value delivered by each stakeholder to the enterprise. Consider the case of Psych-Health, a hospital that is part of a large system of care that provides mental health services to veterans and their families. The stakeholder identification process resulted in the identification of 15 stakeholder groups, ranging from patients and doctors to taxpayers and politicians. The individual value exchange matrices associated with the value exchange between the stakeholder and the enterprise needed to be aggregated in a manner that made it easy for the enterprise leadership team to understand the overall relationship with their key stakeholders. This aggregation can be carried out using a simple 2×2 matrix (as shown in Figure 5-6).

You would expect a hospital to prioritize doctors and patients

Figure 5-5

Assessing Enterprise Value Delivery to a Stakeholder

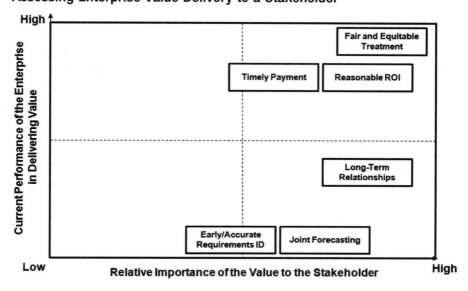

Figure 5-6

Current-State Value Delivery by the Enterprise to Key Stakeholders

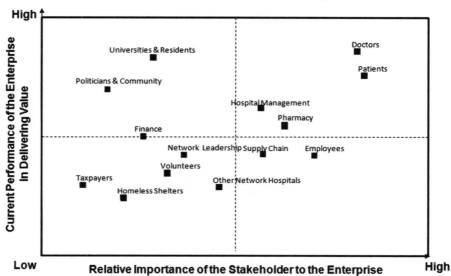

and perhaps even university researchers as stakeholder groups, but this case holds some surprises, including volunteers and homeless shelters. The enterprise leadership team justified the low aggregated values by highlighting that volunteers were of little help in the case of mental health services (though they were invaluable in other contexts, such as caring for terminally ill patients). Similarly, PsychHealth did not receive a lot of patients from the homeless shelters seeking mental health services, and they were not working with any of the local homeless shelters.

To determine the ideal value exchange between the enterprise and its key stakeholders, a simple table can be used to assess the importance of the stakeholder to the enterprise and the expected performance of the enterprise in delivering value to that stakeholder. PsychHealth's ideal value exchange with its stakeholders (shown in Table 5-5) had employees listed both as being extremely important, as well as being provided with sufficient value. A quick look at Figure 5-6 shows that, although patients are important and treated relatively well, they are not the group receiving the highest value from the enterprise. Employees, identified as important to the enterprise, were in reality being provided with low value. These insights enabled PsychHealth to revisit its ideal value exchange and develop the matrix shown in Figure 5-7.

Again, stakeholder centricity is an essential component of lean enterprise transformation. Although the old-school thinking may have been that the primary function of a corporation is to enhance the economic well-being or to serve as a vehicle for the free choices of only the corporation's owners,[12] in today's world, managing all stakeholders is foundational for long-term enterprise performance. Enterprises that focus solely on shareholders can no longer afford to ignore their stakeholders and hope to survive.

To be sure, all stakeholders are not created equal. It is imperative, therefore, to prioritize stakeholders; otherwise, effective analysis is impossible. And the importance of learning directly from stakeholders what they value and how they think the enterprise is performing cannot be overstated. Although a senior leadership team typically clearly understands the value that the enterprise derives from its key stakeholders, they may not always have the same understanding of the reverse.

Using the approach we've described, an enterprise can be ready to satisfice its various stakeholders in the current state and continuously reconfigure its value proposition to meet future expectations.

Table 5-5

Ideal Assessment for Importance and Value Delivery to Key Stakeholders

Stakeholders	Importance to PsychHealth (5 = high, 1 = low)	Value from PsychHealth (5 = high, 1 = low)
Patients	5	5
Doctors	5	5
Employees	5	5
Network Leadership	5	1
Community	3	3
Pharmacy	3	3
Supply chain	3	3
Hospital management	3	3
Universities and residents	3	3
Finance	3	1
Other network hospitals	3	1
Taxpayers	1	1
Homeless shelters	1	1
Volunteers	1	1
Politicians	1	3

Figure 5-7

Expected Value Delivery by the Enterprise to Key Stakeholders

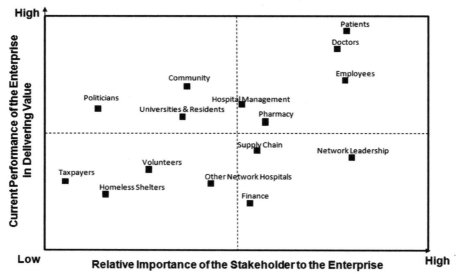

CHAPTER 5 TAKEAWAYS

⚠ Stakeholders must be at the center of any successful enterprise transformation.

⚠ This disciplined process of identifying stakeholders, prioritizing them, eliciting the value exchange, and collectively seeing value exchange enables the enterprise to create a crucial anchor point in its transformation journey.

⚠ Visualizing stakeholder networks using salience and relationships enables the enterprise to better understand the nature and dynamics of value exchange.

⚠ The value exchange analysis must account for bidirectional value flows from the stakeholder to the enterprise and from the enterprise to the stakeholder.

—6—

The Process Architecture Lens

If you can't describe what you are doing as a process, you don't know what you are doing.

W. Edwards Deming[1]

HIGH POWER ENGINES (HPE) is the pseudonym for an enterprise that designs, manufactures, and supports auxiliary power unit systems, miniature jet engines, and environmental control system products. The firm is part of a larger conglomerate, has a modern 225,000-square-foot facility, employs more than 650 people, and most recently generated annual revenues in excess of $250 million. Although successful, HPE has been facing some near-term challenges, including dealing with its large and aging portfolio of existing products and managing a volatile and fast-paced environment. Pressure has been mounting to operate with fewer and fewer resources.

In earlier responses to these challenges, HPE initiated localized, disconnected transformation efforts that resulted in high inventories and high management costs associated with continuously having to "put out fires." Employee morale plummeted, burnout grew, and innovation took a dive.

More recently, HPE's senior leadership team came to understand that successful enterprise transformation is impossible unless you understand the *enterprise processes*—the processes the enterprise uses to create value for its stakeholders. That requires mapping the *enterprise process architecture*—the structure of all enterprise processes together and how they interconnect and interact. So, to avoid repeating its past failures, HPE conducted an analysis of its process architecture to gain a deeper understanding of the dynamics of value creation within the enterprise and avoid implementing transformation projects that add no value or, worse, are detrimental to enterprise value creation.

Process architecture analysis for enterprise transformation integrates ideas from a number of approaches that are widely used by businesses and that include value chain analysis, business process reengineering, value stream analysis, and business process modeling. Each of these approaches is best suited for a specific unit of analysis. We draw on their strengths and avoid their weaknesses to create a method for a less narrow, more robust process architecture analysis that allows you to identify opportunities for transforming the way the enterprise creates and delivers value to its key stakeholders. (In Appendix B, we provide an overview of these other approaches and discuss some of their limitations.)

The approach to process architecture analysis focuses on the architectural interactions between processes from a strategic perspective. It begins with identifying the key enterprise processes and their associated inputs and outputs. From that, you develop an enterprise process architecture that can be analyzed. The critical interactions are identified and analyzed. Those interactions are leverage points—places where the flow of value to stakeholders, if inhibited, can be fixed.

Figure 6-1 shows the overall approach detailed in this chapter.

Identify Enterprise Processes

An enterprise process is a strategic, high-level, cross-functional activity involved in creating and delivering value to one or more enterprise stakeholders. Depending on the scale and scope of the enterprise, this activity may be—drawing again on the approaches discussed in Appendix B—what is typically referred to as:

> ➤ A *value chain*—a chain of activities across multiple organizations through which a family of products or services passes in order, gaining value along the way.

> ➤ A *value stream*—an end-to-end process across multiple organizations that delivers a specific product or service to a customer or consumer.

Figure 6-1

Enterprise Process Analysis Approach

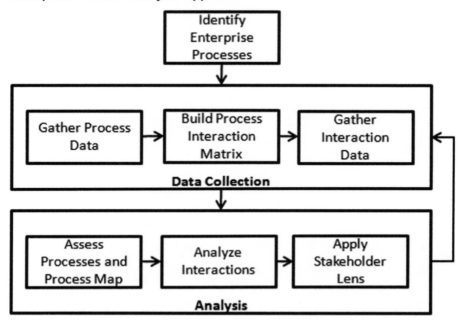

> ➤ A *business process*—a collection of related, structured activities or tasks that produce a specific service or product.

Enterprise processes encapsulate the interdependencies among the activities, people, and organizational structures.

An enterprise's process architecture comprises the set of processes that fall into three groups: Leadership Processes, Lifecycle Processes, and Enabling Infrastructure Processes; the research to determine these three groups was done at the MIT Lean Advancement Initiative.[2]

> ➤ *Leadership Processes* develop the strategic direction, alliances, and resource deployment decisions for the overall enterprise. Ultimately, enterprise executives use Leadership Processes to determine whether a new process should be created or an existing process eliminated.

> ➤ *Lifecycle Processes* are the core business processes of the enterprise. Through these processes, the enterprise adds value to its

products and services over their lifecycles from conception to phaseout.

➤ *Enabling Infrastructure Processes* provide the resources, information, and services required by Lifecycle and Leadership Processes.

Figure 6-2 shows an example of this architecture for a product-focused enterprise; a service-oriented enterprise would have different processes within the three groups. The taxonomy is a starting point for defining the enterprise processes that are specific to your enterprise.

HPE's senior leadership team identified the enterprise processes using these three categories as a starting point. At first, there were three

Figure 6-2

LAI Enterprise Process Architecture

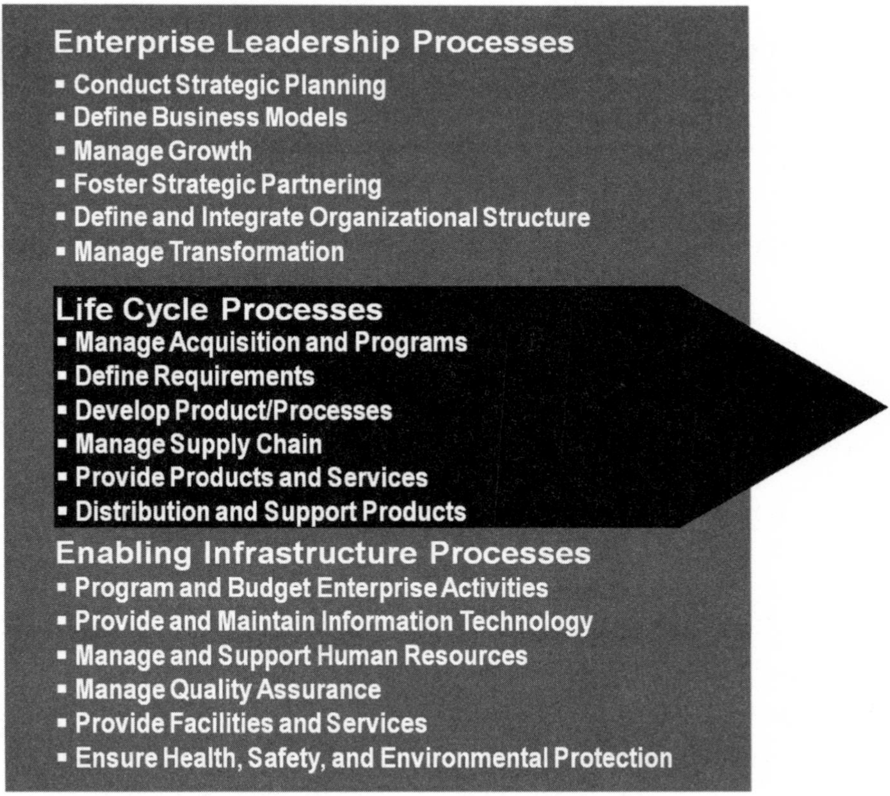

Enterprise Leadership Processes
- Conduct Strategic Planning
- Define Business Models
- Manage Growth
- Foster Strategic Partnering
- Define and Integrate Organizational Structure
- Manage Transformation

Life Cycle Processes
- Manage Acquisition and Programs
- Define Requirements
- Develop Product/Processes
- Manage Supply Chain
- Provide Products and Services
- Distribution and Support Products

Enabling Infrastructure Processes
- Program and Budget Enterprise Activities
- Provide and Maintain Information Technology
- Manage and Support Human Resources
- Manage Quality Assurance
- Provide Facilities and Services
- Ensure Health, Safety, and Environmental Protection

primary Leadership Processes: planning strategy, ensuring strategic communication within and across the enterprise, and planning for leadership succession. Further refinement led the team to expand this group to encompass the constituent subprocesses identified for the strategy planning process: strategic business planning, which focuses on overarching business strategy; strategic supplier planning, which focuses on overall supplier strategy and partnering arrangements; and mergers and acquisitions to support growth goals. Table 6-1 shows the five HPE Leadership Processes.

Most of HPE's five key Enabling Infrastructure Processes are either corporate-specified or outsourced, since the firm is part of a larger conglomerate; they are shown in Table 6-2.

Table 6-1

HPE Leadership Processes

Leadership Processes (Initial List)	*Leadership Processes (Final List)*
↗ Plan Strategy	↗ Strategic Supplier Planning
↗ Ensure Strategic Communication	↗ Mergers and Acquisitions
↗ Plan Leadership Succession	↗ Strategic Business Planning
	↗ Ensure Strategic Communication
	↗ Plan Leadership Succession

Table 6-2

HPE Enabling Processes

Enabling Infrastructure Processes

↗ Provide Financial Services

↗ Manage Human Resources

↗ Improve Quality Systems

↗ Maintain Facilities

↗ Ensure Environmental Health and Safety

For HPE, it turned out that identifying Lifecycle Processes became the major component of developing the enterprise process architecture. The initial identification yielded five key enterprise Lifecycle Processes: interface with the customer; manage programs; engineer parts/products; manufacture parts/products; and identify, manage, and grow suppliers. These, however, were insufficiently detailed to support the data-driven decision making needed for successful enterprise transformation. So the HPE team refined its list and identified 25 subprocesses within these five key Lifecycle Processes; they are shown in Table 6-3.

You cannot successfully analyze an enterprise's process architecture without determining the appropriate level of abstraction. At HPE, a degree of abstraction was chosen that ensured that accurate data could be gathered to support the analysis HPE needed for enterprise transformation. At the same time, it was not so detailed that key enterprise insights would be lost in the thicket. HPE could have continued to specify its Lifecycle Processes down to the individual tasks or activities, but the senior leadership team recognized the importance of developing a process architecture that would allow them to achieve a shared understanding of enterprise dynamics. There is little value, from this perspective, in specifying the subprocess in which, say, Joe on the engineering team enhances the tolerance of turbine blades in engine X and has to interact with Francine, who works on the certification of all turbine components of engine X. What is important, however, is getting to the subset that provides rich enough detail for decision making without creating analysis overload.

As the HPE team went through the process of identifying key enterprise Lifecycle Processes, a significant opportunity for improvement began to unfold. HPE realized that the enterprise's Lifecycle Processes create value in two main ways: developing new products and providing aftermarket services. The processes for both had evolved at different times, and a duplication of subprocesses could be corrected as part of the enterprise transformation.

Collect Enterprise Process Data

Once the enterprise processes are identified, data about them can be collected. We use a template like that in Figure 6-3, which shows the details of the strategic supplier planning subprocess at HPE. Data col-

Table 6-3

HPE Lifecycle Processes

Lifecycle Processes (Initial List)	Lifecycle Processes (Final List)
Interface with the customer	Marketing new OEM program/product
	Develop the business case
Manage programs	Go/no-go decision making
Engineer parts/products	Aftermarket order processing
Manufacture parts/products	Deliver products/parts
	Install products
Identify, manage, and grow suppliers	Manage OEM programs
	Manage aftermarket programs
	Forecast aftermarket demand
	Define requirements
	Develop preliminary and conceptual design
	Develop detailed design
	Test parts/products
	Assess reliability of aftermarket parts
	Certify parts/products
	Assemble preliminary units
	Assemble production units
	Manage product inventory
	Manage aftermarket parts inventory
	Repair aftermarket products/parts
	Develop program sourcing
	Negotiation with supplier
	Provide redline drawings and orders
	Supplier manufactures parts
	Supplier delivers parts

lection using the template involves answering a number of fairly conventional process analysis questions. Who has ownership of the process? What are the inputs to the process, and where do they come from? What actions are taken in the process, and how will it be executed? What are the outputs of the enterprise process and where do they go? The template allows you to go a step further in the data cap-

Figure 6-3

HPE Enterprise Process Data Collection

Enterprise Process: *Enterprise Strategic Planning*			Process Owner: *Jon Chapelle*	
Subprocess: (if needed) *Strategic Supplier Planning*			Subprocess Owner: (if needed) *Dave Stewart*	
Source Originated from	**Inputs** What	**Process** Description	**Outputs** What	**Destination** Where to
OEM Customer After-market Order Processing	Request for Proposals Demand Forecasts	Identify strategic partners for the future, and nurture current partners across the product development lifecycle	Supplier Ranking Annual Awards Select Supplier List Certified Suppliers	Supplier Develop Program Sourcing Manage Product Inventory
Metric Name/ Performance	**Request for Proposals** Clear Requirement/ Poor Supplier Content/ Poor Risk-Sharing/Good **Demand Forecasts** Contractually Shared/ Good Optionally Shared/Poor	**Overall Performance** *Average*	**Supplier Rankings** % Suppliers Ranked/ Average **Select Suppliers List** %Suppliers on Select List / Poor **Certified Suppliers** % Certified Suppliers/ Good	**Resource** Head Count: 5 Cost: $600,000 Key Personnel: Ricardo Mencia Dave Stewart

ture by looking at how the inputs, outputs, and overall process performance are measured (enterprise metrics are the subject of Chapter 7), as well as how financial and human resources are utilized in the process (resources are discussed in Chapter 8).

The data on the inputs, outputs, and the assessment of the measures associated with them are used for analyzing the enterprise process architecture. These data provide the ability to understand performance within a process and the process's potential upstream and downstream impact, but they may not allow us to understand the dynamics of the interactions as a whole. For instance, in the Strategic Supplier Planning process, information from the OEM Customer's request for proposals was being used as a key input. However, the requirements were unclear (*clear requirements* measure) and provided limited insights into what components would be built by suppliers (*supplier content* measure). Given that the overall process performance was rated "average," these data in the process data collection template allow us to do an analysis and identify potential process improvement opportunities.

The data on inputs and outputs highlight specific aspects of the interactions between processes or between processes and stakeholders, but they do not provide a holistic picture. To address this limitation, we gather additional data about interactions. The source and destination information from the process data collection template serves as a starting point for populating an Interaction Matrix, as shown in Figure 6-4. The process interaction matrix provides a simple way of understanding whether there are any interactions between key processes and between the processes and key stakeholders. This explicit identification of important interactions enables you to dive deeper to look at the interactions themselves. The top row in the matrix identifies all key stakeholder groups and enterprise processes, while the first column identifies all enterprise processes. In addition to the process-specific data gathered, the interaction matrix provides process owners and senior leadership with an opportunity to identify any additional interactions that may have been missed. Data are collected on what flows in the interaction, the nature of the interaction, and the quality attributes of the interaction.

We have found that most interactions can be framed effectively in terms of information, material, or resource flows. Given that enterprises interact with the same group of stakeholders in multiple ways, it is important to understand whether the interactions are reactive, proactive, or (in some cases) both. For example, HPE's interactions with legislators through the Ensure Strategic Communications process are both; it is proactive in lobbying for congressional support for new engine programs and reactive to new mandates and regulations from the Federal Aviation Administration.

Figure 6-4

Partial HPE Interaction Matrix

		Stakeholders					Enterprise Processes	
		OEM Customer	After-market Customer	Suppliers	...	...	After-market Order Processing	Define Requirements
Enterprise Processes	Strategic Business Planning	X	X	X				
	Strategic Supplier Planning	X		X			X	X
	Mergers & Acquisitions			X				
	...							

The key attributes of any interaction in which we are interested are:

➤ Stability—interaction occurs regularly, in a well-understood manner.

➤ Timeliness—interaction occurs when expected.

➤ Accuracy—interaction contains the right amount of information, material, and/or resources.

➤ Completeness—no additional information, materials, resources are needed.

Gathering interaction data between the OEM Customer and the Strategic Supplier Planning processes, we can see that information reactively flows to the process and that, although the interaction is on average timely, it is not stable, accurate, or complete. An important opportunity for improvement arises when the interaction crosses the enterprise boundary, either to an explicit process or to a stakeholder group. These interactions are central to the overall process analysis. Figure 6-5 is a template for capturing this information about interactions.

Develop the Enterprise Process Map

Given these data, building an enterprise process map is a matter of connecting sources to destinations. From the data in Figure 6-3, for example, HPE connected the Strategic Supplier Selection process to three other processes and two stakeholder groups. Upstream connections include the OEM Customer and After-market Order Processing process, and downstream connections include Suppliers, Develop Program Sourcing process, and the Manage Product Inventory process.

Enterprise process maps need to be kept simple enough to provide insights into the most important connections between enterprise processes. Typically, that means *not* creating a fully connected map with every process connected to every other process. If an enterprise with 35 processes created a map that showed inputs and outputs for all processes, the 595 connections would be nearly impossible to comprehend.

So how do you determine the most important connections? This is where capturing process-level metrics comes into play. The metrics captured at this point represent how the owner of the process measures the performance of inputs, outputs, and the overall process itself. The owner's metric is based on perception and may not corre-

Figure 6-5

Interaction Data Collection at HPE

Stakeholder Interaction: *OEM Customer - HPE*		
@ Processes: Strategic Supplier Planning		

What Flows in the Interactions?

		Interaction Assessment:
☒	Information	**POOR**
☐	Material	
☐	Resources	

Nature of the Interaction

☒ Reactive   ☐ Proactive   ☐ Both

	Low	Medium	High
Stability	☒	☐	☐
Timeliness	☐	☒	☐
Accuracy	☒	☐	☐
Completeness	☒	☐	☐

Discussion: *The strategic supplier planning process uses information from the OEM Customer's request for proposals as a key input. The information content in the RFPs to support planning is neither stable, accurate, nor complete. We are making "leaps of faith" when we use RFP data.*

spond to the perceptions of others. For instance, the process owner may believe the process provides timely information to suppliers and that the information is of a high quality. The supplier might rate the design information to be of a low quality. In Chapter 7, we discuss creating a systematic approach to measuring performance that serves the overall interests of enterprise transformation. At this point, it is enough to capture this "disconnect" because it is an area that needs further exploration.

When you collect data as part of enterprise process architecture analysis, you are finding the inputs and the outputs of the processes. Each input must be mapped to an output, and vice versa. If any outputs or inputs "dangle"—that is, cannot be connected—they provide information worth knowing. You need to go back and find the connection, have a rational explanation for the absence of a connection, or figure out that the connection might lie outside the enterprise. This is where the knowledge held by the transformation team comes into play. Mapping makes this knowledge explicit.

In HPE's case, mapping the processes identified connections that had been missed, even though the data collection had been quite rigorous. As senior leadership discussed the data, still more connections came to the surface. In this part of the enterprise process architecture analysis, HPE uncovered the duplication of processes mentioned earlier.

Analyze the Enterprise Process Map

The analysis of the process architecture begins with an assessment of the performance of individual processes. During data collection, process-level metrics are gathered on inputs, outputs, and the overall process itself. Poor performance of a process is a starting point for further investigation. When the performance of the process is seen in the context of other enterprise processes, it becomes easy to determine any systemic challenges and bottlenecks.

At HPE, for example, the process for testing products and parts was assessed as being poor, but the certification process for products and parts was deemed to be performing satisfactorily. During discussions, the senior leadership team noted that both OEM products and after-market parts were tested using the same process, but the certification processes were different. The poor performance of the testing process was the result of a tug-of-war between testing OEM products and testing after-market parts. Engineering had ownership of the testing process and a standard process for scheduling all testing activities. However, it was being forced into nonstandard operations due to pressures from the two vice presidents in charge of the respective product lines. During discussions and further analysis, HPE management was able to determine that OEM product testing was being forced to use a nonstandard process because it was not synchronized with product certification activities. Addressing this was critical for the transformation of HPE.

When you analyze the enterprise process architecture as a whole, you are essentially asking three questions:

> ➤ Is the enterprise process architecture designed to achieve the enterprise's strategic objectives?

➤ Are related enterprise processes positively coupled—that is, does increased effectiveness of one enterprise process result in the increased effectiveness of its related enterprise process?

➤ Is the enterprise process architecture as a whole designed to optimize stakeholder value creation and delivery?[3]

If the answer to the first question is no, the enterprise obviously has work to do. Disconnects are gaps that need to be addressed in the transformation plan, so that processes support the enterprise's overall strategic objectives. At HPE, improving Environmental Health and Safety (EHS) was a key strategic objective. When the senior leadership scanned the enterprise process map, there was little on the map beyond the single EHS process. Further investigation, however, showed that the two metrics being used to track EHS performance were both on track and that EHS-related processes showed alignment with the strategic objective. There was no need to map those processes in any greater detail.

With respect to the second question, two related enterprise processes that are not positively coupled present an opportunity for improvement in the enterprise transformation plan. At HPE, clearly there was significant duplication of processes in addressing the needs of OEM and after-market customers. These processes were not positively coupled; what the enterprise learned from building new products for OEM customers was not being transferred to support sustainment operations for after-market customers, and vice versa. In HPE's transformation plan, it might make sense to establish a project to harmonize these two processes and implement some way to improve knowledge sharing.

As for the third question, an ideal enterprise process architecture is optimized to satisfy key enterprise stakeholders. Doing so is an important starting point for designing the enterprise future state and is discussed in greater detail in Chapter 8, where we assess the alignment in the enterprise.

Analyze the Enterprise Process Interactions

Interactions within and across enterprise processes are critical to the success of the enterprise. Enterprises today operate with significantly reduced time, space, and inventory buffers, making operations more tightly coupled than ever and in turn aggravating the problems associated with making changes.[4] So, although processes facilitate what the enterprise does, tight interactions among and between them can also make it impossible to implement new ideas locally and successfully.[5]

Analyzing these interactions, though, is extremely complicated. Leaders need an approach that accounts for and coordinates the interactions among all enterprise processes. This is especially true with respect to value exchange with stakeholders. Every enterprise process must facilitate value exchange with one or more stakeholders. The most crucial interactions can be identified in the interaction matrix when looking at the various stakeholder groups and identifying interactions between them and the identified enterprise processes. In the data collection step, we emphasized the importance of the process owner completing the matrix. During the analysis phase, the senior leadership team must collectively assess whether any stakeholder related interactions have either not been accounted for or have been incorrectly mapped.

Figure 6-6 shows a partial enterprise process map for HPE. It enabled the senior leadership team to see the interactions between HPE's own internal enterprise processes and those of its stakeholders, as well as how these stakeholders interact. For instance, the initial interaction matrix showed that the strategic supplier planning process interacted with the OEM Customer and Suppliers, but the process map shows that after-market Customers interact with the process through the after-market Order Process, thereby highlighting an area for further investigation.

Not every enterprise process lies within the boundary of the enterprise. For example, each customer may have its own Request for Proposal process. Although the process is not controllable by the enterprise, it still needs to be mapped so that its impact on the rest of the enterprise can be understood. For HPE, process interaction with suppliers was particularly crucial. As one senior leader told us:

> In terms of importance to the future of the enterprise and identifying risks and opportunities, this may be one of the top two or three process interactions for us. Ultimately, we have to deal with demand fluctuation and unpredictability in an aerospace market forever changed by the events of 9/11. As our customer demand changes—delivery dates, quantity, quality—we have to reduce lead times and increase quality and capability levels by an order of magnitude in the supply base we are completely dependent on.

Figure 6-6

HPE Partial Enterprise Process Map

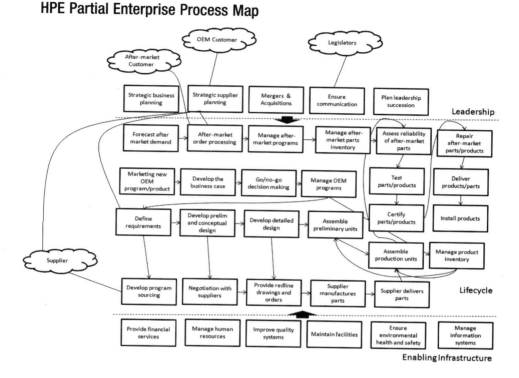

HPE already knew it had problems in its process interactions with suppliers, but only after an enterprise process architecture analysis could HPE see the way forward. During the discussions as part of the process interactions analysis, the vice president of engineering pointed out that a major problem at HPE was that manufacturing never delivered on time. The vice president of manufacturing countered that suppliers never provided the materials his organization needed so that manufacturing deadlines could be met and that the engineering team consistently failed to provide drawings and certifications that manufacturing needed. The interaction analysis highlighted that the problem was not just with suppliers, but internal to HPE—something that could be uncovered only though a structured enterprise process analysis.

Figures 6-7 and 6-8 show two example of this template used by HPE.

Figure 6-7

Interaction Between HPE and Suppliers in the Conceptual Design Process

Stakeholder Interaction: HPE- Supplier		
@ Processes: Develop Prelim and Conceptual Design → Program Sourcing		

What Flows in the Interactions?	Performance: POOR
[x] Information	
[ ] Material	Cross-Boundary Interaction
[ ] Resources	Yes [ ] No [x]

Nature of the Interaction

[ ] Reactive   [ ] Proactive   [x] Both

	Low	Medium	High
Stability	[x]	[ ]	[ ]
Timeliness	[x]	[ ]	[ ]
Accuracy	[x]	[ ]	[ ]
Completeness	[x]	[ ]	[ ]

Discussion: *Ideally we would involve our supplier during conceptual design, but our interactions are poor because we have no effective means of sharing conceptual design information – we have been successful with some selected suppliers but have been unable to replicate it beyond a program.*

Although the information collected may seem to be at a very high level of abstraction, the insights from the interaction analysis drive a significant number of transformation projects. Analyzing your enterprise processes provides valuable information about the current state of the enterprise, in preparation for enterprise transformation. Because you also need to know how well these processes are working, measuring enterprise performance systematically is another crucial piece of the Roadmap. That is the subject of Chapter 7.

Figure 6-8

Interaction Between HPE Engineering and the Manufacturing/Production Process

Stakeholder Interaction: Engineering - Manufacturing	
@ Processes: Assemble Preliminary Units → Assemble Production Units	

What Flows in the Interactions?

		Performance:
[x]	Information	**AVERAGE**
[x]	Material	**Cross-Boundary Interaction**
[ ]	Resources	Yes [ ] No [x]

Nature of the Interaction

[ ] Reactive   [x] Proactive   [ ] Both

	Low	Medium	High
Stability	[ ]	[x]	[ ]
Timeliness	[ ]	[x]	[ ]
Accuracy	[x]	[ ]	[ ]
Completeness	[x]	[ ]	[ ]

Discussion: *In the case of mature programs, our interactions between engineering and manufacturing are stable and timely – however, we are still struggling with accuracy and completeness when it comes to accounting for supplier components.*

CHAPTER 6 TAKEAWAYS

▲ Enterprise processes—Leadership Processes, Lifecycle Processes, and Enabling Infrastructure Processes—are the primary means through which the enterprise creates value.

▲ Identifying and mapping enterprise processes and creating a picture of them together as an enterprise process architecture enables you to see the mechanics of value creation within the enterprise.

▲ Most transformation challenges (and opportunities) can be found in the interfaces and interactions within the enterprise process architecture.

—7—

The Performance Measurement Lens

An acre of performance is worth a whole world of promise.

William Dean Howells[1]

E ACH WEEKDAY MORNING, the chief operating officer of Valero Energy holds a meeting with the plant managers of more than a dozen major refineries located throughout Canada and the United States. In his operations center at the company's San Antonio, Texas, headquarters, the walls feature a series of giant screens with a live display of Valero's so-called Refining Dashboard—Web-accessible gauges and charts that show how each plant and unit is performing to plan. With the data refreshed every five minutes, the dashboard "gives executives timely information so they can take corrective action."[2]

Imagine having that capability to measure performance in real-time at the strategic, enterprise level.

To manage enterprise performance, you must be able to measure it. Every enterprise attempts to measure its performance, usually with the expressed goal of uncovering things that will help increase overall effectiveness and efficiency. In our experience, though, few succeed at translating their measurements into action, as at Valero. Why? The reason has to do not with the effort *per se*, but with the measures that they use.

Some measures are simply ill designed or poorly integrated. However, even if they were useful when first designed and imple-

mented, performance measures tend to grow stale. They often aren't
adapted or updated to meet the enterprise's current realities. More
often than not, they don't produce measures that inform the making
of a holistic picture of enterprise value creation, which can be used to
support decision making at various levels of the enterprise. Instead of
serving the interests of effectiveness and efficiency, they become drivers
of ineffective and inefficient behavior.

In 1991, Robert G. Eccles of the Harvard Business School issued
a manifesto on performance measurement in which he made a bold
prediction: "Within the next five years, every company will have to redesign how it measures its business."[3] Some two decades later, many enterprises are still trying to find better ways of measuring performance.
However, those who have established measurement systems are finding
that, as the enterprise matures, their metrics and the underlying systems must also evolve.

The rate of change in the competitive landscape and the increased availability of information across the enterprise have accelerated the shift away from traditional accounting-based measures to a
broader set that accounts for multiple enterprise perspectives. The Balanced Scorecard (BSC) is one example that has found its way into widespread use. The BSC was adopted in companies throughout the
Western world beginning in the early 1990s after it was described in a
popular article.[4] It blends lagging indicators of performance (financial
measures) with leading indicators of future performance (nonfinancial
measures) to create a holistic perspective on enterprise performance. It
provides a framework for organizing strategic objectives into one of
four categories: financial, customer, internal, and learning and growth.[5]
The intent (although not always the result) of the BSC is to allow an
enterprise to go well beyond a simple checklist of measures to embrace
a more comprehensive system that captures the dependencies between
linked measurements.

Of course, our objective is not to tout the BSC but to highlight
the importance of creating an enterprise ***performance measurement system***—a system of metrics used to gather the performance data and information from throughout the enterprise that are needed to assess
overall enterprise performance. *Metrics* are the objective, quantified information collected to support decision making.

Research has found that the BSC can miss the contributions of
key enterprise stakeholders, especially employees, suppliers, and the
larger community in which the enterprise is embedded. Further, the
BSC framework has been found to have rather unclear provisions for

very long-term measures.[6] Both types of measures are crucial for enterprise transformation.

What matters most in enterprise measurement that supports performance management is not that you create a monolithic system that serves every need. We know of few, if any, enterprises that have anything of the sort. Rather, enterprises tend to have multiple performance measurement systems that focus on specific activities or functions. The key is to integrate the disparate systems to form an enterprise performance measurement system. That integrated system, at a minimum, must allow you to assess effectively how the enterprise is doing in meeting the value expectations of your key enterprise stakeholders by measuring the key components of value identification, value creation, and value delivery in the enterprise.

The Actual Metrics Matter

Obviously, the actual metrics used are at the heart of any performance measurement system. Metrics are the language of communication; they are how you tell others, across multiple levels of the enterprise, how well the enterprise is achieving its objectives. This communication of performance is for control, coordination, and collaboration with internal and external stakeholders. This information helps facilitate coordination across processes, which in turn leads to timely and accurate action that minimizes waste and improves overall performance beyond the individual component being measured.

Whether those who use the metrics understand fully every intricacy of every process does not matter. Metrics that are well designed and well communicated empower the user. They give the user a sense of knowing what needs to be done. They encapsulate the information that a user needs to take action. What you measure is important and valuable because, as two researchers once wrote, "You are what you measure."[7]

Enterprises must make a significant investment in selecting the right metrics and then in training and creating incentives to ensure that they can be used and that they are in fact used. This can be a significant challenge. Enterprises often stumble when designing, selecting, and using metrics.[8] Let's look at some examples.

The use of the inventory turns metric at GammaTech, a major aerospace and defense company, illustrates the problem of a metric that is not used consistently by the entire enterprise. The finance team measured inventory turns by looking back at total average sales divided by average inventory over the 12-month period of the previous fiscal year. The operations team, though, used a forward-looking formula—average orders to be fulfilled in the next 12 months divided by average inventory—to measure so-called inventory turns. The data used for computing the inventory turns metric are drawn from the same source. However, the term "inventory turn" has two different meanings, the metrics measure different things with the same name, and the results often led to contradictory actions. As one senior executive told us:

> Finance ordered the operations team to get rid of existing parts in order to improve the inventory turns. The inventory was required by operations in order to meet their schedule looking forward to the upcoming year. The inventory was reduced, and the operations team ended up spending an additional $60,000 to procure the same components again.[9]

Despite its best intentions in trying to design and select its metrics, GammaTech suffered from having a poorly designed performance management system.

At Procter & Gamble, an internal measure of service was the percentage of orders filled, tracked, reported, and acted on. The company was very pleased by its 99.5 percent accuracy rate until the metric was extended all the way to the store shelf. Then a different picture emerged: Certain products were out of stock between 10 and 14 percent of the time. The original metric was not really measuring what P&G needed to measure—namely, value delivery. Once this was realized, the supply network was redesigned from the store shelf back.[10]

Metrics used by one unit may drive local optimization, but they can come at great cost to the enterprise. When Hewlett-Packard introduced the Color LaserJet printer in 1998, the company noticed that the warranty costs of new printers accounted for about 25 percent of total warranty costs of all HP printers, even though these particular printers represented only about 3 percent of the high-end LaserJet units.[11] Various HP functional units saw warranties in different ways. Service & Support traditionally measured warranty cost, had the most control over how warranty services were delivered, and compiled the most data on product failures and warranty events. Marketing considered a warranty to be a product feature; offering long, attractive warranties made it easier to sell products, which made marketing happy. Conversely, reducing or changing warranties decreased product sales, and marketing would have to work harder. To the R&D and manufacturing organization, a warranty was part of product reliability and quality. These were characteristics over which the organization felt it had control because its teams determined product design and manufacturing methods. Hence, its measure was product failure. Finance served as the arbiter among these other units.

Consider how these different perspectives play out. For example, Service & Support can point to a high number of service requests and claim that the product is unreliable, while R&D and manufacturing can blame the high warranty costs on the inefficient delivery of service and support. This realization led to developing a new definition of warranties that was shared across the functional units.

Some metrics may inadvertently drive counterproductive behavior. For instance, some consumer electronics companies use the warranty call rate (WCR) metric to judge product quality. One company created an incentive for product quality improvement among its employees by giving bonuses for reducing the WCR by a set percentage in the next year. But because the WCR can hardly be influenced within a year's time, managers who knew they would not be able to satisfy the WCR criteria decided to work not for that bonus but instead for another bonus for improving time-to-market.[12]

In 2005, the U.S. Federal Aviation Administration (FAA) established a policy requiring the use of earned value management[13] on its major information technology investments, but a few years later could not ensure the validity of the reported earned value data.[14] Because the data had limited validity, contractors would report data for compliance purposes even if they were not necessarily using those data internally for managing their programs.

A major government agency defined objectives for its transformation that were neither measurable nor actionable. One of the goals was to "do better"—which only led to questions about what constituted doing better. Metrics cannot be at too high a level of abstraction if they are going to be useful.

We've observed several common problems with metrics:

➤ The metrics are defined and/or used differently by different people or organizations within the enterprise.

➤ The metrics do not correctly represent what is being measured or needs to be measured.

➤ The metrics are locally focused at the expense of enterprise performance.

➤ The metrics may inadvertently drive counterproductive behavior.

➤ The metrics are used solely for compliance purposes.

➤ The metrics do not provide information in a way that is actionable.

Select and Structure a System of Metrics

Mistakes like those in the preceding examples can be avoided. You simply need to use a structured process that allows you to select metrics situated within a holistic view of the enterprise and that are easily mapped to the enterprise value proposition. The process starts with a simple litmus test of existing metrics to determine whether they are SMART: strategic, measurable, actionable, relevant, and timely. (This acronym is widely used in business. In some cases, the letters of "SMART" signify different words, but the concept is essentially the same.)

➤ A *strategic* metric, whether it is more or less abstract, can always be linked to an enterprise objective.

➤ Data that are accurate and complete can be collected for a *measurable* metric. (Note that a measurable metric does not necessarily have to be quantitative; it can be qualitative as long as the criteria are clearly defined.)

➤ A metric is *actionable* if it shows a performance trend in a way that makes clear the what, when, and where of that trend. A metric must also be easily understandable across the enterprise.

➤ Enterprises have a tendency to measure everything, resulting in an explosion of metrics that are of limited use and that are in some cases downright confusing. A metric that drives action within the enterprise is *relevant*.

➤ Finally, a metric is *timely* when it reflects the actual state of the enterprise and its performance and when it is accessible to the decision maker so that corrective action can be taken when necessary, without delay.

An enterprise metrics dictionary ensures that metrics are well defined and well understood. It also functions as a communication mechanism within and across the enterprise. If GammaTech had defined "inventory turns" in a metrics dictionary, the company could have avoided the problems that ensued from the term meaning different things to different business units.

To build a metrics dictionary, we use a metrics definition template based on a measure record sheet[15] and design it to make certain that the metrics have SMART characteristics. The sample in Table 7-1 shows how this also captures a metric's connections to the enterprise value proposition: Overall Enterprise Customer Satisfaction (OECS) in the example is an aggregate metric that focuses on the satisfaction of all customers across multiple interactions with the enterprise. It is used to assess both overall performance with respect to customer satisfaction and alignment to the enterprise growth strategy.

Using the template, you first establish the metric's context (objective/purpose, scope, and target). Ideally, the title should be self-explanatory, describing what is being measured. A clear title avoids any ambiguity with other metrics that may be used for similar purposes.

The next sections of the template address the mechanics of the metric. Given that the target is often a benchmark value that represents a trade-off between stakeholder values, crossing the target threshold should result in some action being taken. In the example in Table 7-1, the target is twofold: At least 98 percent of customers rate the enterprise at a 9 or higher in product and service satisfaction, and at the same time the overall customer satisfaction rating is greater than 95 percent.

Identifying who owns a metric and what action the owner is expected to take based on the metric is very important. A metric must be traceable to an owner who is responsible for collecting the required data and preventing the metric from going stale—meaning the metric is no longer driving the right action. Specifying the action allows for effective managerial monitoring and control.

Nike found great success when a metrics dictionary was created as part of a performance measurement system for the company's European operations. Metrics had been documented rather ambiguously before the project, causing communication failures between reporting employees and managers. Using a template increased the quality of the metrics and facilitated more effective communication about metric-related information. The dictionary made stakeholders more aware of performance measurement and enabled Nike employees to leverage reporting into a continuous improvement process by coordinating across various initiatives within the organization.[16]

The Nike example also shows how large a number of metrics an

Table 7-1

Metric Definition Template Example

Title	*Overall Enterprise Customer Satisfaction (OECS)*
Objective/Purpose	Measurement of overall customer satisfaction with the enterprise to ensure alignment with the growth strategy and assess performance of customer services
Scope	Addressing the enterprise, focusing on customer service and product development processes
Target	Rate over 9 in product satisfaction and service satisfaction by 98% of our customers, with an overall score greater than 95%
Formula	Annual survey $\times$ 0.2 + Product satisfaction $\times$ 0.4 + Service satisfaction $\times$ 0.4
Units of measure	Individual ranking on a scale of 1–10, with aggregated ranking in percentages
Frequency	Computed every six months; annual survey measured yearly; product satisfaction measured immediately after purchase, and whenever a complaint or service request is made; service satisfaction measured after every scheduled/unscheduled service
Data source(s)	Survey database: annual survey, postpurchase survey; service information system: service ratings; customer complaints systems: product complaints
Owner/action	VP of shared services: tracking of overall metric as well as the component metrics; initiating review when target is not reached to identify root causes
Comments	This metric is reported on the enterprise dashboard and will be revised based on analysis

enterprise might need. It begins with a handful of metrics at the enterprise level, tied directly to strategic objectives, and the number expands as the metrics are decomposed and spread out into lower levels of the enterprise. For Nike's European operations, more than 100 metrics were ultimately identified and defined. For a larger enterprise, the number of low-level metrics would be even greater.

For enterprise transformation, though, your focus first needs to be on establishing the enterprise-level metrics that are tied to your strategic objectives. In addition to being SMART, these metrics must be easy to communicate and easy to understand across the enterprise.

With so many metrics, organizing them in some useful and manageable way (beyond a dictionary) becomes critical. Most organizations have a hierarchy of measures. Some are enterprise-level metrics, used by the top leadership team to steer the enterprise strategically. Others are used by owners of processes and change initiatives to guide efforts tactically according to individual metrics that are used to monitor and control operations. An effective system of metrics should connect strategic-, tactical-, and operational-level metrics.[17]

Figure 7-1 offers one way to consider the connections between individual metrics, metric sets, and metric clusters as a system. *Metric clusters* are macrolevel indicators of enterprise performance. They are the enterprise-level metrics that provide the leadership team with concise, yet comprehensive, information on performance, and they are used in strategic decision making. Each metric cluster aggregates metric sets and individual metrics. *Metric sets* provide more detailed information about a specific area or process. They are derived from and

Figure 7-1

Architecture of a System of Metrics

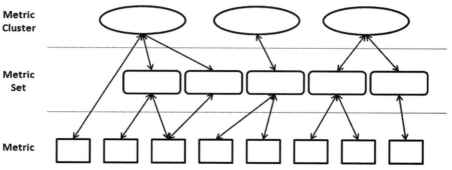

reflect stakeholder values and prioritized strategic choices; they are leading indicators of enterprise performance. *Individual metrics* are tied to an activity or task and are the building blocks for the system.

To illustrate the connections among clusters, sets, and individual metrics, consider the case of human resource metrics (Figure 7-2). A metrics cluster called Human Capital Management might comprise four metric sets: employee engagement, knowledge accessibility, workforce optimization, and learning capacity.[18] These metric sets are mapped collectively over the organizational practices that impact human capital management. The workforce optimization set can be refined further to comprise six metrics that measure whether work processes are well defined, training is effective, working conditions support high performance, high performance is expected and rewarded, hires are made on the basis of skill, and new hires complete a thorough orientation.

Most importantly, the senior leadership team must design the metric clusters, and the clusters should be derived from the strategic objectives and stakeholder values. At a major engine manufacturing company, the key enterprise metrics that were tracked were on-time delivery, delivered product quality, first-pass yields, past-due receivables, and return on invested capital. Each of these represented a key gap in stakeholder needs that needed to be addressed. The metric clusters drove the design and selection of metric sets and individual metrics. In organizations with a rich history of performance measurement, there will also be legacy metrics sets and metrics that influence the design of the metric clusters.

Figure 7-2

Example of a System of Metrics

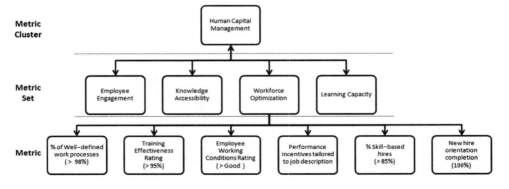

The system of metrics an enterprise uses should capture all the enterprise activities that influence performance.[19] It needs to be designed collectively to ensure that operational actions are connected to and driven by strategic needs.

Ideally, your enterprise will have what we call a *3C system of metrics*: complete, cohesive, and consistent. A *complete* system of metrics has metric clusters that cover all the strategic objectives of the enterprise. A system of metrics is *cohesive* when it has traceability from individual metrics through metric sets to metric clusters that are directly linked to strategic objectives. Finally, in a *consistent* system of metrics, no two related metrics in the system drive contradictory behaviors, and all metrics are used as expected.

Develop and Sustain an Enterprise Performance Measurement System

As you develop, coordinate, and manage individual metrics, metrics sets, and metric clusters, a performance measurement system begins to take shape. Ideally the system will be self-correcting and self-sustaining. In other words, using the performance measurement system will lead to needed changes in the system and will increase buy-in by the system's various stakeholder users.

At Grolsch, the development and adoption of a new performance measurement system for the logistics department was motivated by the need to have a system that served the top management team but that would also help employees at all levels of the enterprise achieve performance improvements.[20] To capture relevant aspects of performance quantitatively in designing its system, Grolsch focused on the identification, documentation, evaluation, and consolidation of existing local knowledge and experience and then on appreciating how it was being used. An understanding of the current state of metrics then served as a baseline to support either reusing as many of the existing measures as possible or creating new metrics as needed. Understanding the current state of metrics meant precisely defining existing metrics, their rationale, the data used for them, the limitations experienced when people used them, ideas for improving them, and ongoing or anticipated changes of information systems that could affect the performance management system. In effect, Grolsch developed a metrics dictionary and then assessed whether it met the 3Cs standard.

The team at Grolsch recognized how difficult it can be to find and use the right metrics. So they supported the logistics department as it experimented to find the appropriate metric at the right level of abstraction. By using metrics the individuals knew worked and experimenting with new ones, Grolsch was able to increase organizational effectiveness and the ability of stakeholders to communicate about measurements. By creating a culture that supports measurement and providing clear visibility into the dynamics of the performance measurement system, Grolsch has also increased the sense of ownership of the system among employees.

The story of Raytheon's Integrated Air Defense Center (IADC) in Andover, Massachusetts, provides an illustration of another lesson for performance measurement systems: Sometimes what works in one part of the enterprise might be a good candidate for expanding into other parts of the enterprise.[21] In this case, Raytheon is phasing it in across the wider enterprise.

Not long after the turn of the millennium, the economic performance of many of Raytheon's business units and programs were in sharp decline. This seriously jeopardized the future of the Andover facility. The company was experiencing a value crisis. Employees would have to be laid off and, without significant improvements, the facility would need to be shut down.

In 2000, the issue was how to cut costs to survive. Then a bold goal was set: reduce costs by as much as 10 percent annually going forward. To meet the objective, Raytheon built on process improvement efforts already underway. It created a Virtual Business System (VBS)—the name Raytheon's manufacturing organization in Andover gave to its performance measurement system—that evolved from a factory floor–level initiative aimed at deploying lean principles and practices. First, in 2002, IADC was reorganized along value streams to improve performance and to continue saving on costs. The Visual Factory initiative was launched in 2004 to consider how decision making could be improved by creating automated real-time display of data on the factory floor. Another major improvement initiative began in 2007 to create new dashboards for assessing the performance of various manufacturing programs that were being revived. The dashboards were specifically aimed at using visual analytics to assist decision makers at the program management office level. In 2008, Raytheon undertook a third extension of VBS, this time targeting the engineering group in an attempt to analyze engineering metrics in a manner that would facilitate the early identification of risks and opportunities. In parallel, Raytheon supported another project to bring the advantages of visibility and communication further upstream in the production process to manage uncertainties in the supply chain.

Figure 7-3 shows how the VBS system evolved at Raytheon to encompass a greater scope across the enterprise. The boundary of VBS has evolved considerably over time, increasing both the scope and number of users of the performance measurement system. It went from an original focus on manufacturing cells to encompass program management, engineering, and supplier management. As more stakeholders joined the performance measurement system, it helped create an environment of transparency and communication to ensure that the actions of one subset of stakeholders was not counteracting the intentions of others and impeding value flow.

The successful evolution of VBS at IADC can be attributed to several factors: It fostered a culture where the root causes of problems were identified without laying blame. As stakeholders understood and became less threatened by VBS, adoption came with less resistance, and stakeholder input was solicited and integrated into the systems. Given the rapid prototype potential of VBS dashboards, developers were able to get feedback quickly and incorporate not only user needs but also user wants. When employees made comments or suggestions, engineers or managers were assigned to address their inquiries and were made accountable for ensuring follow-up. Employees on the factory floor

Figure 7-3

Evolution of VBS Scope at Raytheon IADC

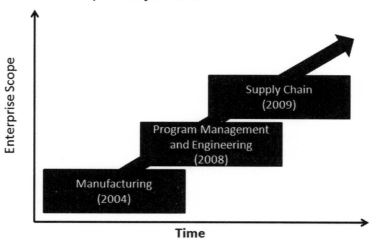

knew they would be heard, and they felt empowered to be proactive and to speak up about process or environmental improvements. Finally, developers actively engaged stakeholders by holding classes to teach employees how to use VBS, and they even ventured into their work-spaces to help troubleshoot whenever possible. Similarly, early adopters were empowered to teach their peers how to use the system and demonstrate the advantages they would accrue.

VBS is not yet a full-blown enterprise performance measurement system, but it is evolving and has the potential to become one.

Performance Measurement Systems and Transformation

The Grolsch and Raytheon examples highlight how important it is to develop an enterprise performance measurement system with SMART metrics that are complete, cohesive, and consistent. Ideally, the system will successfully serve five functions for the enterprise:

➤ *Monitoring* by measuring and recording actual performance
➤ *Controlling* by identifying and facilitating the closing of gaps between expected performance and actual performance
➤ *Improving* by identifying critical opportunities
➤ *Coordinating* by providing information for decision making and enabling communication across internal boundaries and with external stakeholders
➤ *Motivating* by encouraging performance and continuous improvement

An enterprise performance measurement system is linked to transformation efforts in two directions. One is that, in developing a performance measurement system, the task of analyzing the current state of metrics will lead to identifying opportunities to improve the enterprise. Conversely, the analyses, as described in the preceding chapters, that occur in the earlier stages of transformation—strategic objectives, stakeholder values, and process architectures—all inform the design of the enterprise performance measurement system.

To see how an enterprise performance measurement system works to support transformation, let's look at Baylor Health Care Systems (BHCS), a nonprofit integrated health-care provider based in the Dallas–Fort Worth area of Texas. BCHS began in 1903 as a one-building hospital and has since grown to a network of hospitals, primary and specialty care centers, rehabilitation clinics, senior health centers, and affiliated ambulatory surgery centers totaling some 3,000 beds.

In 1999, the BHCS board of trustees established an ad hoc quality measurement review committee tasked with identifying key health-care quality indicators and benchmarks and recommending plans to measure and improve the quality of care. The committee's recommendations included creating a multidisciplinary health-care improvement operations team across all BHCS operating units, introducing performance management incentives linked to clinical indicators, and ensuring that every board member is aligned with the strategic direction of the enterprise.[22]

All three recommendations were implemented through the establishment of a multidisciplinary Best Care Committee (BCC) and the introduction of new metrics linking management incentives to clinical indicators. The Best Care Executive Committee establishes the strategy and agenda for the BCC and ensures that it follows the six aims established by the Institute of Medicine to provide care that is safe, timely, effective, efficient, equitable, and patient centered. The BCC meets every other month to oversee planning, budgeting, execution, and reporting on all activities related to improving quality and patient safety.

"We had always had the perception of being the highest-quality provider in our market, but we wanted to prove it," explains Joel Allison, BHCS president and CEO. "People had always talked about quality, but measuring it was the challenge. As we saw more public reporting, we wanted to make sure that the information on us was accurate, and we wanted to be one of the leaders."[23]

BHCS has translated the six Institute of Medicine aims for health care into four pillars: "people, quality, finance, and service." This framework focuses the BHCS objectives and represents the metric clusters described earlier in this chapter. The quality objectives are measured using 27 metrics across four categories[24] that correspond to our metric sets: acute myocardial infarction, community-acquired pneumonia, congestive heart failure, and surgical care improvement. In addition to these metric sets, the team has metrics and metric sets to gauge additional improvement projects that the Best Care Committee defines. The architecture of the performance measurement system at BHCS is shown in Figure 7-4.

With the right performance measurement system and an understanding of its role in enterprise transformation, we move on to complete the assessment of the current state of the enterprise through an integrative focus on alignment, resources, maturity, and waste—the subject of Chapter 8.

Figure 7-4

Architecture of the Performance Measurement System at BHCS

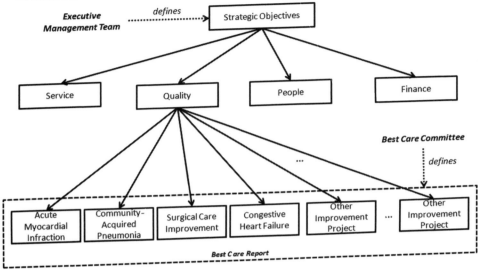

CHAPTER 7 TAKEAWAYS

▲ Metrics, which are essential for successful transformation, must be strategic, measurable, actionable, relevant, and timely.

▲ A performance measurement system comprises metric clusters, metric sets, and individual metrics with explicit definitions and traceable relationships.

▲ A performance measurement system is used not only to monitor and control the enterprise, but also to improve, motivate, and coordinate enterprise performance.

▲ A performance measurement system must be consistent (no two metrics drive contradictory behaviors), cohesive (there is traceability across individual metrics, metrics sets, and metric clusters), and complete (collectively, the metrics cover the key strategic objectives and stakeholder values).

CHAPTER

—8—

The Integrative Lenses

*Give me insight into today
and you may have the antique and future worlds.*

Ralph Waldo Emerson[1]

THE ENTERPRISE, armed with everything you have done so far along the Roadmap, is getting close to the point at which it can establish a vision of its future state. Before that, though, the enterprise must undergo several more elements to a rigorous examination so that the *current* state is clearly articulated. No vision of the future state can be achieved if it is not based on a clear picture of the current state.

Building on your strategic objectives through leadership (Chapter 4) and employing the data from the lenses of stakeholder analysis (Chapter 5), process architecture analysis (Chapter 6), and the analysis of performance metrics (Chapter 7), the next step along the enterprise transformation path is to gauge the current state of *alignment*. Understanding alignment provides a means of understanding the drivers of current-state performance and enables the identification of opportunities for improvement.

The Alignment Lens

Enterprise alignment—consistency among an enterprise's strategic objectives, performance measures, stakeholder values, and enterprise processes—is often the key missing piece to successful transformation. For example, you could have excellent strategic objectives for motivating the transformation, but, absent their alignment with the performance measurement system, the expected results may not be achieved. Similarly, the stakeholder values you have identified must now be linked directly to enterprise processes that provide those values. We have found that assessing the alignment (or lack thereof) of strategic objectives, performance measures, stakeholder values, and key enterprise processes will both increase your understanding of your enterprise and provide you with insights into the actions you can take, as part of enterprise transformation, to improve your enterprise.

This fourth lens is based specifically on the data from the lenses that precede it. We have found it could be quite difficult to get a true, holistic sense of alignment at the enterprise level. So we developed a tool—we call it the *X-matrix*—for assessing the data and creating that picture. We highly recommend you use the X-matrix; we have found it to be very powerful. It provides a very convenient way to display the data from your assessment of the enterprise thus far so that you can see clearly how strategic objectives, enterprise metrics, enterprise processes, and stakeholder values align with one another.

Figure 8-1 shows the template for the X-matrix. The X-matrix has four quadrants. The alignment analysis typically begins with strategic goals and metrics in the top left quadrant. The aim is to understand how well the measures your enterprise collects match the goals you are trying to achieve. Is the alignment strong or weak, or is there no alignment at all? A strong link is indicated by a dark square between the goal and metric. A lighter square indicates a weak link, and white (a blank) is the sign of no link. Misalignment may be an indication that metrics are not in place to track how well the enterprise is meeting strategic objectives.

The process continues through the next three quadrants, moving counterclockwise: metrics and enterprise processes; enterprise processes and stakeholder values; and stakeholder values and strategic goals, respectively. You are depicting the answers to questions such as:

➤ Do metrics flow down through the organization in a logical manner to measure process performance?

➤ Do the processes deliver the requisite stakeholder value?

➤ Do the strategic objectives, as determined by stakeholder value data analysis, represent stakeholder values?

➤ Are they well aligned with the stakeholder values?

Figure 8-1

X-matrix Template

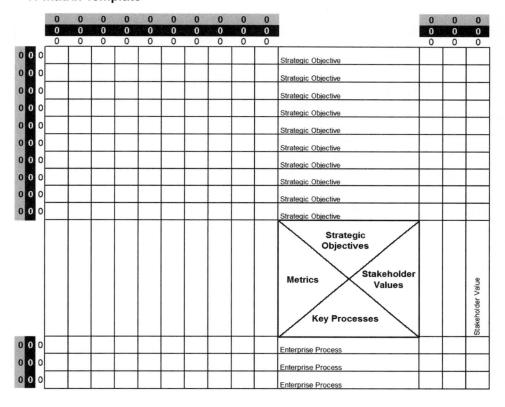

Using the X-matrix makes it possible to see at a glance how all the most important aspects of the enterprise align. It points out what needs to be done as part of the enterprise transformation.

Figure 8-2 shows a completed X-matrix for the upper left quadrant. It shows how well the metrics for a global personal computer developer and manufacturer serve the enterprise's strategic objectives. After we analyzed the metrics and determined which strategic objectives they measure, several issues became apparent. First, the strategic objectives that focus on improving the company's core competencies (such as manufacturing and distribution) have an abundance of metrics to track their performance. The strategic objectives that are new areas of focus, however, have relatively few metrics. For example, there

Figure 8-2

X-matrix of Alignment Between Strategic Objectives and Metrics at a PC Manufacturer

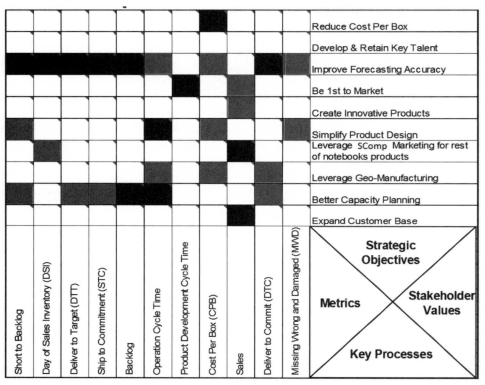

are numerous ways to track the accuracy of forecasts, but very few metrics related to creating innovative products. This indicates that the enterprise needs to do some work to align its metrics with the new strategic objectives, which in this case will soon be defining the future of key new products being introduced.

Another deficiency that Figure 8-2 shows is in the metrics associated with retaining and developing key talent. The enterprise values its employees and treats them quite well, but it still focuses on its products to the exclusion of human resources.

We have found that, although an enterprise does not need to have many of the boxes filled in, it does need to have at least one dark square for every column and for every row. Again, the X-matrix in Figure 8-2 shows that the personal computer enterprise needs to develop metrics for three of its strategic objectives: develop and retain key talent, create innovative products, and leverage geomanufacturing.

Figure 8-3 shows part of a larger X-matrix that compares processes and stakeholder values at the same enterprise. This X-matrix confirms the emphasis on manufacturing and distribution that we found in comparing metrics and strategic objectives. Eight key processes exist to ensure on-time delivery, an important stakeholder value. A number of design processes bring value to the customer through different avenues, including low cost, reliable performance, zero defects, latest technology, and customizability; superior design also benefits manufacturing. However, no key processes bring value to employees.

The software developer ZED used the X-matrix to determine

Figure 8-3

X-matrix of Alignment Between Processes and Stakeholder Values at a PC Manufacturer

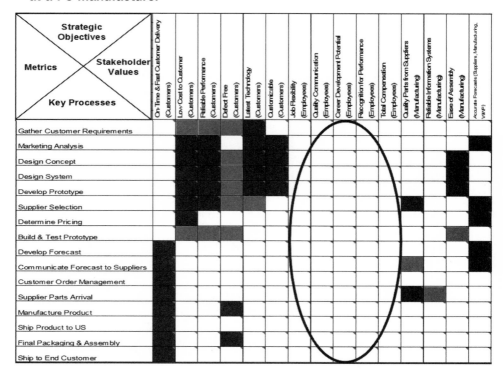

whether its strategic objectives (presented in Chapter 3) aligned with the enterprise's metrics. One of those objectives was to *grow in size*, that is, continue on its growth path in terms of revenue and full-time employees. ZED found that its metrics aligned well with that objective but that another objective, *improve brand recognition*, was less well aligned with metrics. An objective that was so important to the enterprise if it was to "go to the next level," as senior management put it, was a difficult one to measure, especially internally. The enterprise decided to work on enabling capture-and-win ratios as a metric.

The X-matrix analysis for ZED produced some very important information needed for transformation planning when it came to the strategic objective to *focus on larger projects*. A mismatch existed between that objective and the enterprise metrics. A focus on larger projects meant a focus on high-knowledge projects, and, other than counting the number of training modules delivered, ZED had no way to measure any focus on highly knowledge-driven tasks. Clearly, the gap uncovered an opportunity for the transformation plan.

The results of the alignment assessment feeds into the assessment of enterprise waste, which is the last section of this chapter.

The Resource Lens

How does the enterprise use its resources? Does it do so cost-effectively? What are the primary resource leverage points? Every enterprise today should be able to articulate where its resources are being utilized, what it costs to deploy those resources, and how those resources are being deployed. Answering these questions is the aim of this lens.

The purpose of assessing resources is straightforward. For instance, if you are trying to reduce costs, it makes sense to focus on where the biggest costs are, whether it is the cost of people or of materials (the two most common elements in many enterprises) or the cost of something else.

The process architecture lens (Chapter 6) serves as an organizing framework for analyzing the where and how questions on resource allocations. In fact, you cannot complete the resource lens without having done a process evaluation.

To create a picture of the enterprise's costs, you must identify the major sources of cost—for example, direct labor, facilities, overhead, and so on. Distribute these costs between the various categories, and consider how they are allocated between various product lines, if that is appropriate for your organization.

To illustrate how the resource lens works, let's return to High Power Engines (HPE), the enterprise introduced in Chapter 6. Table 8-1 shows the employee head counts associated with enterprise processes at HPE. Even though HPE considers mergers and acquisitions to be a critical enterprise process, no human resources are associated with it.

Head count, though, is not the only component of resource utilization. There are also time and costs. Consider lead time (the total time taken between initiating a process and actually completing it) and value-added time (the time that adds value to the process). Adding these resources to your analysis enriches your understanding of resource utilization. At HPE, the process of negotiating with a supplier has a lead time of 30 days, whereas the actual value-added time is only 12 hours, a ratio of value-added time to lead time of 0.01667.

Costs tend to be measured according to the classical functional and organizational divisions. Breaking down costs in an enterprise is a good way to check whether the enterprise is investing its precious transformation resources effectively. One enterprise we worked with claimed that the hiring and firing of factory workers was one of its core competencies, and the company had spent significant time reducing its direct labor. Yet direct labor accounted for only 10 to 12 percent of the production costs at the prime contractor level.[2]

If you don't truly understand your costs, you will end up wasting your transformation efforts on the wrong things. This effect, unfortunately, is something we see quite frequently. It's not difficult to grasp how much of a wasted effort the wrong focus can be. Consider an enterprise where production accounts for only 17 percent of the histor-

Table 8-1

HPE Leadership Processes Resource Analysis

Leadership Process	Head Count
Strategic Supplier Planning	4
Mergers and Acquisitions	0
Strategic Business Planning	5
Ensure Communication	2
Plan Leadership Succession	2

ical budgetary outlays over the lifecycle of a system.[3] If direct labor affects only 10 percent of the production cost, then the absolute maximum savings that could be realized by eliminating labor is 2 percent of the lifecycle costs. Taking the analysis further, if a maximum improvement of 20 percent is currently achievable from transformation efforts, an emphasis on direct labor results in an impact on lifecycle costs of less than 0.5 percent!

Figure 8-4 shows the enterprise cost breakdown at HPE. You can see three major spending areas: operations, engineering, and customer service. Intuitively, the HPE leadership team knew those were the areas that needed attention. The true power of the analysis comes from integrating all the lenses, rather than looking exclusively through the lens of resources. At HPE, even though the bulk of the enterprise's costs are in operations, those costs are outcomes of design decisions

Figure 8-4

HPE Enterprise Cost Breakout

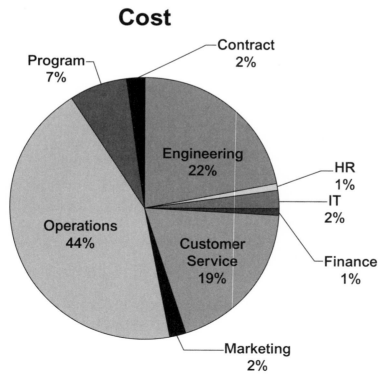

made in engineering. HPE knew this because it had determined its enterprise process architecture. The leadership team made improving engineering processes a key transformation area.

You can learn a lot from a resource assessment and breaking out the costs. For example, if the cost breakout reveals that 70 percent of your material cost comes from suppliers, you would know that cutting material costs requires that you address your supply base, not only your internal cost structures.

Some resource leverage points are related directly to process, particularly in the case of long cycle times, large amounts of resources being consumed, and/or interactions not working as they should. For instance, you may find that resources are consumed through processes where information doesn't flow well or where people from different organizations have trouble working together. This may also help to indicate where (or where not) to focus improvement activities to achieve the most benefits.

Focusing only on the direct cost breakdown is not sufficient. For example, you may commit only 5 percent of the total cost to product design, with materials, labor, and overhead comprising the rest of the commitments, at 50 percent, 15 percent, and 30 percent, respectively. At the same time, the focus of the transformation effort does not have to be on the largest cost component. Rather, what matters is that the true lifecycle costs need to be understood. Deeper reflection about costs reveals that, even though product design is 5 percent of the direct cost, product design has an impact on more than 70 percent of the total lifecycle costs.[4] The same point can be seen in knowledge work such as software development.[5] The enterprise has to focus on the enterprise areas that affect overall lifecycle costs, not just the ones with the highest value.

The Maturity Lens

The sixth lens focuses on assessing *enterprise maturity*—the extent to which an enterprise employs a variety of practices that are key to enterprise transformation. The maturity level assessment is an essential part of understanding the current state. By understanding the maturity of the enterprise, senior leadership can determine which leadership and supporting factors demand focus before embarking on the transformation effort.

The basic concept underlying maturity level ranking involves two steps. First, determine the most important factors in an organization's performance. Then define a series of levels that reflect progressively greater levels of capability as an organization matures in its performance of any given factor.[6]

In our enterprise assessments, we use the LESAT tool, introduced in Chapter 3. LESAT takes you through a guided self-assessment of maturity in three overarching areas of the enterprise. The maturity level assessment highlights key integrative practices at the highest levels of the enterprise. These practices are not all-inclusive, but the list is quite extensive and represents some of the more important behaviors that an enterprise must exhibit to succeed in enterprise transformation.

The first overarching area is *leadership*, specifically leadership for transformation. Through a structured appraisal of several dozen specific practices that derive directly from the Enterprise Transformation Roadmap, we gauge the enterprise's readiness for transformation in terms of strategic integration, leadership and commitment, value stream analysis and balancing, change management, and transformation planning, execution, and monitoring. These practices encompass enterprise strategic planning, the adoption of holistic enterprise thinking, a focus on creating stakeholder value, the development of enterprise structures and behaviors, transformation planning, implementing enterprise initiatives, and nurturing the entire process.

Typically, maturity levels are measured on a scale of 1 (lowest) to 5 (highest). For example, one of the leadership practices we measure is the lean enterprise vision of the leadership. The maturity levels are:

1. Senior leaders have varying visions of the enterprise, from none to well defined.
2. Senior leaders adopt a common vision of the enterprise.
3. The enterprise vision has been communicated and is understood by most employees.
4. A common vision of the enterprise is shared by the extended enterprise.
5. Stakeholders have internalized the enterprise vision and are an active part of achieving that vision.

Again, as we have explained from the very first chapter, the issue of leadership is at the very center of successful enterprise transformation. Assessing the maturity level of leadership practices helps establish whether the new mental model represented by enterprise transformation is shared—ultimately a prerequisite for success. You have to understand not only the actual maturity level of each leader, but also the variability in levels across the leadership to know what steps will be necessary to achieve that shared mental model and then move forward.

The second area we measure is the *maturity of Lifecycle Processes.* This encompasses all the enterprise-level core processes, including requirements definition, product/process development, supply chain management, production, and distribution and support. In this assessment, one of the practices we look at is the enterprise's understanding of downstream stakeholders and how that understanding allows value to flow seamlessly to customers. We measure the enterprise's maturity with respect to incorporating downstream stakeholder values (manufacturing, suppliers, etc.) into product and process design. The maturity levels are:

1. Manufacturing issues are considered late in design.
2. Manufacturing and assembly issues are considered earlier in projects, but in an ad hoc manner, and supplier and cost considerations are limited.
3. Multifunctional teams include some downstream disciplines and key suppliers.
4. The priorities of downstream stakeholders are quantified as early as possible in design and used for process evaluation and improvement.
5. Downstream stakeholders' values in the extended enterprise are quantified and balanced via trade-offs, as a continuous part of the process.

Finally, we measure maturity in terms of the enterprise's enabling infrastructure. This is an assessment of critical supporting processes—such as finance, information technology, human resources, environmental health and safety—embodied in eight practices. Enablers may be organization related or process related. An example of an organization-related enabler is that enterprise stakeholders are able to access financial information that they need. A process-related enabler is that processes are consistent and reusable.

Maturity level measurements involve a number of important diagnostic questions.

> Are common tools and systems being used across the enterprise?
> How well have the financial and accounting systems been integrated with nontraditional measures of value creation?

➤ How well can stakeholders retrieve financial information as required?

➤ Are human resource practices reviewed to ensure intellectual capital matches process needs?

➤ Are Enabling Infrastructure Processes being aligned to value stream flows?

➤ Do processes create the least amount of environmental hazards practical?

➤ Is the information technology system compatible with stakeholder communication and analysis needs?

Something we have observed repeatedly is that the assessment process itself is as valuable as the actual numeric maturity level results. The assessment is a way to begin thinking about strategically important areas, and it always increases the communication among executives who get together for a dialogue about the results. A structured assessment process helps create a common vocabulary for talking about the critical issues in enterprise transformation, and it also helps identify people in the enterprise who might need additional education about key transformation concepts. Nearly every time we go through the process, people in finance and human resources have a sort of awakening as they realize what is required of them to assist and be part of enterprise transformation. Creating a shared picture of an enterprise's maturity along all these practice areas is one way to identify the enterprise-level issues, the largest areas of opportunities, and the biggest gaps that must be filled to capture those opportunities.

The maturity level assessment helps make the next level obvious, too. Sometimes, an organization in the very early stages of transformation and at a low level of maturity may find it difficult to understand not only how to achieve higher levels, but even what those higher levels are. This possibility is part of the reason we have chosen to make the tools very specific, in contrast to some maturity level tools that use generic explanations (e.g., that 1 equals "beginning" and 5 equals "world class").

For example, assessing maturity level helped a multinational aerospace and defense conglomerate that had been actively working on and implementing a new Integrated Product Process Development (IPPD) program. Engineers had been sent to seminars for training, and lean practices were being implemented with stakeholders from manufacturing and suppliers. When we helped them do an enterprise assessment, they were disappointed, but not surprised, that they had failed to reach the highest levels of maturity in areas that had been their primary focus throughout the program.

Closer examination led to a number of key insights. One was that the president of the division was much more strongly committed to the enterprise transformation than some of his direct reports. The reports clearly did not take the initiatives as seriously as he did and thus failed to provide appropriate enabling support. Linked to this was that enabling functions such as finance, information technology, and human resources did not understand their role in supporting lifecycle areas such as product development and manufacturing. The finance organization, for instance, did not see a connection between sharing cost and marketing data and enabling others to make better decisions about new product development and supply chain management. Similarly, the human resources organization had not grasped its imperative to hire engineers who were more flexible and who could see the impact of their design decisions throughout the entire lifecycle. In addition, it was only through this enterprise assessment that the chief information officer began to understand how critical a product data management system was to the enterprise's ability to streamline new product development.

In short, enterprise assessment at the company provided an increased understanding of the critical role played by each part of the organization in enterprise transformation. What had been seen as something being done over in engineering and operations to achieve greater efficiency came to be viewed differently. Everyone, from senior leaders down, came to understand the strategic significance of an integrated, enterprise perspective and the collaboration necessary across the enterprise to achieve the maximum impact from the transformation effort.

In another example, the manufacturing division of a much larger conglomerate was chosen by corporate for a maturity assessment because it had the "best" assembly line. It had already done some good work on improving its operations but had plateaued. What was remarkable is that the maturity level assessment made it possible for the rest of the enterprise to learn that they were the cause and why. When the maturity level scores came in, corporate was surprised that they were so low. The assembly group, though, was not at all surprised. The group's problem all along had been its inability to get its division leadership to pay attention to, support, or even understand what it needed.

The maturity level analysis helped the rest of the division see for itself what the assembly group had been saying, and ultimately it led corporate to an understanding of what the entire company's role needed to be in a transformation effort. By assessing at the *enterprise* level, conventional boundary notions were broken down. People and organizations across the enterprise were able to see beyond the first-order effects of their actions to recognize the implications along the entire value chain.

The assessment served as an indicator of the problems and began to point to solutions. It showed that the manufacturing division was not getting the support it needed from engineering, marketing (in the form of forecasts), and particularly from information technology. With the information from the maturity level and other elements of the current-state assessment, the company developed a vision of the future state of the enterprise and a series of high-priority action items that addressed these shortcomings and that would help achieve the vision. They then sought and received high levels of commitment from senior leadership.

An important thing to remember about measuring maturity level is that not all areas need to be high to achieve goals. For example, if reducing time to market is a key strategic objective, then there ought to be well-integrated product development processes, which would suggest a high level of maturity. In another area, such as distribution processes, it may be fine to have a low maturity level because those processes are not as critical to achieving the strategic objective. Also, because some areas of the enterprise more broadly influence the enterprise as a whole than do others, achieving high levels of maturity in those areas is likely to have a more profound effect on the overall maturity of the enterprise.

We have also observed some very interesting relationships among the three overarching areas. Research on 31 aerospace and defense enterprises in the United States and the United Kingdom found that enterprises with high maturity in the Leadership Processes also exhibited high maturity in their Lifecycle and Enabling Processes. The leadership capabilities of the enterprise were strongly correlated to the change environment created, which in turn was strongly correlated to actual transformation efforts. The research also showed that, when enterprises have high maturity, they had formal information feedback mechanisms, which allowed the enterprise to develop transformation capabilities and to prioritize improvement activities more effectively.

Enterprises with high maturity had followed a transformation trajectory that reflected our Enterprise Transformation Roadmap.[7]

The Waste Lens

The seventh and final lens through which to build an assessment of the current state of the enterprise involves identifying *waste* that can be eliminated. This lens employs data from lenses 2 through 7.

Eliminating waste—an action, process, or activity that does not directly add value for a stakeholder but that still consumes resources—is one of the fundamental tenets of lean thinking. Traditionally, in the lean context, waste has been identified in seven categories: waiting, transportation, overprocessing, inventories, unnecessary motion, product defects, and overproduction.[8] Typically, production waste is assessed in these categories, but for our purposes the seven traditional categories have also been given an information spin.[9] This adjustment was necessary because we've found that, although information plays the same role in the product development value stream that material plays in the manufacturing value stream, this type of waste is all too often ignored in enterprise assessments. Table 8-2 shows the seven traditional waste categories and what they mean in terms of production and information.

To the traditional categories, we've added two additional ones—structural inefficiencies and opportunity costs—to create nine categories of enterprise-level wastes. Table 8-3 shows the nine enterprise-level waste categories and what they mean.

Using your analyses of stakeholders, processes, metrics, alignment, resources, and maturity, the assessment of waste has you look for obvious disconnects. For instance, an enterprise might actually be outperforming in some objectives because there is too much focus on a single area, to the detriment of other areas. Are some areas of strategic importance being neglected? The aim is to find potential sources of waste by identifying the root causes of these disconnects.

➤ Enterprise *processes* may also contain sources of waste. Using the current enterprise process maps and the process resource allocations described in Chapter 6, we look for whether the allocations align with the actual or estimated performance. If not, why not? We also look for sources of enterprise waste in the interactions among processes and stakeholders. Does information flow

Table 8-2

Traditional Categories of Waste

Waste Category	*Production Instances*	*Information Instances*
Waiting	Idle time in which no value is added	Idle time due to unavailable information
Transportation	Excessive movement of materials, tools, parts	Unnecessary movement of paper, people, bits
Processing	Effort expended that does not add customer value	Processing information beyond requirements (e.g., unneeded precision)
Inventory	Accumulations of materials beyond just-in-time requirements	Information that is unused or that is work in progress
Motion	Any human movement that does not add value	Any local human movement made necessary by poor information systems design
Defects	Any item that does not meet specifications	Any erroneous element of data, information, or intelligence
Overproduction	Producing more or sooner than required	Producing, duplicating, and distributing more information to more people than is needed

through the enterprise seamlessly? Are common tools used? Are they effective?

➤ *Structural inefficiencies* waste may be caused by things such as having too many layers of middle management, a tendency to view suppliers in an adversarial way, a lack of interconnectivity and interoperability with partners, or a failure to have mechanisms for determining and sharing customer needs and values.

Table 8-3

Enterprise-Level Categories of Waste

Waste Category	*Enterprise Instances*
Waiting	Idle time due to late decisions, cumbersome and excessive approvals, and unsynchronized enterprise processes
Transportation	Unnecessary movement (including electronically) of administrative information and people; multiple approvals and handoffs
Processing	Effort expended that does not increase value to any of the enterprise's stakeholders; can occur within the workforce, within management ranks, or across the entire enterprise
Inventory	Unnecessary levels of any enterprise resource: capacity, space, workforce, suppliers, information/data
Motion	Any human effort that does not increase stakeholder value
Defect	Erroneous results from defective enterprise processes and decisions
Overproduction	Any creation of enterprise outputs that does not increase stakeholder value
Structural inefficiencies	Waste resulting from inappropriate organizational structure, policies, business model structure, alignment, or strategies
Opportunity costs	Wastes resulting from lost opportunities (e.g., untapped talent in the workforce)

➤ *Opportunity cost* waste may result from remoteness from customers or inappropriate reward/incentive systems. It may be caused by a failure to view knowledge as a corporate asset, or having a workforce that doesn't feel empowered.

These are only a few examples of the many causes of enterprise-level waste.

Waste is often one of the central areas of focus for transformation efforts because the elimination of waste can provide a powerful opportunity for improvement. At a global naval services enterprise[10] with which we worked, the current-state opportunities included cutting non-value-added and/or wasteful steps from core enterprise processes, and the elimination of waste emerged as one of the most important elements of the transformation plan.

As part of the analysis, the team used the enterprise waste categories to develop a detailed list of wastes, which they then clustered into a number of "bins," as shown in Table 8-4.

The team also spent significant time analyzing the core enterprise processes (Chapter 6) to identify wasteful or non-value-added subprocesses. Through this effort, three wasteful subprocesses were identified in the enterprise's supply support processes and one wasteful subprocess in its change implementation process. Mapping the processes revealed possible improvements that could be made and gave the team a chance to interact with additional stakeholders. That, in turn, helped spread out the understanding of what the transformation effort was all about. This example illustrates how much can be learned in the current-state assessment by looking at waste.

Any assessment of waste must be linked to the assessment of maturity level. So we also review where low maturity in Leadership, Lifecycle, and Enabling processes might be contributing to enterprise-level waste. For example, the lack of executive commitment could result in projects that fizzle out due to lack of support. Meanwhile, a lot of wasted effort is expended, and the workforce grows increasingly cynical about improvement efforts.

Bringing the Lenses Together

Going through the steps of the Roadmap to define the current state of the enterprise is necessary for creating the future-state vision (the subject of Chapter 9). These lenses are where the opportunities for improvement are revealed. Each lens generates a list of opportunities for

Table 8-4

Waste at a Naval Services Enterprise

Category	Wastes
Customers	Opportunity costs from leaving fleet isolated from enterprise
	↗ Rework generated by requirement clarifications
	↗ Deployment, opportunity costs for users to generate technical data
	Quality reinspections and audits
	Unclear value proposition to end users
Suppliers	Inventories (people and facility resources)
	Rework generated by uncertain/changing requirements
	Inadequate metrics for efficient performance assessment
Information flow	Excessive reporting, misalignment with strategic objectives
	Multiple fractured/unfused information systems
Processes	Numerous wasteful and/or non-value-added core process steps
	Long wait times on external enterprise process interactions
Leadership	Misaligned strategic goals and enterprise objectives
	Inefficient use of metrics for managing the enterprise
	Poor metrics definition and enterprise linkage
People	Nonaggressive succession planning
	↗ Loss of knowledge transfer opportunity
	↗ Eventual manpower vacuum

change. They inform the future-state vision and ultimately the detailed enterprise transformation plan and associated transformation projects.

Assessing the current state of the enterprise is a catalyst to elevate improvement at the enterprise level and to enable enterprise transformation. It leads to a more holistic understanding of the role of Leadership Processes, core Lifecycle Processes, and Enabling Processes in delivering value. The assessment process is at least as valuable as the actual results.

When the resource consumption and readiness for enterprise transformation are combined with a deeper understanding of enterprise wastes, the initial areas to focus attention on in the enterprise become much clearer. You have a much better idea of where to apply resources in projects that will help achieve the enterprise's goals.

We cannot overstress that assessing the current state of the enterprise means just that—an assessment from a total enterprise perspective, not of individual functional areas. To be sure, traditional functional areas such as manufacturing are assessed, but they are viewed in the context of their place in the enterprise, not as self-contained business units. Achieving a total enterprise perspective also means assessing the strategic elements of leadership and their interrelationships with processes (using what we learned in Chapter 6). So, for example, a key area to assess might be the relationship between engineering and operations. That might entail assessing how well manufacturing and supply chain issues are integrated into the product design process.

In our experience, assessing the current state of the enterprise compels discussion of the critical practices for achieving enterprise excellence. The current-state assessment is an outstanding vehicle for disclosing differences in perception among leadership layers, from senior management on down. Often, we find a high level of commitment to transformation at the highest level of leadership. Then, only one level down, managers are "begging to disagree" with the perception of their bosses. Revealing something that is usually a failure of communication, not of perspective, creates an opportunity for discussion that is more valuable than any scores on any of our assessment tools.

With your results and a clear picture of the current state, you are ready to envision the future of your enterprise, the subject of Chapter 9.

CHAPTER 8 TAKEAWAYS

▲ Resource analysis, which looks at the enterprise cost distributions in terms of people, materials, and other expenses, identifies opportunities for better aligning resource expenditures with the overall enterprise strategic objectives.

▲ Seeing the resource distribution across enterprise processes helps uncover bottlenecks.

▲ An enterprise is aligned when its strategic objectives are reflected in the metrics used to measure performance, when the metrics effectively measure the performance of enterprise processes, when the processes provide value to the key enterprise stakeholders, and when the enterprise's strategic objective reflect the stakeholder values.

▲ Assessing the enterprise's maturity across Leadership, Lifecycle, and Enabling Infrastructure Processes unveils specific gaps in the ability to transform and can serve as a baseline against which to assess future transformation efforts.
    Eliminating enterprise-level wastes provides powerful opportunities for improvement and transformation.

CHAPTER

—9—

Preparing to Transform

First say to yourself what you would be;
and then do what you have to do.

Epictetus[1]

ALTHOUGH A DEEP UNDERSTANDING of the current state provides opportunities for change, the full impact of transformation occurs when there is a vibrant enterprise vision. What makes for a vibrant vision? It must be actionable and evolvable. It must be constructed as a collaborative effort by the senior leadership. And it must engage the entire enterprise in its realization.

Using the characterization of the current state and the opportunities that emerged from your analyses through the seven lenses, you can develop a vision along key dimensions such as organization structure, culture, processes, and knowledge. These diverse strands are then integrated with a refined enterprise value proposition to create a unified enterprise vision that can be communicated successfully to all stakeholders—and for which their buy-in can be won. With an actionable vision, focus can be put on filling the key gaps in the enterprise and capturing the strategic opportunities.

Do not confuse a vision statement with an actionable enterprise vision. Both are important, but they are different. Vision statements are sometimes quite brief, even a single sentence. Some companies print their vision statements on the backs of employee ID badges: "We strive to provide outstanding customer service" or "Our vision is to be the number-one widget company in the world in terms of sales, profitability, and overall customer satisfaction."

What is missing from most vision statements is that they do not spell out what the enterprise looks like when it is "the number-one widget company" or when it does "provide outstanding customer service." The visible component of vision is missing. By contrast, an actionable enterprise vision makes it possible to see the enterprise in a new way and in a new environment. It makes it possible to understand what it feels like to go to work at the "number-one widget company" and to imagine what customers say about the company. The visible part of the statement won't fit on the back of an employee ID badge. It is more dynamic than the vision statement itself, and it conjures up specific images.

In the first half of 2010, the television advertising in the area where we live was inundated with advertisements for a particular cruise ship line. The ad provided a good illustration of the difference between a vision statement and an actionable enterprise vision. We can imagine that the cruise line's corporate vision statement might be something like, "We provide the best vacations on the sea, ever." The TV spot, though, showed what that vacation might look like for the viewer. The ad is from the perspective of a young teenage girl. She is watching her father have the "best vacation." She says that she doesn't recognize him. His behavior is completely unfamiliar to her. He's dancing, having fun, and not checking his e-mail and phone messages. At first, she seems a bit horrified. By the end of the 60-second spot, she's fully engaged in the best vacation.

In a sense, the ad was a vivid description of an enterprise vision. It made visible what a best vacation might look like, and it engaged the girl in that vision. The entire family was transported to an entirely new place, and we don't mean just from point A to point B on a ship. Someone viewing the ad might be motivated to say, "Wow! I can see what a great vacation looks like. I want to be part of that."

There's nothing wrong with a vision statement. It's just not adequate for enterprise transformation. For that, you need a powerful image of what your enterprise would look like and be like in its future state.

Begin with the Current State

All too often, we see enterprises attempting to envision their futures not only without any analysis of their current state, but by starting with a look backward. This is especially true of organizations that have been successful in the past but have fallen on more difficult times.

Everyone yearns for the so-called good old days, and the future-state vision ends up being, in essence, an attempt to recreate the old days. "If we do what we did a few years ago," the leadership insists, "we will be fine."

Obviously, something has changed between those days and the present. The enterprise may have been the direct architect of its own failures, or it may simply have failed to adjust to a changing world, perhaps one with different customers and different customer demands, new technology, and an altered competitive landscape. How could you possibly create an actionable vision of the future without having assessed all those aspects of the present?

Envisioning the future state depends on the clear understanding of how well your enterprise is performing in its current environment, how well your enterprise processes are functioning (both individually and as a total system of processes), and how well your enterprise is meeting the value expectations of its stakeholders. As you answer these questions along the transformation path, using the lenses described in the preceding chapters, you surface, identify, and define opportunities for improving enterprise performance. Typically, an enterprise assessment uncovers numerous such opportunities.

Uncovering those opportunities, though, is not enough for enterprise transformation. Establishing a slew of improvement projects stemming from what is uncovered is also not enough for transformation. To transform an enterprise, you must have an enterprise-wide view of the future state. Each project can then be fit into the plan for realizing that future. Each project can then be about an overarching view of how to compete and deliver stakeholder value.

Transitioning from current-state analysis to future visioning must be handled deliberately. To get started thinking about all the possibilities for the future vision, we find it helpful to review some examples of other enterprise future visions or, better yet, to engage the transformation team in a visioning exercise. Here's an example of a future-state description prepared as part of an enterprise transformation undertaken to develop a system-of-systems systems engineering (SOS SE) capability in the U.S. Army:

> The SOS SE organization leads the synchronization of Army technical efforts and enables delivery of world-class integrated materiel solutions to the Warfighter. It is internationally recognized as the leader in conducting enterprise level trades and providing new advancements in frameworks, tools, databases, and knowledge. Knowledgeable people

collaborating as a virtual team across the Army, using an integrated SOS information technology infrastructure, perform systems of systems analysis and influence the Department of Defense's acquisition process transformation.[2]

Remember that you are setting out to describe an ideal state that is also *achievable*. As we begin to think about an enterprise's future state, we've found it helpful to think about a *pull system*. This concept comes from lean manufacturing, but it can be easily adapted to the overall enterprise perspective. Traditional manufacturing uses the *push concept*, producing large batches of product and pushing them downstream toward the customer, along the way to each downstream process, regardless of whether that process was ready for them. In essence, the pull concept starts at the other end, and in the context of enterprise transformation that other end is stakeholders.

Through the assessment of the current state of the enterprise, you have identified what value has to be delivered to satisfy your stakeholders. If you work backward through all the enterprise Lifecycle Processes and into the Enabling and Leadership Processes, you can trace the flow of value back through the enterprise and determine—at each point along the way—what must be pulled from an upstream process for the enterprise to perform. If you identify the characteristics of how each process must perform to meet the pull from a downstream process, you have created a very useful list of the characteristics of the future enterprise based on an idealistic goal of perfection.

Set Long-Term Goals

For your future vision, the transformation team should work together to create a set of goals for five to ten or more years in the future. The steps to do this are first to agree on the time frame and then think about what you want to have accomplished as an enterprise by that time. The goals should be something the entire enterprise can rally around. They must express what is, on the one hand, difficult enough to achieve that it cannot happen by accident and, on the other hand, something that is not so unreachable that no one is motivated to work toward their achievement.

We like to think of each goal as a Big Hairy Audacious Goal (BHAG, pronounced "beehag"), a term coined by James Collins and Jerry Porras in the mid-1990s. They define a BHAG as "an audacious 10- to 30-year goal to progress toward an envisioned future." We've adapted this time frame to the needs of enterprise transformation, where anything beyond ten years is typically too far in the future to fit into actionable plans.

Collins and Porras go on to explain, "A true BHAG is clear and compelling, serves as a unifying focal point of effort, and acts as a clear catalyst for team spirit. It has a clear finish line, so the organization can know when it has achieved the goal; people like to shoot for finish lines."[3]

The BHAG concept is ideal for enterprise transformation because a BHAG is difficult but achievable. We have found that a good rule of thumb is to create BHAGs that have only a 50 to 70 percent probability of being achieved, unless the enterprise really *stretches* its efforts. In other words, BHAGs should be stretch goals.

Coined by Jack Welch, the former CEO of General Electric, the term *stretch goal* is an objective that you cannot achieve easily through small changes or improvements; instead, you really need to extend, or stretch, yourself to the limit. It takes you and your enterprise beyond your current levels of performance, pushing you to work in different ways to meet targets that are more difficult than usual. Stretch goals take a new mindset. You can't achieve them simply by working harder. This again brings up the important need for leadership to communicate the rationale behind and the achievability of the BHAGs; people in the enterprise will reject the BHAGs outright as being impossible.

A set of BHAGs comprises the elements of an actionable enterprise vision. When we helped part of the U.S. Army along its enterprise transformation journey, this vision statement emerged: "Providing America's warfighters with the decisive edge." Obviously, such a statement is a far cry from what it looks like to be the enterprise that provides that edge. The BHAGs make it more real and very specific; they really stretch the enterprise if they are achieved. Here are the BHAGs that the Army Materiel Enterprise developed[4]; each one is a big, hairy, audacious goal:

> ➤ Equip units to 100 percent of Army Force Generation materiel requirements on time, every time, with a 33 percent cost reduction.

> ➤ Reduce delivery cycle time for requirements by 50 percent.

> ➤ Reduce Operations and Maintenance costs for systems by 50 percent through innovative research, development, test, and evaluation investments that increase reliability and reduce logistics, energy, and total lifecycle costs.

➤ Achieve 100 percent data transparency and asset visibility.

➤ Be a credible organization respected by all.

➤ Develop a skilled, professional, continually improving workforce and be recognized in the *Top 10 Places to Work.*

Articulate What the Future Enterprise Looks Like

When constructing an enterprise vision, your team should consider how it will become part of the enterprise's DNA. Ask what the enterprise will look and feel like when the goal has been accomplished. It is not enough simply to articulate a vision. It must be established in a way that makes it known and internalized by all personnel at every level of the enterprise, so that they can directly relate the vision to what they do on a daily basis.

How do you describe what the enterprise will look and feel like when the vision has been achieved? One good way is to imagine you are a reporter writing about your enterprise after your goal and its vision have been reached. What would you say about the way you do business? What kinds of evidence are there that the enterprise has reached its goal?

Over several months in 2009, we worked with the MIT Center for Biomedical Innovation as it conducted a series of workshops that brought together stakeholders from the broadly defined drug development enterprise in the United States. The workshops included participants from pharmaceutical companies, insurers, relevant U.S. government agencies (National Institutes of Health, Centers for Disease Control and Prevention, Food and Drug Administration), and clinical research services companies. These stakeholders constituted a consortium on new paradigms for drug development, NEWDIGS.[5]

Participants worked to develop a vision of a desired future state for the biomedical "ecosystem." Part of their work involved imagining they were reporters describing the enterprise when the vision had been achieved. Something like this was written for what they called "process future state."

August 20, 2019 (*Wall Street Journal*)—The first product resulting from a new therapeutic development process, a novel anti-cancer drug, has been introduced to the market and has already won great acclaim from patients, private insurance health insurers, advocacy organizations, and government agencies, including the Food and Drug Administration (FDA) and the Centers for Medicare and Medicaid Services (CMS). Lauding the willingness of all stakeholders to work together, Secretary of Health and Human Services Jane Dumont said, "This new paradigm has reduced the translation time from basic research to full medical uptake to four years from seventeen, and has slashed the all-up development costs to $826 million."

One of the hallmarks of the process, which uses the latest Web technology and a significantly improved clinical evidence infrastructure, is that it includes constant, real-time data sharing and complete transparency across the entire value chain and lifecycle between all stakeholders. A major contributor to the success is the new "iHealth" technology, derived from an original FDA real-time data submission tool, that was designed explicitly to monitor outcomes and safety. It also helps link outcomes to payment systems.

Standards development for health information systems has also contributed. Said Secretary Dumont, "This has led to the full application of new science and thinking about clinical trials, including adaptive designs and large observational, staged release."

As one executive involved in the new process explained, "We have succeeded in establishing a learning healthcare system across all stakeholders."

The exercise was used to develop multiple visions of the future state that were particular to various aspects of the enterprise. Something like this was written for the "policy and external factors future state."

August 20, 2019 (*Pink Sheet*)—John Parker, project director at Consumer Best Buy Drugs, announced today that significantly improved outcomes for patients are being realized thanks to a new willingness within the pharmaceutical industry to embrace early collaboration, industry-wide, in drug development, along with innovative risk-sharing payment mechanisms.

With a renewed focus on outcomes, stakeholders and industry are now collaborating to provide services to patients, which increases access to high-quality care and improves overall health.

"The pharma industry has taken a page from other industries that see their products as something more than a single deliverable," Parker said. "Just as no one buys just a cell phone but considers an entire package of the phone and services, drug companies are offering packages, too."

One example can be found among diabetes patients, who are benefiting from overall disease management programs provided by multiple companies that make different products but bundle them together so doctors can offer a unified, and personalized, approach to care that minimizes cost and maximizes effectiveness. Coupled with diagnostic tests that help identify patients most likely to benefit from targeted drugs, the value for all patients is improved and pharmaceutical firms secure market share in a targeted group.

"This is a win-win for everyone," Parker declared. "How do we know it's the right thing? It's been three years since the Clinical Effectiveness Research Institute has disapproved a new drug application." CERI advises regulators on the efficacy and safety of new drug therapies, as well as their overall effectiveness and value to patient populations.

Table 9-1 suggests some specific questions you might address as an imaginary reporter. Remember that your answers are about the future, and what you write should address the opportunities that have been identified for this particular area of the enterprise.

As you think through the questions in Table 9-1, you must consider the implications of achieving the future vision. The vision will affect the leadership and employees of the enterprise. Does it maximize the strengths and minimize the weaknesses of the enterprise? Does the vision challenge the current organizational culture or support it? (The answer to this question will suggest some aspects of the transformation plan.) How will the envisioned enterprise respond to current and future opportunities and threats? Capturing the answers to questions like these is an important element of ensuring that the vision is *evolvable* and that the transformation plan can adapt to both external and internal changes.

Align the Enterprise Infrastructure

At this point, you are nearly ready to develop a transformation plan. The last stop in the Planning Cycle component of the Roadmap, before identifying the gap-closing projects that will be a part of your plan, is to align the enterprise structure and behaviors.

Absent an enabling enterprise infrastructure, including the necessary organization, systems, policies, metrics, and incentives, no vision can be translated into reality. This infrastructure must be in place to support

Table 9-1

Future Vision Considerations

Category	Considerations
Customers	What does the customer relationship look like?
Suppliers	How does the enterprise interact with suppliers/ partners?
Information flow	How is information processed? How is information made available?
Processes	What does the new process architecture look like? How do processes interact with value streams?
Leadership	What are the characteristics of the enterprise leadership? How is enterprise performance measured?
People	What kind of working environment exists for employees? What kind of organizational structure exists to support the enterprise vision?

and drive enterprise transformation. This is also the time to ensure that the enterprise has the change agents in place that you will need to succeed. Although our approach in this book is senior leadership–driven, we have consistently emphasized the importance of leadership at all levels. These change agents are the people who lead the transformation projects comprising your transformation plan.

Aligning the enterprise begins with the *organization*.

Is the Enterprise Organized to Support Transformation?

The first thing to look at is the enterprise's structure, in the broadest possible definition of that term. The main question is whether the enterprise structure supports the vision or needs to change. If the answer is that it must change, you need to think about what those changes ought to look like and begin to design them for the transformation plan. A new organizational structure emerges in the specific context of the vision that the enterprise has articulated.

Let's say, for example, that you have identified as one of your BHAGs to streamline radically your time to market with new products and that you will do so by designing products that are easier to manufacture. You have articulated—perhaps in a faux newspaper article, as part of the visioning—a picture of the environment in which that happens. Now you must look at the existing organizational structure and identify what needs to change.

Perhaps your enterprise is organized with very clear product engineering and manufacturing silos. How do your design, manufacturing, and quality engineers interact? Do they exhibit an over-the-wall mentality, rarely working together or even communicating effectively, but simply handing off work from silo to silo? To achieve the vision of streamlined time to market, you may need to consider how your suppliers and their own manufacturing expertise might be added to the mix to achieve the objective. Maybe you will have people work in virtual teams across functional areas. Or perhaps you will colocate design engineering and manufacturing engineering and even have some supplier representatives working on site as part of a new procurement process.

All such choices imply the realignment of the enterprise's organizational structure. Software developer ZED tackled an objective like this by deciding to reorganize along integrated product and process development (IPPD) lines. Of the six priority recommendations the enterprise identified for its transformation plan, half were specifically about how the enterprise was organized. The plan included creating the position of vice president of innovation excellence, who was directly accountable to the enterprise's board and who was also responsible for quality and processes. The internal "Tendering" organization, responsible for ZED's proposals and contracting for prospective development projects, would be given a greater role in ensuring the consistency and completeness of each tender, as well as responsibility for analytics and feedback intelligence related to tenders.

Perhaps most significant, ZED decided to institute an effective matrix organization with project management practices and a strong project management culture that could underpin the enterprise's growth into a medium-size software business. The enterprise saw this as absolutely crucial to developing the organizational capacity and ability to streamline its projects that were needed to meet its strategic objectives. This wholesale restructuring into a matrix organization was characterized as more suited to the existing "project-based mindset" at

ZED and was expected to capitalize on existing strengths in ZED's open and fast-paced work environment. Meanwhile, management would benefit from a matrix organization in that it would help leaders focus on key stakeholders and projects.

Mindful of the dynamic nature of transformation, though, ZED articulated that its chosen restructuring approach might have to be modified as the enterprise focused more on its products and its product base.

As ZED learned, as long as there is alignment that supports the enterprise transformation plan, you will be on your way to success.

As with all the elements of aligning the enterprise infrastructure, you may uncover additional gaps that become important to your transformation plan. For instance, incentives—or the lack of them—may be an issue. All the changes you are about to make may require that people acquire different sets of skills and communicate in ways that have not been typically found in your enterprise. Do you have the incentives in place to encourage those changes? What rewards and recognition will you implement as part of your enterprise's alignment?

Does the Enterprise Have the Information Systems It Needs?

Information systems are a vital component of every enterprise, and they need to support the vision for successful enterprise transformation. Aligning information systems means determining what might need to be changed, created, or newly acquired. You must ask whether the systems talk to each other in ways that will support the changes to the organizational structure.

Alignment of enterprise information systems provides another opportunity to identify gaps and ways to reduce waste. Take, for example, the enterprise that reorganized along IPPD lines to reduce its time to market. Groups of engineers in different buildings were all using different CAD/CAM applications; they could not share their design drawings electronically. Aligning the enterprise information systems required resolving the incompatibilities among these applications.

Similarly, the same enterprise needed to ensure access to engineering and product data for relevant stakeholders throughout the process, from concept through design and manufacturing, and even into support and maintenance. Engineers needed mechanisms, enabled by information systems, that would allow them to communicate seamlessly and to share these data. Only when the systems were aligned and data were freely shared did the enterprise discover that it was manufacturing three identical gears, with three different parts numbers, in three different ways.

Depending on how you define your enterprise, you'll need to ask a number of questions to align your information systems. What are the information requirements? Do your systems meet those requirements? Are multiple systems attempting to meet them? With the answers, you can rationalize your systems and determine whether any might be integrated or eliminated—which could be a project as part of the transformation plan. You will also need to prioritize which systems you require because they are critical to your transformation and to figure out how to meet those requirements.

Will the Enterprise's Policies Promote Transformation?

Existing enterprise policies are often barriers to the achievement of your vision. It is not necessarily that the policies are bad but that they were devised and were appropriate for an enterprise other than the one you have envisioned becoming. Those policies need to be changed and aligned with the enterprise vision. For example, your vision may be of a more collaborative team environment, but your enterprise may reward individual effort to the exclusion of team effort. Clearly, such a policy will be a barrier to success and needs to be addressed.

Another enterprise we've seen set as an objective to work in partnership with its suppliers, but it had a very strict policy of keeping all data internal and rarely shared information with stakeholders. Still another was the enterprise that set a vision of reducing costs drastically. The objective required empowering stakeholders throughout the enterprise to take action, but the organization had a policy that kept all cost data locked up in the accounting department.

In short, you must examine your enterprise's policies, identify those that will inhibit new ways of acting that support the vision, and take appropriate alignment action.

Are the Enterprise Metrics Appropriate for Transformation?

How will you know when you have achieved your vision? An *actionable* enterprise vision is supported by enterprise-level metrics that measure progress toward achieving the vision.

In Chapter 7, in the context of current-state assessment, we detailed the importance of enterprise metrics and how to design a performance measurement system to support enterprise transformation. Now, having articulated an actionable enterprise vision, you need to make sure that your performance measurements are fully aligned with where you want to be in the future. Your metrics need to be aligned with your BHAGs as part of visioning the future state of the enterprise.

Who Are Your Change Agents?

Every successful enterprise transformation requires its own critical mass of change agents to lead the effort. They are not necessarily all senior leaders. They may be technical leaders, that is, people who have received training in one or another formal change method (e.g., Six Sigma). Or they may just be stakeholders who believe they can help shape the enterprise to be more efficient and effective and who want to commit to the task. Although some help may come by leveraging the knowledge and capabilities of mentors from outside the enterprise, and such assistance may be effective early on along the transformation journey, the enterprise must build its own capabilities. This is the only way to ensure that enterprise transformation becomes embedded in the organizational DNA. Hence, internal change agents must be identified.

Change agents need to enact the transformation at all levels of the enterprise. Identify where your potential change agents are in the organization. Are they spread out, or in only one or two functional areas? Part of developing your enterprise plan may be that you need to move some of your change agents to where they will be needed. If you haven't already done so, this is a good time to establish a Transformation Council, as discussed in Chapter 3. Eventually, everyone in the enterprise becomes a change agent to a greater or lesser degree.

Training and education may be needed to create change agents where they don't exist. Change agents need to be empowered with the authority to make transformational change happen and succeed. You will need to think about what that requirement implies for your organizational structure, incentives, and policies. Sometimes, change agents who see their projects fail and do not see the enterprise adopt the transformation perspective choose to leave and pursue the philosophy they have developed elsewhere.

Once you have aligned the enterprise infrastructure, you are ready to move along the Roadmap and create an enterprise transformation plan—the subject of Chapter 10.

CHAPTER 9 TAKEAWAYS

▲ The full impact of transformation occurs when there is a vibrant enterprise future vision that is actionable and evolvable.

▲ That vision begins with the current state, to ground it in reality, but describes what the enterprise will look like when it has successfully achieved some Big Hairy Audacious Goals.

▲ With that vision articulated, an enterprise engaged in a transformation effort must align its enterprise infrastructure with the goals of the vision and with its enterprise behaviors to ensure that people can carry out the transformation tasks.

▲ Every successful enterprise transformation requires its own critical mass of change agents to help lead the effort.

Transformation Planning

Do not be afraid of taking a big step—
you cannot cross a chasm in two steps.

David Lloyd-George[1]

YOU HAVE GATHERED INFORMATION on the various aspects of the enterprise, from strategic objectives and stakeholder values to enterprise wastes and misalignments. You have analyzed disparate pieces of the information to identify gaps in enterprise performance that needed to be bridged if your organization is going to achieve the desired vision of its future states. Now it's time to turn to the enterprise transformation planning process (Figure 10-1).

The transformation planning process is linked directly to the data and analyses that form the basis for defining and executing transformation projects, and the plan must be traceable to those data. It begins with identifying enterprise *focus areas*—areas in which an enterprise must concentrate its transformation efforts. The next steps are identifying, selecting, and sequencing projects that the transformation team believes will enable the enterprise to transform.

These projects will have been thought through in terms of resources, their relationship to other projects, and expected outcomes. They span the areas on which the enterprise needs to focus, but then they need to be made actionable. As the action steps are developed for each project at this strategic level, an overall transformation plan be-

Figure 10-1

Enterprise Transformation Planning Process

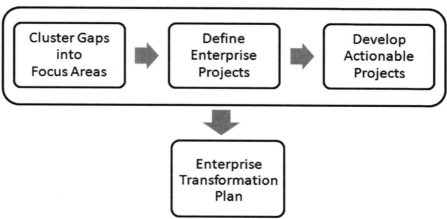

gins to emerge, with associated short- and long-term projects, the structure and sequence in which they will be executed, and how the transformation will be governed.

To see how the transformation planning process works, consider the case of ChipDesign, a semiconductor chip manufacturing company that faces significant challenges stemming from growth and from changes in its core technology. For example, ChipDesign uses a 200-mm-diameter wafer for building chips, whereas most of its competitors are using either a 300-mm- or a 450-mm-diameter wafer process. Using a larger-diameter wafer drastically reduces the cost of manufacturing chips. But ChipDesign's challenge is made even greater by the fact that upgrading existing facilities to handle the larger wafer is prohibitively expensive, even more expensive than building an entirely new facility.

Despite its technological disadvantage, ChipDesign has been able to secure new contracts to produce additional chips. So its transformation efforts have to focus on remaining competitive by lowering costs and improving output without changing the underlying technology.

The transformation challenge for ChipDesign is to create an enterprise agile enough to address the immediate needs of customers and also meet future needs in a changing environment. ChipDesign needs a long-term strategy that will allow it to maximize utilization of its production capabilities over the next ten years. In addition, the senior leadership team has to deal with an enterprise culture that assumes that change takes a long time. Even if product development takes a year or two, the ability to manufacture the product, once it is developed, typically takes three to four years. Most people associate this time stretch to the stringent conditions for semiconductor chip manufacturing.

To address these issues, ChipDesign's leadership team has undertaken an analysis that leverages all seven lenses as the basis for developing a transformation plan.

Identify Focus Areas

Focus areas are the levers of enterprise transformation. They emerge as a result of the discrete analyses described in earlier chapters, the synthesis that reveals gaps that need to be closed, and the opportunities that are uncovered and that can be exploited to close those gaps and move the enterprise from the current state to its desired future state. Clustered together, these opportunities constitute enterprise focus areas.

Your comparison of the current state and the future vision will identify the processes and functional areas that require the most attention. We've found that you need to answer a big question: Based on what you know about the current state of the enterprise, why isn't the future state currently achieved? In other words, what keeps the enterprise from having its future *now*? Typically, the answer to this big question can be found by revisiting the current-state assessment. Articulate the disconnects between stakeholder values and stakeholder value delivery by the enterprise. Ask whether the enterprise strategic objectives align with the value that stakeholders pull through the enterprise. You must also revisit the metrics. How do they measure enterprise performance? Do they do so in a way that allows you to gauge progress that supports achieving the vision?

You will already have identified the wastes that are evident in the enterprise. Can they be eliminated? What will it take to do so? Look at interactions in the enterprise, too. How can they be streamlined?

This exercise will help you state quite specifically what is imperative to get the enterprise from its current state to its future state. Articulate the top five or six highest-priority, highest-impact areas on which to focus. Determine whether the effort will require additional resources, skills, competencies, or technologies. Figure out a realistic time frame for achieving the enterprise transformation. You will be well on your way to having what is needed for an enterprise transformation plan.

The ChipDesign team used a template (Figure 10-2) to capture information about the 30 gaps and opportunities that had been identified earlier. A key part of the value of this template is that it establishes traceability to the analysis lenses that acted as the source(s) for uncovering the gaps, making any plan traceable to real data. The gap in Figure 10-2 concerns the uses of nonstandard processes for managing test wafers at ChipDesign. In chip manufacturing, given the significant costs of poor quality in production units, test wafers are used at various stages of the production process to verify and validate process and product quality. As many as three test wafers may be used for a single production wafer.

For ChipDesign, reducing overall enterprise costs is a key strategic objective, making understanding test wafer usage—one of the major drivers of overall enterprise cost—critical. As ChipDesign's senior lead-

Figure 10-2

Gap Identification Template

Gap: P2
Description: Our processes for managing test wafers are non-standard, have significant variation, and are increasingly becoming costly.
Root Causes: -Each product line manager specifies their own test wafer stocking policy - Process allows for escalation, and therefore use of more expensive test wafers -Test wafers are managed by suppliers, and there is no clear-cut way of knowing the true impact of our stocking policy - Our inventory management system does not capture required data
Source: (Circle Appropriate Source(s))  Alignment   Enterprise Maturity   Resources   Waste
Data Traceability: ChipDesign senior leader interviews, TestManager interview; ChipDesign Verification and Validation Process Data; Wafer Cost Metric

Stakeholder Values   Process Analysis   Performance Measurement

ership gathered data, they realized that they lacked a standard process for managing the use of test wafers. Product line managers (each of whom controls the development of a specific chip) basically define their own process for using test wafers. They have control over the type of test wafers used as well as amount of test wafer inventory needed for production. The analysis of stakeholders, processes, and metrics showed that a number of product lines were using the highest-quality, most expensive test wafers to meet their manufacturing deadlines because the actual test wafers they wanted were not in inventory. Without a standard inventory management process, it was difficult to identify the root causes of the increase in costs due to inefficient test wafer usage.

In the context of the enterprise vision, this gap became an opportunity for improvement. Depending on the nature of the gaps, a large number of opportunities may be identified. It is important to point out that, in our context, gaps and opportunities have a one-to-many relationship in both or either direction. In other words, an opportunity can address more than one gap, and a gap can be addressed by multiple opportunities. The focus areas emerge when these opportunities are clustered together to maximize the coverage of gaps and to enhance the connection between gaps and opportunities.

ChipDesign's CEO knew that transforming the enterprise was necessary to remain viable into the next decade. She knew she had an advantage in that the enterprise culture focuses on data-driven decision making. On the flip side, that same culture is risk averse and resistant to change anything that works. The transformation planning process would enable her to leverage the data-driven decision-making culture to overcome resistance to transformation.

The vision developed for ChipDesign centers on transforming the enterprise to be able to meet the needs of today by maximizing the effectiveness of how it currently creates value and creating new capabilities for the future. The vision articulates the need for reducing total enterprise cost by 20 percent in the next five years. In addition, the vision calls for an annual increase in R&D investments of $200 million over the same time frame. The senior leadership feels that the needs of today can be met through a combination of people, processes, and technology, while future needs will be met by creating new strategies and developing human capital.

Clustering ChipDesign's opportunities and gaps led to the emergence of four focus areas: *growth, people, operational excellence,* and *information integration,* as seen in Tables 10-1 and 10-2. Other typical

Table 10-1

Developing ChipDesign Focus Areas (I)

Focus Area	Gaps Addressed
Growth	SV1: We do not currently have a growth strategy that will allow us to remain competitive into the next decade.
	SV4: Employees have little to no clue about long-term plans of the enterprise, with respect to either technology or processes.
	SV6: Our decision-making processes are slow and disjointed.
	A1: Our functional structure prevents knowledge sharing between product lines, something that is essential for our long-term competitiveness.
	A2: Every product line owner believes that his or her issues have the highest priority. When it comes to growth, we need a shared understanding of our strategic objectives.
	A3: Our strategic objectives are misaligned with our stakeholder values (e.g., growth and learning)
	P4: Our enterprise culture is based on "thick walls" separating departments; as a result, we have information that exists in silos across the enterprise.
People	SV2: Our learning programs currently do not effectively support the development of human capital to meet future needs.
	SV4: Employees have little to no clue about long-term plans of the enterprise, with respect to either technology or processes.
	A1: Our functional structure prevents knowledge sharing between product lines, something that is essential for our long-term competitiveness.
	R2: The sudden spurt in growth has seen us recruit a lot of people who will simultaneously be eligible to take sabbaticals, thus creating a personnel crisis when more than two people are not available.

(continues)

Table 10-1 (Continued)

Focus Area   Gaps Addressed

A3: Our strategic objectives are misaligned with our stakeholder values (e.g., growth and learning)

P5: There are no formal knowledge-sharing mechanisms in place between shifts in the enterprise. What little sharing that is happening is almost exclusively due to personal relationships among middle managers.

P4: Our enterprise culture is based on "thick walls" separating departments; as a result, we have information that exists in silos across the enterprise.

Legend: Stakeholder Values (SV); Processes (P); Performance Measurement (PM); Enterprise Maturity (EM); Alignment (A); Resources (R); Wastes (W).

focus areas for enterprises we've worked with include *leadership, enterprise processes, suppliers, customers,* and *policy.*

A crisply defined future state vision makes the gaps in current-state performance easier to see and understand. Once the focus areas are identified, the transformation team can define multiple **enterprise projects**—projects that affect the enterprise as a whole and enable the enterprise to transition from its current state to its desired future state.

Production is one of the enterprise processes at ChipDesign, but the process analysis highlighted that only 35 percent of the cycle time is value added. If a significant part of the remaining 65 percent of the cycle time can be improved, the overall operational excellence of the enterprise will improve dramatically.

We pointed out earlier that there is significant resistance to change anything at ChipDesign perceived to be working. Individual product line managers feel that the system, though not perfect, functions well enough for them to create and deliver quality chips to the customer. The analysis revealed, however, that a critical part of the production process—the use of test wafers—is completely ad hoc. Chip-Design does maintain an inventory of test wafers. However, the process of determining which test wafer types to use, in what quantity, applied to which process step, and at what time has long been determined using a nonstandard, highly labor-intensive process. Again, all the product

Table 10-2

Developing ChipDesign Focus Areas (II)

Focus Area	*Gaps Addressed*
Operational Excellence	SV3: Plant workers have little visual feedback on the performance of the process they are executing. SV5: Suppliers are currently providing us with very poor documentation and support. A1: Our functional structure prevents knowledge sharing between product lines, something that is essential for our long-term competitiveness. R1: We do not have a clear understanding of the true costs of nonstandard test wafer usage. P1: Our yield rate makes it difficult to target the new products segments that will enable us to remain sustainable. P2: Our processes for managing test wafers are nonstandard and have significant variation that is induced by product line workloads. P3: Our preventive maintenance process is at its infancy and still needs to be standardized. PM1: Each group uses its own metrics, and there is little agreement among the groups on the enterprise metrics. W1: Suppliers' test wafer restocking process is not pulled by our processes. W3: Significant wastes are induced by the setup process, as well as by in-process waiting. W4: We need greater collaboration among the functional groups.
Information Integration	SV3: Plant workers have little visual feedback on the performance of the process they are executing. SV7: There is a general lack of awareness of our transformation efforts.

(continues)

Table 10-2 (Continued)

Focus Area	Gaps Addressed
	SV8: Our employees do not have a shared understanding of the knowledge and tools needed to make our transformation successful.
	A4: Our information systems are disconnected. Each functional area and in some cases each product line has its own legacy information systems that don't talk to each other.
	W2: Information flows across the enterprise are broken down—across shifts, across product lines, and across functional groups.

Legend: Stakeholder Values (SV); Processes (P); Performance Measurement (PM); Enterprise Maturity (EM); Alignment (A); Resources (R); Wastes (W).

line managers do it their own different ways. ChipDesign does have a software program that monitors the available quantity of test wafers for each product line and creates a notification when the quantity drops below a fixed minimum level. However, an emphasis on lowering costs has resulted in people ignoring the recommendation of the software program unless a cheap test wafer is available. This behavior drove nonstandard operations because other personnel in a shift had to orally communicate their needs, adding unnecessary work. Although this approach potentially optimizes local costs, it also results in stockouts for other product lines and production shifts, in turn resulting in those lines and shifts using more expensive test wafers, driving up overall enterprise costs.

When assessing stakeholder value exchange with the suppliers who provide the test wafers, it became clear that ChipDesign could not accurately assess test wafer performance. There was limited understanding of when and how suppliers deliver the test wafers. Part of the reason was that the information used for supplier management was stored in a different system than the one used for managing production operations—and the systems did not talk to one another.

Kirk Norström, ChipDesign's executive vice president for production, recognized that a standard process for managing test wafers could result in two key outcomes: (1) a reduction in overall enterprise cost by 10 percent and (2) an increase in the availability of the correct test wafer to 95 percent. Even though the inventory levels would not fall dramatically, the overall impact on the enterprise would be transformative.

Project leaders had to have responsibility, authority, and accountability over their functional areas and, at the same time, grasp the enterprise-wide impact of the project. Identifying key personnel is a critical success factor, and giving them the same kind of responsibility, authority, and accountability over projects is necessary. The VPs from production and supplier management were ideal. Kirk felt the project could be executed by a small team of six people, despite its far-reaching potential to change dramatically the way the enterprise operated. The right team, he believed, could carry out an effective analysis, maintain a strategic perspective, and still account for operational realities. The team's collective knowledge of ChipDesign production, supplier management, and information technology capabilities fit the bill.

Figure 10-3 is a template for capturing the information about an enterprise project. It is filled out for ChipDesign's project to create a standard process for managing test wafers—the example we continue through this chapter. With the template, you can standardize how projects are specified. The eleven boxes capture all the relevant information.

➤ The *Developers* (box 1) identifies the senior leader who defined the enterprise scope of the project.

➤ The project is given a pithy *Title* (box 2) that captures the purpose behind undertaking the project.

➤ The *Focus Area* (box 3) shows where the project has impact.

➤ The *Project Description* (box 4) expands on the title to provide a rich description of the project intent—the big idea being tried out.

➤ Another purpose of the template is to ensure there is documentation of the assumptions made in defining the project. *Gaps to Be Addressed* (box 5) should be identified using some type of coding system, or gap numbers, as we call them. In ChipDesign's case, gaps were coded as P (related to processes), A (related to alignment), and SV (related to stakeholder value).

➤ *Expected Outcomes* (box 6) should include both tangible and intangible outcomes; an example of the latter is to "raise company morale."

Figure 10-3

Enterprise Project Definition Template

Enterprise Project Definition Template

1. Developer(s): *Kirk Norström (EVP Production)*

2. Title: *Define a standard process for managing test wafers*

3. Focus Area: *Operational Excellence*

4. Description:
Our costs associated with the use of test wafers are significantly higher than our competitors. Furthermore, we are unable to identify the root causes of the significant variations in our use of test wafers across product lines. We are utilizing 'human glue' as a means of locally optimizing the utilization of test wafers but at the enterprise level, we have constant stockouts, product lines and other shifts are left with incorrect wafers. We have no visibility into how and when our supplier is delivering and managing wafers.

5. Gaps to be Addressed: P2 – *No standard process for test wafers;* **A4** – *Information systems do not contain the same information;* **SV6** – *Decision making is slow and disjointed.*

6. Expected Outcomes: *The measurable outcomes of this project are:*
- *Reduce test wafer inventory by 10%*
- *Ensure availability of appropriate test wafers at 95%*
- *Reduce enterprise cost by 10%*

7. Related Ongoing Effort(s): *We currently have a number of initiatives underway:*
-ERP/PDM integration project (ongoing) – does not currently account for supplier managed inventories
-Standard preventive maintenance (proposed as an enterprise project)
- We also have a major challenge in that we have to make major deliveries of new chips in the next year

8. Timing: *(Circle One)*

Short Term – < 1 Year   Mid Term – 1 to 2 Years   Long Term – > 2 Years

9. Candidate(s) for Leadership:
Steve Ive (VP, Production) and
Jony Jobs (VP, Supplier Management)

10. Supporting Agencies: *This will need coordination with the process engineering team, as well as the product development teams.*

11. Resources Required: *This will require pulling people from three groups: production, supplier management, and information technology.*
The new team will probably require 2 people from each of the teams, plus system development costs.

> ➤ Enterprises today tend to be involved in multiple change initiatives, which raise the distinct possibility of duplication of effort or, even worse, directly contradictory efforts. In the *Related Ongoing Effort(s)* section (box 7), all such related efforts are captured so that, when it comes time to develop the transformation plan, decisions can be made about which to execute and which to kill.

> ➤ Some enterprise projects are short term and will demonstrate results within a year (or even sooner), while the impact of long-term projects may not be seen for several years. In either case, the *Timing* is made explicit in box 8.

> ➤ In earlier chapters we have talked about the importance of distributing leadership across the enterprise, as well as the difficulty of ensuring that leaders are provided with responsibility, authority, and accountability for their actions. In the *Candidates*

for Leadership section (box 9), the transformation team identifies individuals who can serve as change agents and who have the requisite domain knowledge to develop an implementable transformation plan.

➤ By their very nature, enterprise projects span functional and potentially organizational boundaries. In the *Supporting Agencies* section (box 10), the transformation team identifies other relevant individuals and organizations that need to be involved or engaged in the project. At a minimum, this section should identify the key stakeholders who have to participate in and are impacted by the project.

➤ In box 11 is the identification of the *Resources Required* in the project in terms of time, money, and people.

Depending on the nature of the desired future state and the ability of the enterprise to commit sufficient resources to the planning and execution of the transformation effort, more enterprise projects might be identified than can be executed. The selection and sequencing of enterprise projects becomes critical for transformation success.

Overall, the specification of projects avoids some of the most common pitfalls that undermine transformation efforts: the lack of leadership commitment and inadequate resourcing of projects.

Select and Sequence Enterprise Projects

In our experience, enterprise projects typically number between ten and fifteen. Fewer than ten is rare, although some enterprises may have only a handful of big projects. More than fifteen can be unmanageable, and the transformation team will need to down-select to a manageable set based on enterprise-specific selection criteria such as the number and nature of gaps addressed, the expected impact of the project, and alignment with the enterprise vision. The transformation team may decide to prioritize some projects over others because they will demonstrate success in the near term or because they satisfy key stakeholder needs. Whatever the criteria, the transformation planning process cannot proceed unless the team reaches a consensus on which enterprise projects to select.

The ChipDesign transformation team identified twelve projects across its four focus areas. These projects represent a consensus the team achieved about what required the greatest attention. Figure 10-4 shows the twelve projects.

Once they selected a manageable set of enterprise projects, the ChipDesign team developed a dependencies diagram to capture the expected sequence of execution. Figure 10-5 shows the dependencies

Figure 10-4

Enterprise Projects Selected at ChipDesign

Growth	People	Operational Excellence	Information Technology
Develop a human capital growth program	Increase awareness of transformation through communication	Develop a standard maintenance process	Harmonize legacy systems to create an integrated system
Define growth strategy & technology roadmap	Educate all employees on our transformation approach and tools	Define a standard process for managing test wafers	Develop a new performance measurement system
Create a cross-functional organization	Define common metrics across functional groups	Establish a knowledge sharing process across shifts	Develop new means of sharing information – both visual and Internet-based

Figure 10-5

Enterprise Project Dependencies Diagram

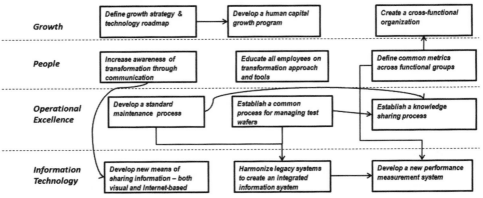

among selected projects based on project prerequisites. These could be the successful completion of another enterprise project; for instance, developing new processes for preventive maintenance and managing test wafers should happen before developing an enterprise information system that integrates them. Another dependency might be a function of the trade-off in resource allocation between projects, where one project might need the change agents from another project to become available. Developing a dependencies diagram provides another chance to refine the projects that have been selected, including the opportunity to redefine some projects if necessary. ChipDesign brought a number of dependencies to the surface with its diagram.

Mapping the projects against the focus areas and charting the dependencies among them begins to develop a visual representation of the expected transformation trajectory. The project descriptions from above, together with the diagram, represent strategic decisions by the transformation team. However, the final decision on what to execute, and how, is yet to come—as part of developing a detailed transformation plan.

Develop Actionable Projects

Members of the enterprise transformation team may have defined the enterprise-level transformation projects, but enterprise change agents translate them into actionable projects. Change agents are identified in the project descriptions and are selected for their knowledge of the problem being addressed and the context for that problem.

The set of subprojects that result from analyzing an enterprise project fall into three categories that unfold on a continuum.

➤ *Just-do-it* (JDI) projects must be executed for enterprise transformation efforts to progress. The solution to a problem addressed by a JDI project is already known; it's just a matter of doing it.

➤ *Improvement events* (IEs) are carried out to gain greater insight into a perceived problem, and typically they are between a day and a week in duration. The conclusion of an IE often results in identifying other projects that are needed: perhaps a JDI project or another IE project.

➤ *Change projects* (CPs) are larger combinations of JDI and IE projects carried out to achieve a discrete objective, with measurable outcomes.

Kirk Norström, ChipDesign's EVP of production, initiated the so-called catch ball process by handing the enterprise project to develop a standard process for managing test wafers (Figure 10-3) to his two candidates for leadership, the VP of production and VP of supplier management. At the same time, he provided them with the requisite resources to refine the project and make it actionable. These change agents developed a set of five subprojects (Figure 10-6) to get them to the point where they could establish a standard process: two JDIs, two IEs, and one CP. These all corresponded to what the data used to develop the enterprise project description suggested and to their views of what would be needed to sustain the transformation: mapping the test wafer inventory; creating the baseline for the current test wafer management processes, developing a new inventory management strategy; defining the new test wafer management process; and, finally, deploying the newly developed process across the enterprise.

Each of the subprojects can be specified using the template in Figure 10-7. Like the enterprise project specification template (Figure 10-3), it captures the project context and execution logistics. The template is a concise expression of the project's expected impact and its degree of difficulty. It includes a crisp elevator-pitch justification for the project, along with expected costs and savings. Key personnel associated with the project are all identified. For the specific project shown in Figure 10-7, the director for production was recommended as the owner because of his responsibility for eventually defining the standard process. He staffed the project with key stakeholders from product lines, shift managers, and a "black belt"-trained expert from the con-

Figure 10-6

Making the Enterprise Project Actionable

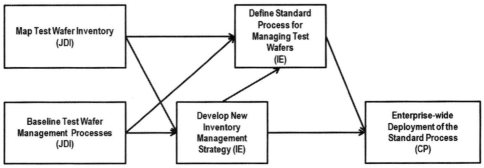

Figure 10-7

Template for Defining Subprojects

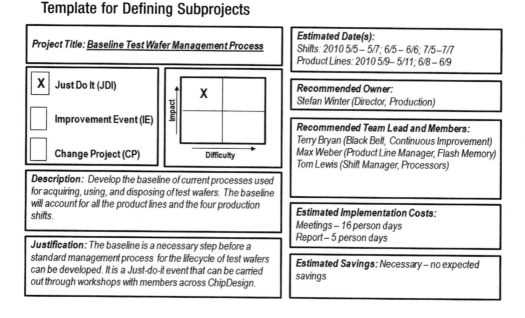

Project Title: *Baseline Test Wafer Management Process*	**Estimated Date(s):** *Shifts: 2010 5/5 – 5/7; 6/5 – 6/6; 7/5–7/7* *Product Lines: 2010 5/9– 5/11; 6/8 – 6/9*

X Just Do It (JDI)

☐ Improvement Event (IE)

☐ Change Project (CP)

Impact ↑   Difficulty →   X

Recommended Owner:
Stefan Winter (Director, Production)

Recommended Team Lead and Members:
Terry Bryan (Black Belt, Continuous Improvement)
Max Weber (Product Line Manager, Flash Memory)
Tom Lewis (Shift Manager, Processors)

Description: Develop the baseline of current processes used for acquiring, using, and disposing of test wafers. The baseline will account for all the product lines and the four production shifts.

Estimated Implementation Costs:
Meetings – 16 person days
Report – 5 person days

Justification: The baseline is a necessary step before a standard management process for the lifecycle of test wafers can be developed. It is a Just-do-it event that can be carried out through workshops with members across ChipDesign.

Estimated Savings: Necessary – no expected savings

tinuous improvement team. The latter's role was to capture, consolidate, and analyze the data collaboratively with other team members.

This project was classified as a JDI because it was a necessary prerequisite to developing the standard process. The expectation of low difficulty reflected that the product line owners and the shift managers had locally well-defined internal policies about their test wafer management processes and that they had sufficient documentation from their previously executed projects to develop an effective baseline of how test wafers were acquired, used, and disposed of. The expectation of high impact came from the view that a baseline would enable the team to define requirements that matched operational realities, potentially resulting in less disruption due to changes.

The team decided to baseline the processes for product lines and shifts separately to achieve the maximum ability to see multiple perspectives, as seen from the schedule for execution. The team also built in a review date with key stakeholders to increase buy-in on the baseline.

Documenting and sharing the transformation team's assumptions creates the opportunity for enterprise change agents to challenge those assumptions effectively and make the case for any alterations to projects they feel may be necessary. This catch ball process helps create alignment across the multiple levels of the enterprise regarding the nature of the projects that need to be executed. Done properly, the result is increased enterprise-wide buy-in regarding the why and how of transformation.

Develop the Transformation Plan

The transformation plan integrates all the plans for actionable projects developed by the enterprise change agents. The transformation team resolves conflicts among projects and ensures the feasibility of the overall plan. With a single, integrated master transformation plan, you can set explicit milestones for progress on transformation objectives and resources can be allocated as needed. The analysis of the resourcing profile and dependencies between projects required to develop the transformation plan provides a first-pass test of project feasibility.

Enterprises mistakenly believe that their ability to execute *regular* projects automatically means they can effectively manage the execution of their transformation projects. But there are important differences in the nature of the work. Transformation projects are cumulative in nature, and success is achieved when *all* the projects perform as expected and the enterprise successfully manages unintended side effects. This requires governance—an important element of the transformation plan that is all too often left out of the discussion.

In the case of ChipDesign, the CEO carried out regular reviews of the four focus areas and the projects associated with them as part of her monthly executive meetings. In addition, she initiated a quarterly review of transformation progress with the Transformation Council, which provided an opportunity to revisit any key interdependencies and make any additional resourcing decisions. Each of the focus area owners was responsible for tracking the progress of enterprise projects within their portfolio through a monthly review. In essence, ChipDesign was consistently tracking the progress of the four focus areas and the twelve underlying enterprise projects and making the necessary course corrections (as seen in Table 10-3).

The governance that needs to be put in place for effective transformation is an extension of the Transformation Roadmap. Projects need to be tracked as they are executed. In our experience, monthly project reviews are called for, but each enterprise will need to figure out its own best timing scheme that allows for effective tracking of the

Table 10-3

ChipDesign Transformation Governance

Focus Area	Enterprise Project	Focus Area Governance
Growth	Define growth strategy and technology roadmap	
	Develop a human capital growth program	
	Create cross-functional organization	Tracked during monthly focus area meeting
People	Increase awareness of transformation through communication	
	Educate all employees on our transformation approach and tools	
	Define common metrics across all functional groups	Tracked during monthly focus area meeting
Operational excellence	Develop a standard maintenance process	
	Develop a standard test wafer process	
	Establish a knowledge sharing process across shifts	Tracked during monthly focus area meeting

(continues)

Focus Area	Enterprise Project	Focus Area Governance
Information technology	Harmonize legacy systems to create and integrate system	
	Develop a new performance measurement system	
	Develop new means of sharing information, both visually and Internet based	Tracked during monthly focus area meeting
Transformation Plan Governance	CEO monthly senior leadership meeting—Progress on each focus area Enterprise Transformation Council—Quarterly review of complete plan	

Table 10-3 (Continued)

progress of tactical plans against expected outcomes. Enterprise change agents have to review all the enterprise projects on a regular basis, making themselves available as required to remove obstacles or barriers to progress. The enterprise transformation team as a whole needs to review progress on enterprise transformation objectives at least quarterly. Each review, at each level, enhances the efficacy of the overall transformation and allows those involved to account for any changes to the operational environment that may have occurred along the way. The reviews provide a platform for reflecting on the transformation effort as a whole and for taking corrective action as needed.

Armed with a transformation plan that makes sense and has been accepted throughout the enterprise, the enterprise is now ready and able to enter the Execution Cycle of the Transformation Roadmap—the subject of our next chapter.

CHAPTER 10 TAKEAWAYS

▲ Transformation plans must be traceable to the data collected and analyses performed as part of understanding the enterprise's current state.

▲ Focus areas, the levers of enterprise transformation, provide solutions for the gaps that need to be filled and for capturing the opportunities to exploit to move the enterprise from its current state to its desired future state.

▲ Enterprise projects enable the transition from the current state to the desired future state. They must be selected and sequenced to maximize the enterprise-wide benefits.

▲ Once enterprise projects are identified, getting input from people at the next level down in the enterprise not only builds alignment and learning, but also defines the subprojects that will make it actionable. Communicating the assumptions and data used to develop enterprise projects enables people at the next level in the organization to understand the context and to further develop the enterprise projects. Additionally, the process also creates greater enterprise alignment.

▲ The transformation governance structure that is put in place has to ensure not only the monitoring and control of progress, but also make it possible to reassess strategically the overall direction and constituent projects.

CHAPTER

$-11-$

Executing the
Transformation Plan

Knowing is not enough; we must apply!

Johann Wolfgang von Goethe[1]

T HE LAST TWO BOXES of the Transformation Roadmap comprise the *Execution Cycle*. Some of the activities in those boxes were covered in Chapter 10. Here, we address what it takes to ensure that implementation can succeed and yield positive improvements. We look at what needs to happen throughout the enterprise, both in terms of specific activities and at the level of how the enterprise "thinks" about itself.

This is when enterprise transformation is diffused throughout the entire enterprise, not only through improvement projects but also in terms of the day-to-day communication and day-to-day *being*. Now is when you are remaking your enterprise as one in which enterprise thinking is becoming second nature—or, at least, beginning to move the enterprise on its way to that point. Because what happens at this stage is synchronized with the enterprise's strategic plan, the stage is set for reentering the Roadmap at the Strategic Cycle in an everlasting process of enterprise transformation and improvement.

Figure 11-1 shows the Execution Cycle of the Enterprise Transformation Roadmap.

Successful execution of the enterprise implementation plan thus forms the basis for further improvement.

Figure 11-1

Enterprise Transformation Roadmap Execution Cycle

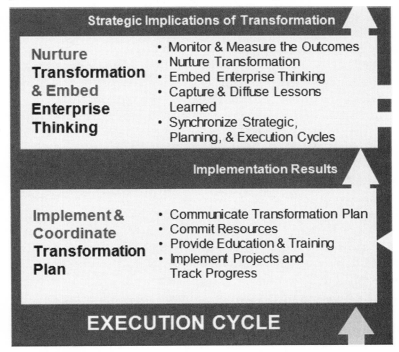

Communicate the Transformation Plan

The importance of communicating not only the intent of the enterprise to transform, but also the actual transformation plan, cannot be overstated. This communication needs to take place across the enterprise and to the extended enterprise where appropriate.

Every possible communication channel should be employed. Staff meetings are opportunities to convey plans and provide updates on progress. Enterprise newsletters should regularly cover news of the transformation. Enterprise leaders can give speeches at locations throughout the enterprise, on a regular basis, to offer clear explanations of the transformation plan to enterprise stakeholders and to demonstrate its implementation through examples. Senior leaders, as well as enterprise employees and other stakeholders, can communicate and promote the transformation plan through media and events such as conferences, interviews, and meetings with clients and customers. It is also important to identify network leaders (informal, trusted leaders who may not have formal titles) and bring them onboard. They can serve as critical, informal conduits for communicating the transformation.

The importance of communication really comes to the forefront in the implementation of the transformation plan.[2] The enterprise needs to hear about the transformation from senior leadership, not as unsubstantiated (and often negative) rumors that might convey incomplete or false information and, worse yet, become roadblocks.

Communication about transformation may be programmatic or participatory.[3] *Programmatic* approaches emphasize the top-down communication of transformation to generate stakeholder alignment—often the case when you are beginning your transformation journey. *Participatory* approaches focus on involving all stakeholders to generate ideas for improvement; this approach is ideal once enterprise thinking has been embedded as part of the transformation effort. We recommend putting in place a hybrid approach that allows the enterprise to evolve from purely programmatic communication to include participatory communication as the transformation progresses. All communication, regardless of the mode, should emphasize building mutual understanding and trusting relationships.[4]

Delta Airlines' restructuring efforts in 1994 are a good example of the hybrid approach to communication in an enterprise transformation.[5] The company had a no-layoffs policy but had to downsize to remain competitive. So Delta created a program, "Leadership 7.5," to cut the cost to fly one seat one mile from 9.4 cents to 7.5 cents by 1997. To help prevent fear from spreading throughout the enterprise, a special toll-free number was established; employees could call into this Delta Newsline to leave comments, ask questions, and provide feedback on the state of the transformation. On the day of the restructuring announcement, there were 6,000 calls; the number reached 14,000 by the end of that week. To manage the information requests from middle managers and supervisors, a special communications center was established to ensure that people across the enterprise got accurate information about the transformation efforts. Delta's senior leaders also went out into the field, conducting facility tours and holding open forums to respond to questions. This enabled them to disseminate accurate information across the enterprise and create alignment for the transformation effort.

The objective in communicating about transformation is to make it a *habit*. Anything the enterprise does can be turned into a communication channel about transformation. Even internal training courses can provide an opportunity to talk about transformation and the implementation of the plan.

The ideal is when *all* enterprise stakeholders understand the transformation plan, actively participate in its implementation, and *promote* the plan outside the enterprise.

Provide Education and Training

Continuous enterprise learning develops the transformation capabilities of an enterprise. For this reason, education and training are front and center in the Execution Cycle. Some training will be very specific: For example, an enterprise may need employees to become proficient in certain methods to carry through a particular improvement project. Other education will be more generally about enterprise thinking and transformation as concepts, but in the real-life context of the transformation unfolding in the enterprise.

An enterprise that is successfully training and educating its internal stakeholders as part of a transformation effort is providing programs, including refreshers, on a just-in-time basis that serves the needs of specific transformation projects. The education and training curriculum supports the enterprise in its need to have stakeholders who possess the skills necessary for transformation efforts and to achieve specific goals.

Take, for example, the North Shore–Long Island (NY) Jewish Health System. Michael J. Dowling, its president and CEO, places great emphasis on quality when talking to new employees as part of their orientation. He explains to them the quality improvement dashboard, which lays out the organization's quality measures, performance targets, and results. As Dowling puts it, "Quality is not a department. It's not just one process. It's not just the responsibility of people with designated quality titles. It is everyone's business. You want it to be part of the DNA of the organization." This dedication to quality is what won North Shore–LIJ Health System the 2010 National Health Care Award.[6]

Similarly, at Baylor Health Care System (BHCS, introduced in Chapter 7), the Accelerating Best Care training program focuses on providing all practitioners with a common baseline for carrying out improvement efforts. The first objective of the program is to have a cultural impact on participants by creating a sense of urgency about the so-called quality chasm (on which the BHCS objectives for healthcare improvement are based) and the need to adopt health-care improvement methods. As of 2009, the core six-day program had graduated more than 600 change leaders, including clinicians, nurses, and administrators.[7]

The Baylor program provides experiential training in tools of health-care improvement that integrates knowledge from a variety of sources, including lean, Six Sigma, Toyota Production System, and so on. The objective is to create a shared vocabulary and instill the use of a common toolbox. The training program itself covers team building, feedback skills, process modeling, data system design, Pareto techniques, statistical process control, and cost-quality relations, all in the context of enterprise transformation. Also, domain-specific training modules cover customer service skills, safety, equity, and chronic care.[8]

The BHCS leadership team recognized that not everyone could take the full course and has created a portfolio of programs that include an accelerated one-day version of the program aimed at frontline caregivers, a half-day introduction to quality improvement for practicing physicians, a version targeting residents, and shorter customized versions for special settings such as nursing homes and home care.

As Baylor shows, a common vocabulary of transformation is necessary throughout all training and education. This means that the terms of enterprise transformation—for example, "enterprise," "stakeholder," "alignment," and so on—are used and understood the same by everyone throughout the enterprise, regardless of the site at which programs might take place or projects may unfold. This commonality of vocabulary facilitates successful transformation efforts and continuous enterprise learning.

An enterprise with education and training that are not coordinated with the needs of the transformation plan must change course and develop programs that support the plan. In the most advanced enterprise transformations, education and training are part of a human capital development program, with a focus on skills and capabilities that support the ongoing needs of the extended enterprise transformation plan.

Implement Projects and Track Their Progress

Implementation of the enterprise transformation plan developed in Chapter 10 is about flowing down into the specific actions, programs, and projects. If you have gotten this far, you have a plan that has been translated into the details necessary to make that happen.

You will also need to track progress at the project level, preferably in real time. Successful transformation requires that actual outcomes be assessed against the goals set out in the transformation plan. An effective project management process is important; it enables everyone to understand the progress of projects and provides a way to gauge how you are doing in the context of enterprise-level milestones and targets. Project management should, of course, include providing feedback to the enterprise-level leaders about project progress.

The NAVAIR AIRSpeed program is one of the most successful instances of the Navy's overall transformation effort. The program uses a "deployment management system" that tracks the complete lifecycle of a project from idea generation to completion. This so-called environment not only captures all the required documentation about projects, including deliverables and status, but also allows for resourcing decision making and executive review through reporting and data visualization systems.

Your own system for tracking, tuned to enterprise transformation, enables you to make local assignments of responsibility and accountability for improvement success, which in turn enables fast corrective action at the local level within individual projects.

Monitor Overall Transformation Progress

Tracking project progress and monitoring *overall* transformation progress are linked, but they are not the same. Whereas the former is done at the local, project- and initiative-specific level, the latter requires the active participation of enterprise leaders. Further, overall transformation progress is judged not by improvements achieved by specific projects, but by the aggregate benefits of everything making up the transformation effort.

Monitoring overall progress requires regular reviews that are documented and disseminated to all the relevant stakeholders. These reviews provide enterprise leaders an opportunity to address deficiencies in the transformation plan. You may find, for example, that your implementation of an integrated product development process is severely hampered by the lack of a product data management (PDM) system that allows for the sharing of engineering data. You may then choose to accelerate the PDM implementation schedule.

How you monitor is up to your enterprise to determine. It may be that you derive a way to measure transformation implementation plan progress against enterprise-level milestones and success criteria. If so, this needs to be done for *all* projects, not just for some. We sometimes find that enterprise leaders benefit from using a formal methodology to analyze the overall progress of all transformation projects, which allows for making modifications as learning unfolds.

Optimally, you will be able to conduct an aggregated review across all projects. This permits the reallocation of resources and the adjustment of plans to ensure ongoing alignment with strategic objectives. If you can engage your stakeholders in the extended enterprise (e.g., suppliers, shareholders) in monitoring with you, collaboratively, you will be functioning at the highest level of capability and able to adjust the plan proactively to achieve extended enterprise objectives.

Nurture the Transformation and Embed Enterprise Thinking

As enterprise thinking becomes part of the foundation of daily activity in the enterprise and the transformation plan moves forward, the improved performance becomes a strong driving force for future strategic planning by enterprise executives. To ensure that this can happen, senior managers must be actively involved in monitoring the progress of enterprise transformation at all levels. You need to make sure that the stakeholders involved in transformation are being challenged to build on and sustain the improvement efforts and that the level of support and encouragement is appropriate.

Nurturing the transformation process is about ensuring executive-level involvement. Several indicators reveal whether an enterprise is doing a good job nurturing transformation. One is that enterprise leadership and management are actively supporting and involved in ensuring the success of improvement projects. Another is that the positive actions and the effort taken are recognized and rewarded, even when improvements are not fully successful. Finally, enterprise records include information about improvement projects and outcomes that make it possible to track improvement and create incentives for achieving improvements. When enterprise leaders are in constant harmony with the pulse of transformation and proactively inspire transformation ownership throughout the extended enterprise, success is becoming pervasive.

If you find a low level of support for the transformation effort from enterprise leadership, corrective steps must be taken to make that support greater and more widespread. Enterprise leaders must be providing encouragement and support for, and recognition of, the transformation efforts. Ideally, enterprise leaders and managers work actively to identify and remove barriers. Teams and individuals who successfully implement improvements are being recognized and rewarded. Enterprise leaders, managers, and other members of the organization continually emphasize and encourage the transformation.

Clay Jones, the CEO of Rockwell Collins, has continually evangelized about the role that Lean Electronics™ plays in the enterprise's long-term success. For example, speaking of the challenges of implementing the next generation of air traffic control systems, he said, "[O]ur commitment to applying Lean will allow us to continuously improve at a pace that corresponds with the changing needs of our industry, while also reducing costs, increasing customer satisfaction, and positioning us to capture new business."[9]

This emphasis is not restricted to the CEO. LeeAnn Ridgeway, the vice president of material operations for Rockwell Collins Services, has also emphasized the use of Lean Electronics™ in her group. Reflecting on her group's long transformation journey, she highlighted how Lean Electronics™ enabled Rockwell Collins Services to go from a 44 percent on-time delivery to customer request rate in 2001 to achieving 90 percent on-time delivery by 2005.[10] The journey, though, did not stop there—every year, her group refreshes its improvement plan and aligns the new projects with overall group goals, which are in turn aligned with the business unit goals and through that to the enterprise goals.

Speaking about the success of Rockwell Collins Services, Ridgeway said:

> The strategy that worked for us was to start with smaller projects, record the progress the teams made, share the success, and then move on. We also created a culture along the way of open and honest reporting and accurate, data-driven decision making. Communicating the team's progress and involving all affected people in the process is most important.[11]

When transformation has become fully embedded in the enterprise, local organizational boundaries cease to be obstacles to an enterprise perspective. Management and training foster a sense of place for all employees within the broader enterprise, and actions (and consequences) span boundaries. You know enterprise thinking has become embedded when enterprise thinking is both verbalized *and* enacted.

Another clear sign that enterprise thinking has become embedded is when continuous improvement becomes institutionalized. A continuous improvement process challenges people to tackle the root cause, rather than the symptom. It engages the enterprise in applying the enterprise transformation principles in Chapter 2 to all enterprise systems and processes, utilizing the lessons learned. These are the indicators that continuous improvement has been institutionalized.

This part of the Roadmap is especially critical for the executive leadership of the enterprise, for whom the entire Roadmap is intended. Their leadership will largely determine whether the enterprise can succeed in making enterprise transformation a part of its everyday business. This is also when their actions as leaders really come into play. Do they talk about transformation at staff meetings? Do they take every opportunity to imbue enterprise thinking around the enterprise as they engage in management by walking around?

As you think about nurturing the transformation, think about how you nurture children. The same principles apply. Children are best nurtured when they are given unconditional support for making genuine efforts, even if they fail. They are encouraged whenever they try to tackle something difficult, and their parents help break down the barriers in the way of success. In an enterprise setting, this can be done generally and also specifically by senior leaders becoming mentors, in a sense, for improvement projects.

In a very real sense, embedding enterprise thinking is about making it part of the organizational culture of the enterprise. Culture is "the specific collection of values and norms that are shared by people and groups" in the enterprise "and that control the way they interact with each other and with stakeholders outside the organization."[12]

Every enterprise has a unique culture. However, making enterprise thinking a part of that culture typically means taking on the aspects of it that support and perpetuate the silos. The most successful enterprises succeed in imbuing the notion that everything the enterprise does should be seen holistically, that is, as having enterprise-wide ramifications. Further, an ongoing culture of enterprise thinking is one in which transformation is not a one-off dramatic change but an *integral* part of the way people think and act in the enterprise.

The power of culture cannot be overstated. In the aerospace industry, the culture of "higher, faster, farther" has resulted in each organization involved in developing an aerospace platform focusing on maximizing the capabilities of its individual component. From a platform perspective, every so-called local function has concerned itself with its own interests. It has been driven by its own cultural paradigms (what the organization is about), organization and power structures, symbols, rituals and routines, and even stories and myths—the components of a culture. This has precluded taking an enterprise perspective. In the U.S. Navy's F/A-18E/F Super Hornet project, a conscious effort was made to establish a mindset of the "airplane is the boss" to help overcome this fragmentation in a very large extended enterprise. By shifting the cultural paradigm to establish a new boss, the Super Hornet became a model of enterprise-level integration for future efforts.[13]

In a culture of enterprise transformation, improvement becomes an ongoing, ever present activity. Even though enterprise transformation is led by the senior leadership, in this culture everyone is engaged with transformation and with improvement all the time. And everyone readily sees that sustained improvement. It is what takes you back into the Strategic Cycle of the Roadmap in a continuous cycle of transformational change to make the enterprise better and stronger.

Capture and Diffuse the Lessons Learned

When you capture and diffuse the lessons learned along the road to transformation, you ensure that the successes you achieve will lead to more successes. The enterprise learns what works—the best practices—and what doesn't work, and learning the lessons creates greater effectiveness for improvement projects, as well as helping eliminate the need to reinvent anything.

The United States Army provides one of the best-known examples of a structured reflection and review process for capturing and diffusing lessons. The After Action Reports (AAR) were initiated in the mid-1970s to capture lessons learned from simulated battles at the National Training Centers, and they were institutionalized after the first Gulf War.

Although AARs are a military application, the ideas behind them have wide applicability to other enterprises. The essence of an AAR is built around answering four simple questions:

➤ What did we set out to do?

➤ What actually happened?

> ➤ Why did that happen?
> ➤ What are we going to do next time?

In earlier chapters, we showed you project description templates that can be used in transformation planning. Tracking systems like those discussed earlier in this chapter should provide a coherent answer to the AAR's second question of what took place. Real learning takes place when you answer the last two AAR questions.

When we worked with GameDevCo, a software company, we found that its team had developed its own version of after-project reflections, called "Retrospectives," that comprised a set of checklist questions. However, nothing about Retrospectives generated any usable lessons, and so it had no impact on the company's future practice.[14]

By contrast, at IndiaCo, every project deviation required a root cause analysis and the dissemination of the lessons across the other teams.[15] Rather than issue a policy directive, the IndiaCo senior leadership team made this analysis a part of the regular project management workflow, with forms and tools to make the reporting process easier. In addition, IndiaCo instituted project manager sessions to review the lessons learned and to ensure that there was common awareness of the best practices.

In the most successful transformations, there is a specific focus on both capturing and learning from transformation implementation, both within and outside the enterprise. Incorporating lessons learned explicitly into the formulation of new initiatives can then become routine. Often, this involves setting up forums for sharing project implementation experiences with others in the organization. This includes not only what went well, but also what went wrong. It also helps to make the process for capturing and diffusing lessons learned easy.

Capturing and diffusing lessons could also involve attending conferences and seminars where you have the opportunity engage with others involved in similar transformation projects.

Adjust and Align the Planning and Execution Cycles

After you have been monitoring progress for some period (usually several months), you will likely find you need to make some adjustments to the plan to align to its actual execution. Some projects may need to be accelerated, while others may need more resources assigned to meet schedules or desired outcomes. The adjustments may necessitate pushing projects out to a later date. You may modify your education and training strategy based on better understanding of organizational needs. Experiences in project implementation and other lessons learned may provide you with better estimates of resources (both time and people) required. This may require a change to the transformation plan.

Consider again an enterprise in the midst of implementing an integrated product development process, something it deems to be a critical enterprise project to achieve its strategic objective of reducing its time to market. In its monthly status reviews, the enterprise discovers a number of impediments to successful implementation. The most serious is the lack of a capability to share data across different parts of the engineering organization, including manufacturing engineering. Also, the team discovers that they need the company's key suppliers integrally involved in the design process and want to bring them onto their team sooner than originally planned. Another impediment they discover is the lack of engineering personnel with expertise in manufacturing.

For this enterprise, these impediments would necessitate several changes to the transformation plan. First, the product data management (PDM) system for sharing engineering data, already in the plan but not scheduled to begin until the following year, was moved up in priority to begin the very next quarter. This meant moving another information technology project to improve the human resources benefits system back a quarter, because of resource constraints. A second change involved adding some of the key component suppliers to the product development team immediately, rather than sticking to the original plan of bringing them in six months later, after the initial design took place. Third, the team decided to accelerate the cross-training of engineers with manufacturing, not only for the immediate project team, but in preparation for future integrated product development teams. One of the lessons learned from the current team was that this exchange of knowledge was a critical success factor for team success.

Adjustments of this sort are fairly typical as the enterprise engages in its transformation projects. The leadership team must stay attuned to the project teams, recognizing when they need to step in to provide assistance that is beyond the project teams' own boundaries. In summary, it is critical to ensure alignment across all enterprise projects, while recognizing that periodic adjustments have to be made.

Reentering the Strategic Cycle

As your enterprise executes the transformation plan, many of the results will have effects at the strategic level. Thus, by its very nature, transformation takes you back into the Strategic Cycle of the Roadmap—especially in the context of an organization fully imbued with enterprise transformation thinking. For such an enterprise, where continuous improvement has become the order of the day, following the Roadmap repeatedly is the norm. In fact, imbuing enterprise thinking means you do and must do transformation as a cycle. Your enterprise, in essence, has no choice.

We find it useful to reevaluate transformation goals on a regular basis, with a full-blown assessment at least annually. Goals may well change. For instance, your enterprise may have set as a strategic objective to reduce overall costs by 10 percent in three years, and the transformation plan calls for multiple projects to achieve that objective. What if you learn, though, that your chief competitor is reducing costs by 25 percent, and that the reduction is giving them a competitive advantage. Your own strategic objectives need at least to be revisited.

Rockwell Collins has been on its transformation journey for more than a decade. One of the key contributors to the company's success has been the ability to assess accurately the current state of the enterprise and to make any necessary strategic adjustments. For example, when the enterprise leadership team recognized the slowdown in the economy, they knew that they had to refresh their transformation efforts.[16] To that end, they identified four enterprise focus areas:[17] (1) reenergize Lean Electronics; (2) refresh lifecycle value stream management; (3) update processes for selecting, onboarding, and developing first-time leaders; and (4) ensure goals are aligned across the enterprise. As illustrated in Chapter 2, each of these areas is something Rockwell Collins had focused on previously and in which the company has seen progress in. Equally important is that all of the focus area sponsors were drawn from the enterprise leadership team, as shown in Table 11-1.

Remember, transforming an enterprise is an ongoing process that takes not months, but years. In fact, you're never really done. The environment is always changing, and an enterprise imbued with transformation thinking works constantly to adjust, realign, relevel, capture, and recapture and recapture again opportunities to become even better.

Table 11-1

2010 Enterprise Focus Areas at Rockwell Collins

Reenergize Lean Electronics

Sponsor: Kent Statler, executive vice president of Rockwell Collins Services

To position Rockwell Collins for long-term success, we must engage every employee in the practical, day-to-day application of Lean. This initiative will reinforce clear expectations, provide meaningful education opportunities, and promote ongoing awareness to ensure that continuous improvement is always top of mind.

Refresh Lifecycle Value Stream Management (LCVSM) process

Sponsors: Greg Churchill, executive vice president and chief operating officer of Government Systems, and Kelly Ortberg, executive vice president and chief operating officer of Commercial Systems

Rockwell Collins' Life Cycle Value Stream Management (LCVSM) process enables our company to make smart decisions about our portfolio of products, systems, and services. This initiative will ensure employees understand the value of the LCVSM model, as well as clarify roles and responsibilities within the model to improve business performance.

Update processes for selecting, onboarding, and developing first-time leaders

Sponsor: Ron Kirchenbauer, senior vice president of Human Resources

Effective leadership is critical to the success of our company. This initiative will build on the development opportunities available through the School of Leadership to improve the efficiency of how we prepare and equip new entry-level leaders at Rockwell Collins.

Ensure goals are aligned

Sponsors: Nan Mattai, senior vice president of Engineering and Technology, and Jeff Moore, senior vice president of Operations

As an enterprise, we need to make certain that the specific goals and objectives for each business and shared service are aligned appropriately to drive success. This initiative will ensure that improvement in one process or organization does not adversely affect another.

CHAPTER 11 TAKEAWAYS

⚠ By executing the transformation plan, transformation is diffused to the entire enterprise, both through improvement projects and through day-to-day communication and activity.

⚠ It is critically important to communicate not only the intent to transform, but also the actual transformation plan, both across the enterprise and to the extended enterprise.

⚠ Continuous enterprise learning develops the transformation capabilities of an enterprise.

⚠ Successful transformation requires that actual outcomes be assessed against the goals set out in the transformation plan, and progress needs to be tracked.

⚠ Enterprise leaders need to be actively engaged in monitoring the overall progress of enterprise transformation and to make adjustments in the plan as necessary. This is key to nurturing the transformation and embedding enterprise thinking throughout the enterprise.

⚠ Capturing and diffusing the lessons learned along the road to transformation ensure that the success achieved will lead to more successes.

CHAPTER

−12−

Enterprise Transformation from Inception to Implementation

Arriving at one point is the starting point to another.

John Dewey[1]

S TAYCOOL ENGINEERING CORPORATION is a profitable, rapidly growing company with three value streams from which it generates its revenues. Founded as a research and development firm, the company eventually began to produce commercial products in the areas of thermal control and energy conversion. More recently, the company has been designing and manufacturing more complicated refrigeration products for the U.S. Department of Defense (DoD).

Successful and profitable, StayCool remains relatively small. The company's founder and president directs day-to-day operations. He has been facing the challenge of growing the company, creating management systems for effective leadership, and acting as the visionary for future products in StayCool's commercial line, leading proposal writing for innovation projects, and coleading the DoD product development teams.

The president realized that StayCool needed to rethink how it does business and indeed how it sees itself from a holistic perspective. This chapter follows StayCool through the Roadmap as it engaged the entire enterprise in the strategic, planning, and execution cycles and set off on enterprise transformation. StayCool engaged its senior leadership, employed the seven lenses of current-state assessment, developed a transformation plan, and set off on implementation. The enterprise thus affords us an opportunity to see the entire Roadmap in action.

StayCool may not be in your industry. It may be much larger or smaller than your enterprise. However, the challenges StayCool has faced will, we believe, resonate in almost any enterprise, as will its transformation journey.

Background on the Enterprise

StayCool, founded in 1986, is fortunate to have a highly motivated group of employees who work in a fairly open culture. The natural barriers between departments are considerably weaker than in many similar companies. However, the different departments are not well integrated, particularly with respect to product development, which results in substantial rework and leads to a good number of designs being completed scrapped. Not long before we began working with StayCool, the company instituted its first-ever cross-functional teams for two newly developed products.

In essence, StayCool is an R&D-oriented company that has hit it big with a successful product. At the core of its culture, though, is the emphasis on research and engineering and all that entails. The successful product has resulted in manufacturing being added to the company's required core competencies, and now StayCool needs to "transform" as a way to account for the new capability it needs to build.

Revenue from StayCool's three sources were $36 million in the most recent complete fiscal year. Table 12-1 shows the breakdown of StayCool's workforce by functional area and highlights the growing competency in manufacturing in addition to its strong roots in R&D.

The company's engineers are kept busy with 40 active research contracts and product development. The progress on both research contracts and product development is unsteady as engineers shift back and forth among projects, usually working to meet external deadlines.

StayCool has long had a relatively simple management structure, as shown in Figure 12-1. Except in the accounting department, standards are rarely used in the company. There are no systems of con-

Table 12-1

StayCool Workforce Summary

Department	Employees	Notes from Analysis
Engineering	57	Includes the CEO, is considered to be slightly understaffed
Engineering Administration	4	
Machining	5	Stable department size
IT	3	Actively looking for another employee
Marketing	7	Down one person due to a termination in September that has yet to be filled
Production	22	Includes one part-time employee
Accounting	10	Stable department size
General Administration	3	Stable department size
Total Employees	111	

Figure 12-1

StayCool's Management Structure

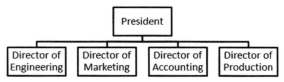

tinuous improvement. The few existing performance metrics are based on throughput: quality, inventory, lead time, employee satisfaction, and customer satisfaction play an insignificant role. This is one of the key gaps that StayCool needed to address.

Strategic Issues

StayCool Engineering had been facing a number of strategic and organizational challenges (Table 12-2) before deciding to follow the Roadmap. These challenges stemmed from the nature of the company's business, the multiple areas of focus, and StayCool's rapid growth.

The first challenge was the *segmentation of the company*. Founded as a research firm doing government contract work, the company grew

Table 12-2

StayCool's Strategic Issues/Challenges

Strategic Issue/Challenge	Details
Segmentation of the company	Separation among three divisions creates problems to overcome.
Focus	SBIR proposals lead to work outside company core competencies. Commercial product development is chaotic. Military product work lacks clear development goals and committed resources.
Resource allocation	Linked to problem of focus Too much firefighting Needs policy
Managing rapid growth	How to avoid stifling the creativity and agility that allowed past success?
Manufacturing and inventory planning	Too much inventory Need to focus on overall cost, not unit cost
Communication	Need for more formal communication Need to create awareness among employees

as it formed its commercial refrigeration products division. This division was largely separate from the engineering division, having begun as a spin-off from one of the company's early Small Business Innovation Research (SBIR) contracts with a product that had been proven by engineering. As StayCool continued to grow, the separation between these two groups grew even wider. The divide has been further exacerbated by the fact that today each of the three divisions has its own building, making it even more difficult for employees to interact across divisional lines.

Clearly, this segmentation has been a significant strategic challenge for StayCool as the company continues to grow as a manufacturing firm and has to focus more of its engineering resources on the commercialization of products. Senior leadership was motivated to explore enterprise transformation in large part because they realized the need to address the integration of their divisions as a critical factor for successful growth.

The second challenge has been overall *focus*. StayCool secures its research contracts through the U.S. government–sponsored program, Small Business Innovation Research (SBIR). Although only 10 percent, give or take, of StayCool's total revenues come from SBIR contracts, this R&D work has produced each of the products the company has successfully sold through its commercial and military divisions.

Submitting proposals for any contract that StayCool thinks it can win provides great potential for short-term earnings. However, the company winds up working on such a wide variety of research topics that focusing on the core competencies of thermal control and energy conversion is difficult. Meanwhile, the product development process for commercial products is often chaotic and lacks a clear long-term strategy. Ideas are developed into products with scant attention to how they might fit with an overall company vision. In addition, StayCool's military products lack clearly defined development goals and committed resources. Development efforts sometimes sit idle for months, and development times are approaching ten years for some products.

Segmentation and focus speak to StayCool's identity problem. Ask just about anyone at the company, and she or he will wonder aloud whether StayCool is a manufacturing firm or an R&D company. This type of response often occurs when companies that start out with an R&D focus suddenly have a hugely successful product that makes people sense a shift to having to manage revenue streams.

Linked to the focus problem is a third challenge: *resource allocation*. One of StayCool's greatest strengths is the intellectual capacity of its employees and its ability to solve a vast array of problems for its customers. StayCool has made a reputation by consistently delivering quality research through the SBIR program and is often awarded contracts that fall outside their core competencies and strategic focus. These same engineering resources are also responsible for product development activities and are usually working on a number of different projects simultaneously. Because of the timed nature of the SBIR contracts, the company often uses the all-hands-on-deck approach of reassigning individuals from product development work to SBIR work with approaching deadlines. This tactic sacrifices work on product development, which has no fixed external deadlines. There is no guarantee that a person starting a project is the one who completes it. As the company grows, StayCool knows that decisions need to be made about how to allocate resources in a way that is better aligned with strategic goals.

That StayCool has this resource allocation problem is not surprising. Absent a clear resource management policy, companies often find themselves in this predicament. The old approach of throwing resources at a group of so-called techno-cowboys who need to fight fires all the time just to get jobs done is no longer working.

Fourth, *managing rapid growth* presents its own set of challenges. With large growth comes the challenges associated with managing an evolving and growing company while not stifling the creativity and agility that has fostered past success. Rapid growth also presents Stay-Cool with the challenge of staffing for the future. Finding the appropriate mix of talented individuals from different engineering backgrounds that meet the needs of the company is seen as a particularly significant challenge.

Fifth, as StayCool entered the commercial products business, it began to experience the challenge of *manufacturing and inventory planning*. As manufacturing practices emerged to meet the company's day-to-day needs, there was a growing recognition that refinements were necessary so that StayCool could rid itself of what was becoming massive amounts of inventory. StayCool's senior leadership began to see the need to break from its convention of focusing on unit cost and begin to look at overall cost.

Finally, in the context of all of the other challenges, *communication* came to the fore as an overarching issue. Since its founding, Stay-Cool has relied on information dispersing somewhat informally through the organization. With growth, though, this approach, which works well in very small organizations, has not served the company well. Clearly, except for the senior leadership, most StayCool employees of the company were largely unaware of the state of the business as well as its goals, objectives, and future vision. As the company continues to grow, developing a formal communication process to align the efforts of the organization will be crucial.

These strategic challenges, for StayCool, articulate the case for enterprise transformation. The senior leadership recognized the urgency of doing something to meet these challenges. He set out to articulate a set of strategic objectives that could form the basis for beginning with the Roadmap, conducting a data-driven assessment of the current state of the enterprise, and creating an actionable transformation plan that would take StayCool to the next level in its growth and success.

Strategic Objectives

Enterprise transformation began at StayCool Engineering at a moment that the senior leadership characterized as a "critical impasse" in its history. Transitioning from a traditional research and development firm with a small presence in commercial products to a company where 90 percent of its revenues come from the manufacturing and sale of commercial and military products required more attention to strategic objectives than ever.

StayCool's senior leadership identified four strategic objectives (Table 12-3) as key to the company's future success as a manufacturer, product developer, and researcher.

➤ The first was to *increase StayCool's R&D stature in critical fields.* Increasing the firm's stature in the fields of heat transfer, energy conversion, and thermal control, where StayCool already was a well-respected leader, would help the firm maintain its competitive advantage and grow the number of government product contracts that it can win.

➤ To support its increased stature in the SBIR community, StayCool also needed to *expand its commercial product line and revenues from these products.* StayCool set a specific objective of growing revenue to $20 million from these products within five years. Doing so would allow StayCool to win more contracts and make it a respectable force in thermal products. The additional revenue would provide StayCool with the cash flow necessary to pursue larger R&D projects and employ a larger sales force.

Table 12-3

StayCool's Strategic Objectives

Strategic Objective	Details
↗ Increase R&D stature in critical fields	↗ Heat transfer ↗ Energy conversion ↗ Thermal control
↗ Expand commercial product line and revenue from commercial products	↗ $20 million within five years
↗ Increase revenue through design and manufacture of military products	↗ Leverage relationship with strategic partner
↗ Leverage diesel generator technology to expand military sales	↗ Build on SBIR research contracts

➤ StayCool saw a significant opportunity for profitability in the military sector, and it set out to win more contracts quickly. To aid this objective to *increase revenue through the design and manufacture of military products*, StayCool looked to leverage its relationship with a marine container designer and manufacturer to win future business.

➤ Finally, StayCool looked to *leverage diesel generator technology to expand military sales*. StayCool has invested a significant amount of resources in developing a diesel generator in conjunction with a number of SBIR initiatives. To expand the firm's sales and revenue, StayCool hoped to leverage that technology and, once a final contract has been reached, expand its generator technology through the completion of eight SBIR proposals in this field of study.

The senior leadership felt that these four strategic objectives would serve to increase StayCool's revenue while bolstering the company's position in the SBIR community. Ultimately, by increasing the firm's commercial and military products, senior leadership believed

StayCool would not only increase revenues but increase the company's attractiveness for future SBIR contracts by being a model firm.[2]

StayCool's Stakeholder Lens

With a leadership team firmly committed to enterprise transformation, StayCool set out into the Planning Cycle of the Roadmap and began its stakeholder assessment. The team identified six stakeholder groups: employees, customers, suppliers, strategic partners, society, and leadership. As is sometimes the case, the StayCool assessment team had to rely in part on interviews with internal people who are closest to external stakeholder groups to gather data. This works as long as the organization is aware of and accounts for the potential limitations, including the possibility of low data fidelity and the introduction of internal biases.

Here we show the assessments of three stakeholder groups as examples: employees, strategic partners, and customers. The stakeholder assessment of the employee group revealed that StayCool enjoys a good relationship with its employees, in a family-like work atmosphere in which employees are generally very happy. Further, the team found that all the employees surveyed were very happy with their compensation and benefits. The primary employee concern was a lack of communication from leadership.

Table 12-4 shows the employee value exchange with the Stay-Cool enterprise.

The employee stakeholder assessment revealed that one of the challenges for StayCool going forward will be to maintain the current level of employee satisfaction as the company grows. To achieve this goal, StayCool needs to design formal mechanisms to ensure the future satisfaction of employees, such as performing and responding to employee satisfaction surveys. Given StayCool's history as an engineering company, it was not surprising to see that the freedom provided to employees to pursue research/engineering efforts was rated highly. The company's rapid growth, coupled with a lack of formal policies for managing resources, had put increased pressure on employees on the production front to ensure that production projects were completed on time. In addition, employees felt that the flexibility they once enjoyed (that had been partly due to the nature of the work they were doing) had given them opportunities to learn and explore new areas. Creating learning opportunities is something that StayCool would have to put in place to retain its key researchers.

Table 12-4

StayCool Employee Value Exchange with Enterprise

Value Expected from the Enterprise	Employees	Value Contributed to the Enterprise
↑ Job variety ↑ Job stability ↑ Salary ↑ Benefits ↑ Good co-workers ↑ Feedback ↑ Learning opportunities/ challenges ↑ Sense of accomplishment ↑ Low-pressure job ↑ Respect ↑ Opportunity for advancement ↑ High level of responsibility and freedom ↑ Tools availability ↑ Communication of company goals	↑ Hourly workforce ↑ Salary workforce ↑ Executives	↑ Time ↑ Skills ↑ Knowledge ↑ Social networks ↑ Attitude ↑ Motivation ↑ Ability to develop professionally

Clearly, leadership communication needed improvement. Notably, when we asked the enterprise leaders to identify the value of senior leaders, they listed resource allocation, strategic direction, vision, goals, metrics, and product ideas. Not a single leader mentioned communication, even though it is embedded in all of those other values.

Figure 12-2 shows how employees perceive StayCool's value delivery.

StayCool's one strategic partner stakeholder is the marine container company mentioned earlier, Atlantic Marine Containers (AMC). This partner acts as the commercialization agent for StayCool's military refrigeration units. AMC integrates StayCool refrigeration units into refrigerated containers that are then sold as a package to the military.

Figure 12-2

StayCool's Employee Value Delivery

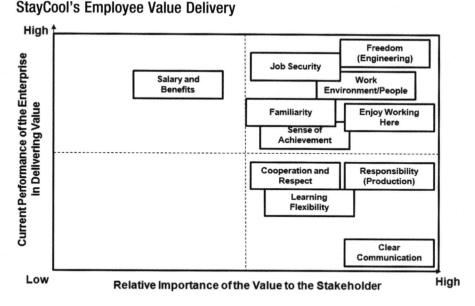

The relationship between the two partners is excellent because their capabilities are complementary and both are needed to provide a high-value product to the customer. The level of collaboration is extensive and the value exchange flows without major blocks. Table 12-5 shows the value exchange with this strategic partner.

Figure 12-3 details the value delivery.

Table 12-5

StayCool Strategic Partner Value Exchange with Enterprise

Value Expected from the Enterprise	Strategic Partners	Value Contributed to the Enterprise
Refrigeration unit (product) (quality, schedule, volumes) Technical support	AMC	Marketing expertise with military Risk and reward sharing Container for refrigeration unit

Figure 12-3

StayCool's Strategic Partner Value Delivery

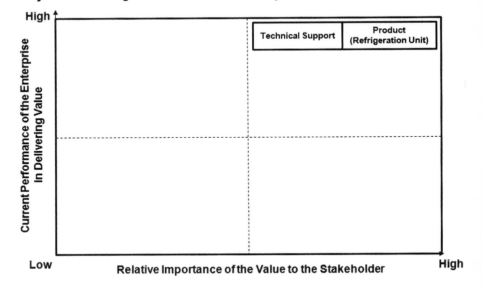

StayCool's customers include both the government (military and SBIR), as well as commercial users such as refrigeration technicians and distributors. The value expected from the enterprise by its customers is well defined. Table 12-6 shows the value exchange with customers.

Figure 12-4 details the customer value delivery.

The facets of value that customers most value are the innovation and quality of the company's products and services. Due to the formal communications required by government contracts, StayCool has an open and robust feedback channel with this customer that provides the clear communication of issues and opportunities. The feedback channels with commercial customers, however, are extremely limited. To gain an understanding of how StayCool's products are performing, the company relies on marketing call feedback—which is highly informal and often gathers limited information.

The component of customer value delivery that requires immediate work is attention to customers' needs. The gap between current performance and the relative importance to the customer in this element is related to the lack of direct communication channels between

Table 12-6

StayCool Customer Value Exchange with Enterprise

Value Expected from the Enterprise	Customers	Value Contributed to the Enterprise
Proposals New products Complete product line Good pricing On-time delivery Good quality Customer satisfaction Product support Published papers Fulfilled research objectives	Government Refrigeration Technicians	Needs and requirements Payment feedback New ideas for products

Figure 12-4

StayCool's Customer Value Delivery

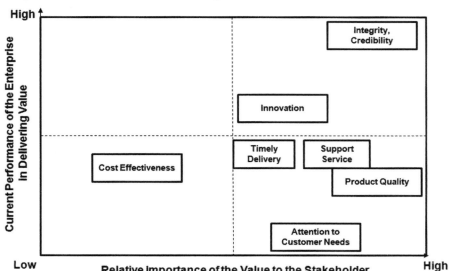

the company and its customers/end users. Adding to the perception of low product quality is the lack of quality control practices in Stay-Cool's manufacturing division.

StayCool's Process Architecture Lens

Figure 12-5 shows the high-level process map for StayCool that was created as part of the current-state assessment. The central strategic element of StayCool's business is the completion of SBIR work. Almost the entire technical staff was hired to perform SBIR-funded R&D. Once StayCool became a firm that earns nearly 90 percent of its revenue from product development and manufacturing, the centrality of SBIR work began to create some strategic issues.

The analysis of StayCool's enterprise processes was broken into three parts, corresponding to three main revenue streams: SBIR work, commercial products, and military product development. Here we present the most important observations about two of the three divisions: SBIR research and commercial products.

Figure 12-5

StayCool's Current-State Enterprise Process Map

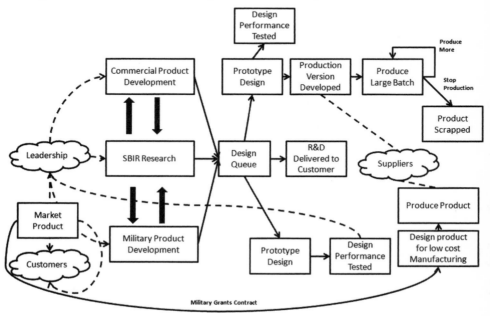

Figure 12-6 shows a detailed process map for SBIR research. The analysis revealed several problem areas, which could be opportunities for improvement projects as part of enterprise transformation. One was that the proposal writing period is very chaotic. The limited time window and lack of consideration of other work essentially bring all other nonessential work to a halt. This process has a serious impact on all other work flows in the company.

The internal and external review process does a good job of creating a quality standard for StayCool submissions. However, these internal quality checks are not formalized, and their results are not used as key metrics to gauge proposal quality. The process of submitting proposals to the company's controller is uncoordinated. A large percentage of proposals are sent to the controller at the last minute, which create quality problems as proposals are rushed through the system.

More broadly, the actual process of performing research and de-

Figure 12-6

StayCool's Current-State SBIR Research Process Map

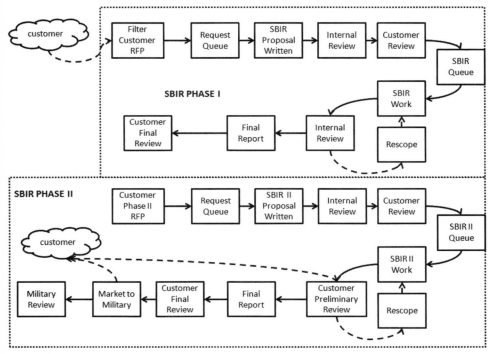

velopment often creates trade-offs with other organizational initiatives, usually product development. This results from the fact that key engineering resources such as electrical engineers can be scarce. In general, the interactions in this phase are informal and unstructured, making planning for resource allocation difficult. Further, the number of active contracts far exceeds the number of engineering staff. Thus, the engineers/scientists are involved with several different projects, and progress tends to be unsteady as engineers shift back and forth among projects to meet deadlines.

Here, the senior leadership team realized that, if StayCool scheduled work so engineers could concentrate on only one project at a time, the SBIR work could be condensed. This change would eliminate the significant waste involved with juggling projects. When an engineer has to drop a project to address another project, the first project requires time to restart, often a day or more.

The process of submitting final reports was seen as a lost opportunity to contribute to StayCool's institutional knowledge, because the only communication at the end was to the project's sponsor. At this phase in the enterprise process analysis, StayCool immediately began to discuss implementing a knowledge capture system for the engineering staff to stop further losses of valuable knowledge.

Knowledge came up in another process too, and the lack of a knowledge management system was seen as causing significant wastes. Engineers often end up redeveloping what StayCool has done before. Furthermore, long-term development/production relationships are not established with suppliers, and their expertise is not utilized during the development. In fact, several other problems were uncovered in the process of performing research and development and submitting deliverables. Design standards are not used to ensure manufacturability. Because the engineering staff at StayCool are primarily research engineers, designs typically are focused on maximizing the technical capability, rather than on delivering required capability at low cost. StayCool found it needed to develop design standards to ensure that design for manufacture (DFM) principles are followed. Additionally, the company lacked a robust prototype testing process, which resulted in designs that did not always meet performance requirements.

Finally, the analysis came to processes associated with the commercial products division. Figure 12-7 shows a detailed process map for commercial products, which result from knowledge generated during the research process. Ideas come mainly from StayCool's president, sometimes as the result of informal customer feedback provided to the

Figure 12-7

StayCool's Current-State Commercial Products Process Map

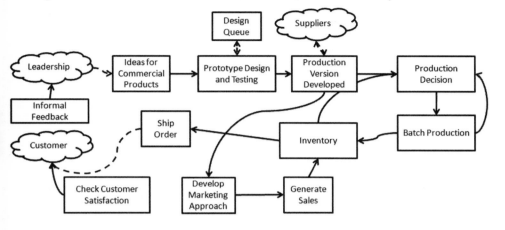

president by the marketing department. This link to customers, though, is weak and leads to many missed product opportunities.

The product development cycle was found to be longer than needed in many cases, usually because engineers are continually pulled away to perform SBIR work. Designs tend to be picked up and put down many times before completion. There was also no link to customers during product development. Although the marketing director is made aware of the product being developed, the customer/end user is completely ignored. Similarly, interactions with suppliers is minimal during this process. Supplier relationships are short term and are used very little during the product development process.

Product manufacture is not linked to customer demand. The StayCool leadership realized that, as with military products, a tighter link to the customer would allow manufacturing issues to be uncovered earlier and resolved faster.

Marketing and sales processes suffered from the absence of a formal feedback process with customers. As a result, the company does not know what problems the customers may be having with a product, and ensuring that a product will meet the needs of the customer is almost impossible. The customer is not included or considered until after development is complete and the product has been produced.

Senior management discussed its belief that designing and producing a product and trying to sell it is cheaper and easier than researching what the customers/end users want in advance. The analysis brought to the fore that this approach can be very wasteful and ignores a very important stakeholder, the customer.

Other problems with the commercial products processes were that the sales department did not work to assist the production department in achieving level production. In fact, there was no link between the two departments at all. Further, 10 percent of all orders shipped in the order fulfillment process were incorrect.

StayCool's Performance Measurement Lens

Metrics and a performance measurement system were largely lacking at StayCool. The team was able to document a few metrics for StayCool's production, R&D, and sales departments. In manufacturing, only recently were any metrics beyond throughput-based incentives used. Until then, employees had been rewarded based simply on their throughput. The production system was uncontrolled, and employees would manufacture the products that were the easiest to produce to maximize their incentives. The result was low quality, high overall cost, and enormous inventories. These throughput-based incentives were discarded in favor of a better system that is still under development.

A tardiness/absentee metric has recently been established for the manufacturing staff. Previously, some individuals on the production staff were late more than 90 percent of the time. Now, tardiness has decreased dramatically.

In research and development, the primary performance metric is the number of proposals each engineer writes for SBIR grants. An engineer is given a goal during his or her annual review of how many SBIR proposals need to be written during the next year. Typically, new hires are required to write one SBIR proposal during the next calendar year, intermediate engineers are required to write two, and senior engineers have a target of three. There is no reported company-wide goal for SBIR proposals.

StayCool ensures the quality of its proposals through an internal review process in which proposals are reviewed by other engineers for quality and format. This review process is informal, however, and qualitative values are not given, nor are the results recorded. StayCool also rewards principal investigators (PIs) if they keep a project under budget. For PIs with multiple projects, though, the absence of a penalty for going over budget makes this incentive less useful than it might otherwise be to the enterprise.

StayCool gauges its performance by targeting an engineering backlog of 1.2–1.9 years. The engineering backlog is defined as the number of worker-years it would take to complete all work that Stay-Cool currently has in-house and that has not been started.

Marketing metrics for commercial products are based on the number of sales calls made per day. Marketing employees are expected to call 70 customers every day. Customers include wholesalers and other refrigeration companies identified by StayCool as current or potential customers. A detailed incentive plan is used to reward the telemarketing staff. Currently, the incentive plan includes all possible outcomes. For example, leaving a message provides an incentive of $0.02, while placing an order has an incentive of $0.49. The large number of different outcomes makes tracking actual performance difficult.

StayCool's Alignment Lens

The StayCool team used the X-matrix templates (see Chapter 8) to assess the alignment between the enterprise's strategic objectives, metrics, processes, and stakeholder values. Figure 12-8 shows the overall scores.

Several problems were uncovered, including a misalignment between strategic objectives and stakeholder values. The assessment revealed that stakeholder values were actually either *strongly* aligned with objectives (especially those related to SBIR work, the company's founding backbone) or not mapped at all (the newer areas of StayCool). The situation was critical with respect to employee relationships and the work environment areas. Although the company had done an excellent job maintaining a highly motivated workforce and a healthy work environment, it obviously needed explicit and consistent strategies to continue to deliver those values as the pace of growth intensified. StayCool realized that it was at risk of diluting its enterprise culture and losing top talent if it could not deliver those values consistently.

The analysis found further that the alignment between metrics and strategic objectives was weak and in some instances nonexistent. The existing metrics were either too general or failed to capture the required progress that would lead to achieving StayCool's objectives. Alignment between key processes and metrics was also a significant area of concern. The X-matrix made it clear that StayCool needed to generate an improved set of metrics to measure the effectiveness of its processes. In fact, only one metric had a strong alignment with enter-

Figure 12-8

StayCool's Alignment

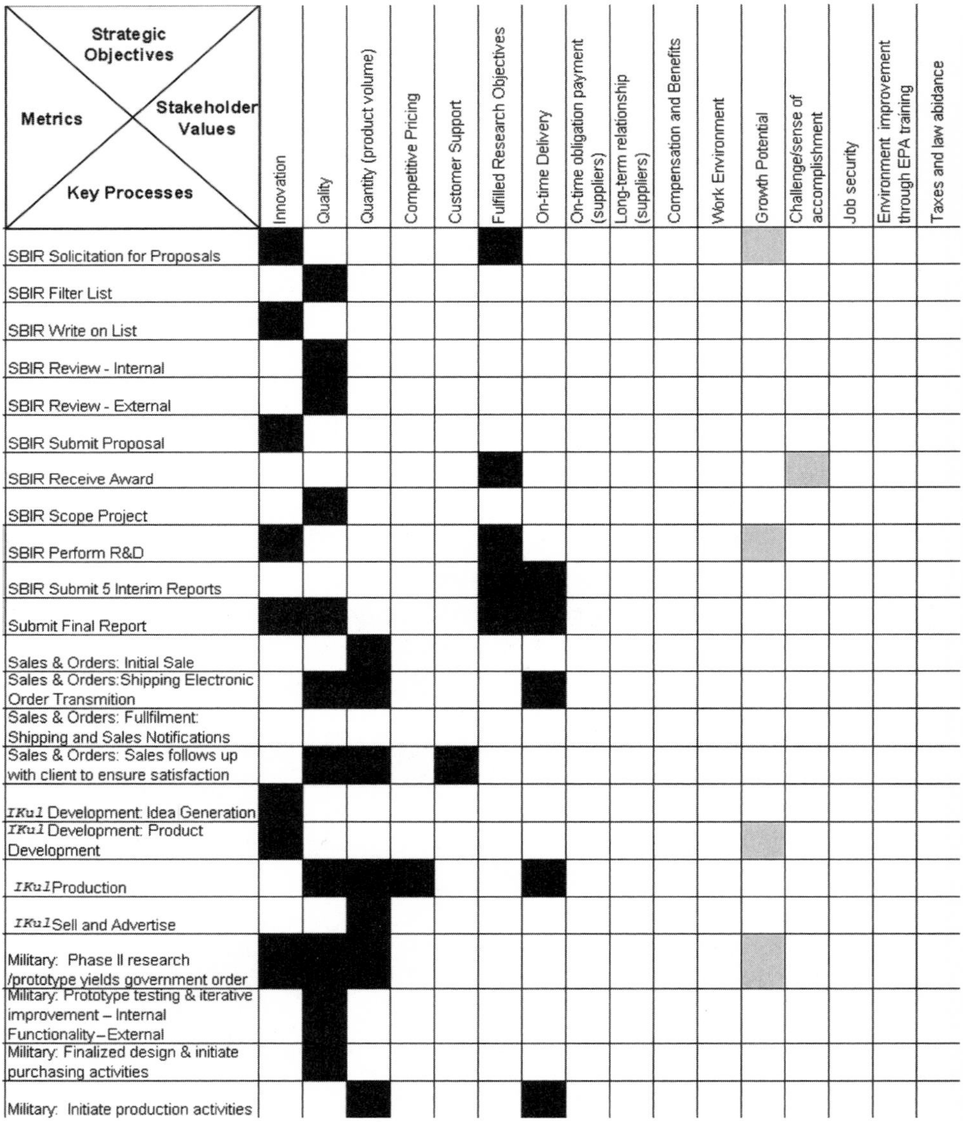

Key Processes \ Metrics / Stakeholder Values / Strategic Objectives	Innovation	Quality	Quantity (product volume)	Competitive Pricing	Customer Support	Fulfilled Research Objectives	On-time Delivery	On-time obligation payment (suppliers)	Long-term relationship (suppliers)	Compensation and Benefits	Work Environment	Growth Potential	Challenge/sense of accomplishment	Job security	Environment improvement through EPA training	Taxes and law abidance
SBIR Solicitation for Proposals	■					■						▨				
SBIR Filter List		■														
SBIR Write on List	■															
SBIR Review - Internal		■														
SBIR Review - External	■															
SBIR Submit Proposal	■															
SBIR Receive Award						■							▨			
SBIR Scope Project		■														
SBIR Perform R&D	■						■					▨				
SBIR Submit 5 Interim Reports						■		■								
Submit Final Report	■					■										
Sales & Orders: Initial Sale			■													
Sales & Orders: Shipping Electronic Order Transmition			■				■									
Sales & Orders: Fullfilment: Shipping and Sales Notifications																
Sales & Orders: Sales follows up with client to ensure satisfaction			■		■											
IKul Development: Idea Generation	■															
IKul Development: Product Development	■											▨				
IKul Production			■				■									
IKul Sell and Advertise			■													
Military: Phase II research /prototype yields government order	■		■									▨				
Military: Prototype testing & iterative improvement – Internal Functionality–External		■														
Military: Finalized design & initiate purchasing activities		■														
Military: Initiate production activities			■				■									

prise processes: the SBIR metric to track the number of proposals written.

Similarly, key processes and stakeholder value alignment lacked explicit strategies to support value generation for employees, suppliers, and the community. Although StayCool does deliver value to all of its stakeholders, formal process definition was yet to be done.

StayCool's Resource Lens

StayCool's cost structure reflects the composition of the firm. As Figure 12-9 shows, 26 percent of the company's expenses are employee related (direct labor and benefits) and general expenses and overhead account for 24 percent of StayCool's costs. Significantly, running the commercial products business had also begun to be a sizable cost source for

Figure 12-9

StayCool's Costs

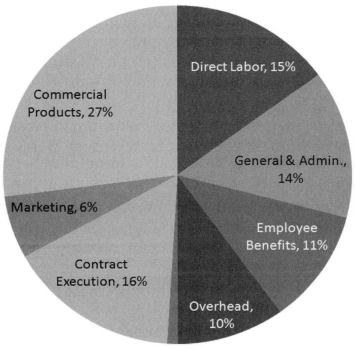

StayCool at the time of the analysis. The analysis of this cost break-down told senior leadership that they would have to pay significant attention to the cost of goods sold as the enterprise grew as a commercial and military product manufacturer. Future expenses of procuring raw goods, managing inventory, and manufacturing products would require careful management.

StayCool's Maturity Lens

The LESAT was completed by StayCool's president and the heads of engineering, finance and human resources, and IT and computing. Having a diverse group of senior leaders each complete the LESAT is a good thing: It typically results in a useful dialogue about the results and is a positive step in the direction of developing a shared mental model of the enterprise. At StayCool, this diverse group provided interesting responses that did indeed provoke a useful discussion.

As is so often the case, StayCool set for itself the goal of achieving the highest possible scores in every category of the LESAT. The current state in most categories, however, was a 1 or 2 out of 5 (5 being the highest). Although having perfection as a goal is good, it is rarely realistic, and some aspects of the LESAT are more important than others, depending on the particular enterprise. For StayCool, what mattered most was to prioritize for itself what mattered most.

StayCool's LESAT scores clearly reflected that it was in the very early stages of transformation. Overall, the highest average scores were seen in the areas that address commitment, support, employee empowerment, and resource allocation. Leadership scores reflected that there was most definitely support for transformation at the highest levels of the enterprise, with resources and time allocated to make changes. There did, however, appear to be some variation among the leadership team in terms of what they wanted to do. Absent a clear vision, there can be a disconnect about improvements and how transformation will be implemented.

In the LESAT section dealing with *leadership*, we found strong concurrence. Figure 12-10 shows the LESAT leadership scores. Enterprise strategic planning maturity questions garnered average scores between 1 and 2 for all questions. These answers were justified because StayCool has yet to document and formalize an enterprise transformation plan, even though there had been much discussion and the leadership team showed obvious intent. Leadership scored higher in adopting an enterprise paradigm, demonstrating the commitment to

Figure 12-10

StayCool's Current Maturity in Leadership/Transformation Processes

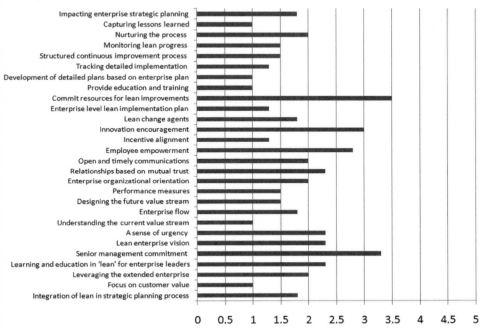

and support for transformation. These scores might have differed if the LESAT was administered to less senior members of the company.

Scores with respect to the value stream were quite low, which appeared to reflect the highly segmented character of StayCool. This suggested how critical it would be for management to understand its current value stream as it began its lean transformation. Results for developing a lean structure and behaviors had varied scores. Although employees were empowered and encouraged to innovate, there was little alignment with incentives to support these behaviors. Again, metrics and an aligned reward and recognition system would be extremely important for StayCool.

The last three sections of the LESAT *leadership* maturity assessment, which all deal with introductory stages of transformation, showed considerable variation. With respect to creating and refining a transformation plan, the absence of a plan led, not surprisingly, to a low score. However, the score was very strong for committing resources for improvements. This once again showed that management was ready and willing to make the transformation but needed to understand how to achieve it. The early stage of transformation led to extremely low scores for implementing initiatives, as well as low scores for the focus on continuous improvement.

Figure 12-11 summarizes StayCool's *lifecycle* maturity. Here again we saw the effects of an empowered workforce that has a high utilization rate but that lacks the focus on growth and performance management. Varied scores in the section on developing product and processes reflected that the customer's value and downstream stakeholder value were not being taken into consideration in the design of the product and processes. Procurement scores, also low, indicated StayCool's ongoing challenge to come up with a process for managing its supply chain. StayCool was moving in the right direction, though, having created a position to deal with procurement.

Production scores were also relatively low. A new production

Figure 12-11

StayCool's Current Maturity in Lifecycle Processes

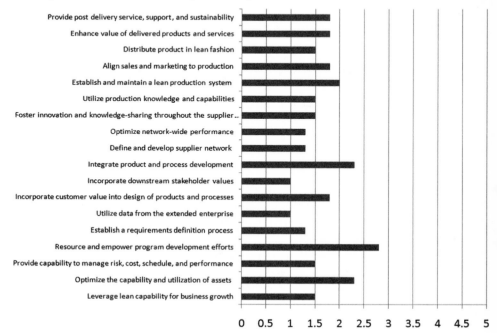

manager with a background in lean manufacturing made immediate changes upon his hiring, including cleaning up the manufacturing area, optimizing the line to be more productive, eliminating safety hazards, initiating the development of standard work, and developing and implementing metrics around people, attendance, and performance. These measures, though, were only a beginning. Some improvements were also reflected in the scores for distributing and servicing products, mostly resulting from efforts to align sales with production so that feedback from the customer (by way of sales) can be communicated to manufacturing.

StayCool scored highest on the *enabling* sections of the LESAT, as Figure 12-12 summarizes. The results showed that the company was ready for change and open to it. Management was very much on board with the initiatives and excited about implementation. StayCool's financial system was configured so that the changes required to support the business structure could take place without violating contractual requirements, including being able to pull the information needed (required for a metrics system to be implemented). Process standardiza-

Figure 12-12

StayCool's Current Maturity in Enabling Infrastructure Processes

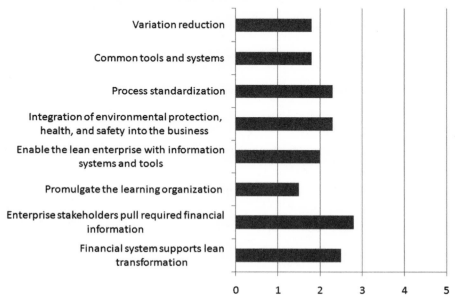

208 BEYOND THE LEAN REVOLUTION

tion was starting and showed every sign of continuing to grow in all areas of the company. Finally, due to the size of the company, implementing common tools and systems was proving to be easy.

Meaningful metrics will help improve the results of a LESAT for StayCool or any other enterprise. At StayCool, the plan was to develop metrics to show everyone how the business is doing and how each and every person helps contribute to the bottom line. A significant part of this had to include deciding how leadership would communicate the continuous improvement.

StayCool's Waste Lens

The transformation team identified various sources of waste. With customers, one source of waste was the opportunity cost of not performing market studies before investing in product development and production. The firm held years' worth of supply of some products, for which there was no demand, sitting in the production facility. The lack of customer feedback also caused a waste: a delay in the flow of information that StayCool receives on product quality and features.

Supplier-related wastes flow from the unrealized savings from having only an ad hoc rather than a structured purchasing process. The lack of communication and interaction between the R&D and Product organizations caused an information waste.

Process waste was found in:

➤ The absence of clearly defined information and product flow processes that go across the enterprise.

➤ The ineffective use of manufacturing facilities.

➤ The lack of information systems to store and share lessons learned from previous R&D and production experiences.

➤ Production planning done without regard for actual demand.

➤ The absence of clear processes and specifications in the design and testing criteria for military products, resulting in a highly iterative process with unnecessary rework and long cycle times.

Leadership-related wastes were uncovered in the absence of a formal enterprise Planning Cycle, which means that StayCool has no way to define and revise its vision and strategic objectives. Instead, the company is always reacting to business without having planned the best way to execute. The absence of an enterprise performance measurement system exacerbates the leadership problems.

Finally, resource management at StayCool does not allow for efficient R&D project execution. Hence, waste results from engineering resources jumping from project to project or to proposal writing mode as deadlines approach. Highly qualified engineers are StayCool's most valuable asset, and a considerable amount of their time is lost as a result of the inefficiencies in executing R&D projects.

StayCool's Future-State Vision

Having understood the current state, the senior leadership turned to the task of articulating a vision of StayCool's future state. They knew that they had to focus on growth. With the intellectual capital Stay-Cool had gathered over the years, they recognized that they had a tremendous advantage over competitors but they could lose the edge if they didn't exploit it through growth in the next five years. At the same time, they were struggling with a simple fact: They really did not have the planning, communication, and infrastructure to transition from being an organization centered on research and development to one that had a more balanced portfolio with stable distribution across commercial products, military products, and research.

The senior leadership described their vision for StayCool's portfolio as follows:

> Today, StayCool's refrigeration products are in 80 percent of all U.S. service bases, and have at the same time been recommended as the primary product of choice by the Restaurant Association of America. We have matured our technology to be dual use, so that changes in the commercial market due to business cycles are offset by the defense market, and *vice versa*. Today, our portfolio is evenly distributed across core research, military product development, and commercial product development. In addition to our research funding through the SBIR program, we have been able to partner with the MIT Sloan Automotive Laboratory to obtain National Science Foundation funding to develop the next generation of portable diesel engines.

StayCool's leadership also understood that people were at the core of the company's success. Yet StayCool's evolution into a new competency area, manufacturing, had increased tensions among its employees. The bold steps they were taking in their transformation would increase the workforce, putting StayCool's unique family-like culture and high employee satisfaction at risk. The leadership team described its vision regarding its people as follows:

> In the recent rating of best places to work, StayCool was ranked third by the American Society of Heating, Refrigeration and Air Conditioning (ASHRAC). Our key researchers are on the editorial boards of the *International Journal of Refrigeration*, the *Journal of Heat Transfer*, and the *Journal of Thermal Science and Engineering Applications*. In addition to our CEO, two of the research group heads have been elected to the National Academy of Engineering. In a profile of our work environment, *HRM* magazine described StayCool as an enterprise with a startup-vibe and well-oiled processes and infrastructure.

StayCool's Focus Areas

Having followed the Roadmap and completed the current-state assessment, the senior leadership at StayCool identified five focus areas for its transformation effort:

➤ Enterprise-level Planning

➤ Knowledge Management

➤ Employee Satisfaction

➤ Communication

➤ Relationship Management

These focus areas were derived from the 25 gaps/opportunities that had been identified from insights gained through the current-state analysis lenses and the exercise of articulating the future-state vision. Senior leadership believed that focusing transformation projects on these areas would enable them to manage their growth effectively from being an R&D-centric enterprise to having the more balanced portfolio articulated in the StayCool future-state vision. They wanted to achieve the transformation without losing the company's R&D-driven culture and while ensuring that employees continued to remain extremely satisfied with the enterprise.

Table 12-7 details the first focus area, *Enterprise-level Planning*. StayCool recognized that the company had to establish a formal enterprise planning methodology as a means of both determining their strategy going forward and putting in standard processes in manufac-

Table 12-7

Enterprise-Level Planning Focus Area

Focus Area	*Gaps/Opportunities*
Enterprise-Level Planning	SV3: Our growth into product development (both commercial and military) has reduced the learning flexibility that came from R&D work; this is affecting our ability to grow human capital.
	P1: Product development processes are ineffectively integrated, leading to substantial rework and often completely scrapped design.
	P3: Our policies for managing work distribution between research contracts and product developments are not working.
	P4: The production process for commercial products uses significant batching and are unconnected to customer demand, resulting in large inventories (even worse for products not selling in the market).
	P5: Manufacturing does not have an effective quality control system, leading to the perception of poor quality among our stakeholders.
	P6: Military development work is highly unsteady due to an all-hands-on-deck mentality for meeting critical SBIR deadlines or other project deadlines.
	PM2: No measures on proposal quality or learning.
	PM1: Incentives are misaligned, leading to individual behaviors that are not aligned to maximize enterprise value: Manufacturing employees are rewarded based on throughput metrics; principle investigator incentives are based on percentage under budget.
	PM3: No enterprise-wide performance management system is in place.
	A1: We are only now beginning to implement cross-functional teams.
	A3: The current performance measurement system is inadequate for truly measuring and understanding enterprise performance.

turing and product development. One of the challenges the company would have to address as part of its planning process was developing a new incentive structure that was effective for the functions, at the same time tracking overall enterprise value delivery.

StayCool had always known the importance of its intellectual capital and the role its employees play in creating and building knowledge. Given the company's initial small size, tacit knowledge sharing and face-to-face meetings were easy. However, with the proposed growth, the senior leadership knew that they needed to put in place a formal knowledge management strategy and figure out new ways of enhancing collaboration. (One of the enterprise projects focuses almost exclusively on designing physical spaces for collaboration.)

Another challenge the leadership team recognized related to the diversity of the "languages" that would be spoken at StayCool—those of manufacturing, product development, and research. Rather than forcing everyone to become trilingual, they decided to develop a training program that would make everyone bilingual—fluent in their functional area and fluent in transformation.

This transformation would have to be accompanied by explicit changes to the policies that governed how people worked and how the enterprise would ensure that employees remain enthusiastic about coming to work.

Table 12-8 details the *Knowledge Management* focus area. Table 12-9 details the *Employee Satisfaction* focus area. Table 12-10 details the *Communication* focus area. Even in the current state, communication with StayCool's key stakeholders at StayCool was not effective, whether leaders were talking to employees or the enterprise was communicating with customers and suppliers. To execute on the growth vision, Stay-Cool would have to share its vision across the enterprise and create the necessary infrastructure that would enable the enterprise to bring customers and suppliers inside the enterprise boundaries.

Table 12-11 details the *Relationship Management* focus area.

Having identified these focus areas and the associated gaps and opportunities for improvement, StayCool developed a transformation plan that included 13 projects that spanned the focus areas (see Figure 12-13). As of this writing, the transformation effort, based on that plan, has begun to show results. With the structured governance system StayCool has put in place—the CEO does a quarterly review and the enterprise project champions track projects on a biweekly basis—the enterprise is well on its way to achieving its vision.

Table 12-8

Knowledge Management Focus Area

Focus Area	*Gaps/Opportunities*
Knowledge Management	SV3: Our growth into product development (both commercial and military) has reduced the learning flexibility that came from R&D work; this is affecting our ability to grow human capital.
	P1: Product development processes are ineffectively integrated, leading to substantial rework and often completely scrapped design.
	P3: Our policies for managing work distribution between research contracts and product developments are not functioning.
	PM2: No measures on proposal quality or learning.
	EM2: No common vocabulary across the enterprise when it comes to transformation.
	W3: R&D and product development do not communicate effectively.

Revisiting Transformation Through the Seven Principles

StayCool's journey, following our Enterprise Transformation Roadmap, was based on the seven principles of enterprise transformation introduced in Chapter 2. These principles (Table 12-12) establish the foundation for successful transformation, and every step on the Roadmap is grounded in the principles.

StayCool's CEO recognized that the company had to grow—indeed, that it was growing. He did not have the luxury of stopping the growth so that StayCool could fix, incrementally, all the functional disconnects and morph the enterprise culture to one that equally embraced research, product development, and manufacturing. He realized

Table 12-9

Employee Satisfaction Focus Area

Focus Area	*Gaps/Opportunities*
Employee Satisfaction	SV1: Lack of communication from leadership
	SV2: We need to be concerned about our ability to keep or increase the current employee satisfaction level.
	P3: Our policies for managing work distribution between research contracts and product developments are not functioning.
	P6: Military development work is highly unsteady due to an all-hands-on-deck mentality for meeting critical SBIR deadlines or other project deadlines.
	A2: Proposal writing is not always aligned to our strategic objectives; the ability to win a grant supersedes alignment.

that the only approach that would work was to *adopt a holistic approach to enterprise transformation.*

Although the particulars may be different, the challenges Stay-Cool faced are generally the same as those that every enterprise faces. Senior leaders have a choice to make: They can either lead their enterprises through unconnected changes that may remedy some things and meet some of the challenges. Alternatively, they can step back, take a holistic view, determine the real current state of the enterprise, and build a response that addresses where the enterprise really needs to be and how it is going to get there in the context of its enterprise value proposition.

StayCool did not have the rich history of change of, say, a company like Rockwell Collins. Yet its leaders recognized the importance of developing one transformation *program*, not a series of possibly discordant events. That is the holistic approach in action.

Where does the enterprise begin its transformation journey? It

Table 12-10

Communication Focus Area

Focus Area	*Gaps/Opportunities*
Communication	SV1: There is a lack of communication from leadership.
	SV4: There is very little communication on the vision and direction of the enterprise other than what employees hear through their own informal networks of friends and colleagues.
	SV5: We are unable to pay effective attention to customer needs because we do not have effective feedback or communication channels with those stakeholders.
	EM1: We have a strong desire to transform the enterprise, but no vision regarding where the transformation will take the company.
	EM2: No common vocabulary across the enterprise is available when it comes to transformation.
	W3: R&D and product development do not communicate effectively.

must begin with the leadership and with our second principle: *Secure leadership commitment to drive and institutionalize enterprise behaviors.* Without senior leadership commitment, the changes you initiate across various levels of your organization may do some good, but you will not be able to capture the enterprise-level impacts that these localized changes can have. Without senior leadership commitment that is based on holistic enterprise thinking, your enterprise will not enjoy the space needed to allow transformation efforts to flourish and achieve their larger effects on overall performance. As new policies and work practices are deployed as part of a transformation plan, the senior leadership commitment and engagement overcome the temporary drops in

Table 12-11

Relationship Management Focus Area

Focus Area	*Gaps/Opportunities*
Relationship Management	SV5: We are unable to pay effective attention to customer needs because we do not have effective feedback or communication channels with these stakeholders.
	SV6: Our suppliers would like to have longer-term, established relationships, but currently we are unable to establish them.
	P4: The production process for commercial products uses significant batching, and is unconnected to customer demand, resulting in large inventories (even worse for products not selling in the market).
	P5: Manufacturing does not have an effective quality control system, leading to the perception of poor quality among our stakeholders.
	P6: Military development work is highly unsteady due to an all-hands-on-deck mentality for meeting critical SBIR deadlines or other project deadlines.
	PM1: Incentives are misaligned, leading to individual behaviors that are not aligned to maximize enterprise value: Manufacturing employees are rewarded based on throughput metrics; principle investigator incentives are based on percentage under budget.
	W1: There is significant opportunity cost in not carrying out market studies prior to the start of product development and production.
	W2: We have an ad hoc procurement process, which in turn means we are in some cases waiting for specialty parts from our suppliers (since we don't have long-term relationships with them).

Figure 12-13

StayCool Enterprise Projects

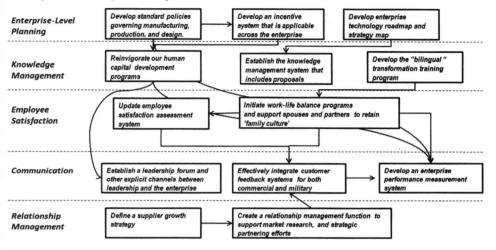

Table 12-12

Enterprise Transformation Principles

↑ Adopt a holistic approach to enterprise transformation.

↑ Secure leadership commitment to drive and institutionalize enterprise behaviors.

↑ Identify relevant stakeholders and determine their value propositions.

↑ Focus on enterprise effectiveness before efficiency.

↑ Address internal and external enterprise interdependencies.

↑ Ensure stability and flow within and across the enterprise.

↑ Emphasize organizational learning.

performance that may occur during these important changes. The senior leadership guidance keeps the enterprise on course to ensure that the fruits of the transformation efforts are harvested.

StayCool's transformation was supported not only by the CEO, but by the leadership of all the functional areas and the three cross-functional value streams.

We pointed out in Chapter 1 that your enterprise value proposition effectively captures why your enterprise exists—its reason for being. Our third principle emphasizes the need to explore in expanded detail exactly what value is exchanged with your key stakeholders and to assess the performance of that value exchange: *Identify relevant stakeholders and determine their value propositions.* The need to transform comes into even sharper focus when you assess your current state and realize that the enterprise value proposition is misaligned with the values of key enterprise stakeholders.

The key is to look at the bidirectional flow of value between the stakeholder and the enterprise. The analysis of StayCool's employee value exchange unveiled a fundamental issue with which the leadership team was struggling: how to balance the need to provide freedom for R&D work while maintaining execution discipline. StayCool always managed to deliver products to customers on the expected delivery date, but it wasn't until StayCool performed a Stakeholder Analysis that the leadership understood the impact this tactic had on its people. The Stakeholder Analysis of customers surprised the StayCool leadership team too. There had always been an assumption that the business would be just fine as long the final delivery dates were met. However, a detailed look at the customer value exchange analysis told a very different story: Attention to customer needs was very important, but very low.

StayCool, perhaps like your enterprise, realized it had work to do to align its value proposition with the values of its multiple stakeholder groups. After all, StayCool, like every other enterprise, exists because it has unique value to create for its stakeholders. That led StayCool to our fourth principle: *Focus on enterprise effectiveness before efficiency.*

Effectiveness and efficiency are not a trade-off in enterprise transformation. Rather, this principle is about reflecting on whether you are doing the right things before determining whether you are doing those right things the right way. For StayCool, as perhaps for your enterprise, the leadership realized that, to be effective, the enterprise had to grow in a manner that would allow for keeping the research-driven focus. That was the right thing; doing it the right way meant *not* doing research simply for the sake of doing research. Another right thing to do was to grow the use of the company's products and services; one of the right ways was to leverage existing relationships. StayCool also realized that it had neither the right processes in place on the manufacturing side, which created perceptions of poor quality, nor the right policies for managing resource distribution, which led to employee dissatisfaction. Once the team figured out the right things to do, it could make process and policy fixes part of the transformation that would improve both efficiency and effectiveness for the entire enterprise.

That overall enterprise perspective highlights our fifth principle: *Address internal and external enterprise interdependencies*. Enterprises do not exist in isolation. They are part of a fluid ecosystem in which both internal and external interdependencies are constantly evolving. The lenses of current-state analysis make it possible to put this principle into action.

At StayCool, for example, the process architecture lens (Chapter 6) indicated that the enterprise's most effective value stream—winning SBIR funding—could be improved dramatically. The firm needed to establish a common internal proposal review process and create a shared knowledge repository accessible to all proposal writers. Further, the lens revealed a problem StayCool encountered repeatedly: Personnel who started a project were not necessarily the ones who finished a project.

Our sixth principle emphasizes the need for smooth information and resource flows: *Ensure stability and flow within and across the enterprise*. What was revealed by StayCool's process architecture lens certainly speaks to this important principle. Perhaps at your enterprise, like at StayCool, a major portion of the value is created with knowledge work. People need to be able to work on projects for sustained periods to make a tangible contribution. The absence of stability all too often means that people end up constantly reinventing the wheel. People and knowledge not flowing within and across the StayCool enterprise meant that overall performance suffered.

StayCool embarked on a transformation journey to overcome the challenges the enterprise had uncovered and to capture its many opportunities. Taking a holistic approach, it assessed the current state of the enterprise and created a transformation plan. At the heart of any transformation effort is the ability to capture lessons learned and to diffuse that learning—and StayCool aimed to do so. Our final principle is targeted at building an enterprise that may make many mistakes but that does not make the same mistake twice: *Emphasize organizational learning*.

We know there is no cookie-cutter answer to transformation. Every enterprise will embark on the journey and measure success differently. The key to success is whether the approach you take is based on a true and rich picture of your enterprise. In this book, we have provided a framework and tools for analysis, as well as a foundation for tailoring and implementing a transformation plan that works specifically for your enterprise because it is based on your current state.

As we have seen again and again, an enterprise that embarks on a transformation journey employing these seven principles can, in fact, become a whole that is greater than the sum of its parts. Like StayCool, your enterprise can transform from a disjointed organization to an enterprise that lives up to its value proposition and creates value for all its stakeholders.

Lean Enterprise Self-Assessment Tool: Case Studies

T HROUGHOUT THIS BOOK, we have shown examples of how enterprises have used the Lean Enterprise Self-Assessment Tool
(LESAT) to conduct various aspects of the assessment of the current state before creating a plan for enterprise transformation. In this
Appendix, we present two full case studies that show how LESAT is
used and what results are obtained from the analysis.

These cases derive from data and information obtained while
researching U.S. firms within MIT's Lean Advancement Initiative consortium, but each case is actually a composite from multiple participants. The names of the companies and individuals are fictitious. The
exact data and corporate information do not reflect any specific firm
that participated in the MIT research. The data have been modified so
that each case illustrates a particular management issue associated
with enterprise transformation.

The cases were originally prepared by Cory R. A. Hallam, at the
time a doctoral candidate at MIT, in October 2001. We have made some
minor alterations for their publication in this book. They are as relevant today as they were when first constructed.

Case 1: Advanced Composite Aerostructures Incorporated

Advanced Composite Aerostructures Incorporated (ACAI) is a Virginia-
based company with annual revenues of US$400 million. ACAI pro-
duces nonprimary composite structural components for commercial

221

aircraft and spacecraft manufacturers, as well as in-service replacement parts for Department of Defense (DoD) customers. The company employs 2,200 people, has in-house staff for marketing, finance, human resources (HR), product design, engineering, manufacturing, and customer support, as well as a base of 225 suppliers. ACAI is very functionally oriented, managed by a president and executive committee representing each of the functional groups.

Since 1994, they have made sporadic attempts at becoming lean, mostly driven by several shop floor managers intrigued by the concept after attending a conference on lean manufacturing. The company achieved several successes in manufacturing between 1994 and 2000. It created several component production lines that were able to produce in single-piece flow, mainly due to cellular reorganization of the production process. The lead time on these components dropped by 58 percent, and work in progress (WIP) was cut from weeks of inventory to hours of inventory. Although these successes were applauded by the director of manufacturing, little change to become even leaner has taken place elsewhere in the company.

The same shop floor managers who had initially driven lean subsequently left the company after becoming frustrated by the demands placed on them by financial tracking systems, expediters, MRP systems, warehouse managers, and purchasers that were not allowing the value-delivery process to become even leaner. Faced with the issue of winning new contracts and hiring new managers who spoke the language of lean, ACAI's president decided to create a new position, vice president of lean, with responsibility for hiring new managers and coordinating the lean production system. After a lengthy search, a suitable candidate was found, and David Stonegarth filled the position.

The new vice president was familiar with the work that the Massachusetts Institute of Technology's (MIT) Lean Advancement Initiative (LAI) had been doing on lean transformation. After a lengthy review of ACAI's past efforts, David informed the ACAI president, Steven Jameson, that enterprise transformation was the logical next step for the company. After all, many of the issues identified by the managers who had left the company were related to the entire organization, not just to the manufacturing function. The new vice president of lean proposed that ACAI use MIT's Lean Enterprise Self-Assessment Tool (LESAT) to identify and assess the company's strengths and weaknesses with respect to creating a lean enterprise at ACAI. Jameson agreed on the condition that Stonegarth could assure him it would require minimal time from ACAI's executive staff, as he didn't want to burden them with extra paperwork.

LESAT Sessions

Stonegarth, the vice president of lean, spent months getting the executives of ACAI to agree to a date on their schedules when they would all be available for a one-hour meeting. Using the briefing material provided by MIT, he gave an hour-long overview of the LESAT tool and provided instructions for the managers to complete the assessment on their own—a task he said would take no more than two hours. He then explained that a follow-up meeting would be held to discuss the assessment results.

The ACAI executives left the meeting with their LESAT books in hand and with instructions to get their results to Stonegarth within three weeks. Over that period, Stonegarth fielded calls from executives with questions about what was meant by terms such as "extended value stream," "enterprise flow," "designing the future value stream," and so on. By the end of week three, only four of the 12 participants had returned their assessments.

Calling the executives, Stonegarth was repeatedly told that they were very busy and would get to it when they had a chance. Finally, after pleading with the president for some support, the executives were forced to complete the assessment and Stonegarth received all the data. With some compilation and number crunching in an electronic spreadsheet, he had the assessment results and was ready to organize a postassessment discussion session for the executives.

LESAT Results

Based on the LESAT assessments done by the 12 participants, Stonegarth compiled the current-state LESAT *averages*, as presented in Table A-1. (The full current-state LESAT results may be found at the end of this case study, Tables A-2, A-3, and A-4.)

With these data in hand, Stonegarth prepared to present the results to executive management. For the briefing, he first reviewed the purpose of the LESAT tool, and then reminded the executives of the definitions associated with the five levels of the capability maturity model used in the assessment. (The general maturity capability levels may be found at the end of this case study, in Table A-5.) He presented the general results shown in Table A-1 as his high-level summary. Most of the data seemed to suggest a general awareness of lean, with infor-

Table A-1

ACAI LESAT Averages

Section I: Lean Transformation/Leadership		Average = 1.8
I.A	Enterprise Strategic Planning	1.7
I.B	Adopt Lean Paradigm	1.4
I.C	Focus on the Value Stream	1.7
I.D	Develop Lean Structure and Behavior	2.4
I.E	Create and Refine Transformation Plan	1.7
I.F	Implement Lean Initiatives	1.2
I.G	Focus on Continuing Improvement	1.5
Section II: Lifecycle Processes		Average = 2.3
II.A	Business Acquisition and Program Management	2.2
II.B	Requirements Definition	2.3
II.C	Develop Product and Process	2.6
II.D	Manage Supply Chain	2.0
II.E	Produce Product	2.7
II.F	Distribute and Service Product	2.4
Section III: Enabling Infrastructure		Average = 1.9
III.A	Lean Organizational Enablers	1.8
III.B	Lean Process Enablers	2.0

mal approaches deployed in a few areas that enjoyed varying degrees of effectiveness and sustainment.

Seeing these results, one executive commented: "I have to say that I am quite shocked with how low we scored on this tool, since we have been doing lean for seven years at ACAI. Is this LESAT tool measuring the right aspects of our business, or were we overzealous in extolling the gains achieved by our previous lean improvements in manufacturing? I thought we would have performed much better on this assessment."

Stonegarth then explained that the LESAT tool was aimed at assessing *enterprise*-level lean transformation, of which the previous efforts at lean manufacturing were only a small subset. If one considered the items of the assessment related to the manufacturing elements of the enterprise (such as Section II.E.2 in particular), ACAI was scoring significantly higher than in areas such as strategic planning (Section I.A).

At this point, Elizabeth Hartley, ACAI's director of engineering, spoke up. "David, based on the results you just discussed, I question the validity of this tool. While we scored low in strategic planning, we all know that each functional manager does strategic planning for his or her functional group for both an annual plan and a five-year outlook plan. Our functional organizations are definitely better than a 1.7. How can we score low on enterprise strategic planning when everyone in the enterprise's executive management does strategic planning for his or her respective function?"

This point raised several additional questions about the tool that were focused very much on what each functional group was doing. Many of the executives were convinced that their functions should have scored much higher than the overall average suggested. The discussion focused on the issue of functional assessment versus enterprise assessment for quite a while.

By then, the executives were struggling with the many interfunctional issues that had come up, in addition to the overall low scores of the LESAT. Stonegarth suggested that they review the line items in the LESAT assessment that scored very low to frame the discussion and help everyone understand why ACAI had gotten these particular LESAT results.

At the end of the scheduled hour, the president made an executive decision. "Folks, there is obviously more to this assessment than meets the eye. We have scored very low on this first assessment, but I am confident that we could do much better the next time around. I suggest that as an enterprise we need to increase all of our scores to a level 3 by the next review period in six months. Then we can set a goal of level 4 and 5 for the next year to make sure we have a world-class ranking.

"David, we need to understand the root cause of these low scores."

The executive committee commended Stonegarth's effort for organizing the assessment process and concluded the meeting. Stonegarth returned to his office, sat down at his desk, and contemplated his next steps for carrying out a full enterprise analysis of ACAI.

Tables A-2, A-3, and A-4 present ACAI's full current-state LESAT results.

Tables A-5 presents ACAI's generic capability maturity levels.

(text continues on page 232)

Table A-2

ACAI LESAT Results for Section I: Lean Transformation Leadership

Roadmap Link	Lean Practice	State	Mean	Range
I.A Enterprise Strategic planning	I.A.1. Integration of lean in strategic planning process	Current	2.0	3
	I.A.2. Focus on customer value	Current	1.7	3
	I.A.3. Leveraging the extended enterprise	Current	1.4	2
I.B Adopt Lean Paradigm	I.B.1. Learning and education in lean for enterprise leaders	Current	1.3	2
	I.B.2. Senior management commitment	Current	1.4	2
	I.B.3 Lean enterprise vision	Current	1.5	3
	I.B.4. A sense of urgency	Current	1.3	2
I.C Focus on the Value Stream	I.C.1. Understanding the current value stream	Current	1.4	2
	I.C.2. Enterprise flow	Current	2.0	1
	I.C.3. Designing the future value stream	Current	1.2	1
	I.C.4. Performance measures	Current	2.0	2

Table A-2 (Continued)

Roadmap Link	Lean Practice	State	Mean	Range
I.D Develop Lean Structure and Behavior	I.D.1. Enterprise organizational orientation	Current	2.3	2
	I.D.2. Relationships based on mutual trust	Current	2.6	3
	I.D.3. Open and timely communications	Current	2.6	2
	I.D.4. Employee empowerment	Current	2.5	1
	I.D.5. Incentive alignment	Current	2.0	2
	I.D.6. Innovation encouragement	Current	3.0	2
	I.D.7. Lean change agents	Current	1.8	2
I.E Create and Refine Implementation Plan	I.E.1. Enterprise-level lean implementation plan	Current	1.2	3
	I.E.2. Commit resources for lean improvements	Current	2.0	1
	I.E.3. Provide education and training	Current	2.0	2
I.F Implement Lean Initiatives	I.F.1. Development of detailed plans based on enterprise plan	Current	1.2	1
	I.F.2. Tracking detailed implementation	Current	1.2	2
I.G Focus on Continuous Improvement	I.G.1. Structured continuous improvement process	Current	1.1	2
	I.G.2. Monitoring lean progress	Current	1.2	2
	I.G.3. Nurturing the process	Current	1.9	1
	I.G.4. Capturing lessons learned	Current	1.6	2
	I.G.5. Impacting enterprise strategic planning	Current	1.8	2

Table A-3

ACAI LESAT Results for Section II: Lifecycle Processes

	Lean Practice	State	Mean	Range
II.A. Business Acquisition and Program Management	II.A.1. Leverage lean capability for business growth	Current	1.3	2
	II.A.2. Optimize the capability and utilization of assets	Current	1.3	1
	II.A.3. Provide capability to manage risk, cost, schedule, and performance	Current	3.0	2
	II.A.4. Resource and empower program development efforts	Current	3.2	2
II. B. Requirements Definition	II.B.1. Establish a requirements definition process to optimize lifecycle value	Current	2.1	2
	II.B.2. Utilize data from the extended enterprise to optimize future requirement definitions	Current	2.4	1
II.C. Develop Product and Process	II.C.1. Incorporate customer value into design of products and processes	Current	2.8	2
	II.C.2. Incorporate downstream stakeholder values into products and processes	Current	2.8	2
	II.C.3. Integrate product and process development	Current	2.2	1

Table A-3 (Continued)

	Lean Practice	State	Mean	Range
II.D. Supply Chain Management	II.D.1. Define and develop supplier network	Current	1.9	1
	II.D.2. Optimize network-wide performance	Current	2.0	2
	II.D.3. Foster innovation and knowledge-sharing throughout the supplier network	Current	2.0	1
II.E. Produce Product	II.E.1. Utilize production knowledge and capabilities for competitive advantage	Current	2.0	1
	II.E.2. Establish and maintain a lean production system	Current	3.4	2
II.F. Distribute and Service Product	II.F.1. Align sales and marketing to production	Current	2.2	3
	II.F.2. Distribute product in lean fashion	Current	2.5	1
	II.F.3. Enhance value of delivered products and services to customers and the enterprise	Current	2.5	1
	II.F.4. Provide postdelivery service, support, and sustainability	Current	1.7	2

Table A-4

ACAI LESAT Results for Section III: Enabling Infrastructure

	Lean Practice	State	Mean	Range
III.A. Lean Organizational Enablers	III.A.1. Financial system supports lean transformation	Current	1.1	2
	III.A.2. Enterprise stakeholders pull required financial information	Current	1.6	3
	III.A.3. Promulgate the learning organization	Current	1.5	2
	III.A.4. Enable the lean enterprise with information systems and tools	Current	1.8	3
	III.A.5. Integration of environmental protection, heath, and safety into the business	Current	3.1	2
III.B. Lean Process Enablers	III.B.1. Process standardization	Current	2.0	2
	III.B.2. Common tools and systems	Current	2.0	1
	III.B.3. Variation reduction	Current	2.0	2

Table A-5

ACAI Generic Capability Maturity Level

Capability Maturity Level	Generic Definition
Level 1	Some awareness of this practice; sporadic improvement activities may be underway in a few areas.
Level 2	General awareness; informal approach deployed in a few areas with varying degrees of effectiveness and sustainment.
Level 3	A systematic approach /methodology deployed in varying stages across most areas; facilitated with metrics; good sustainment.
Level 4	Ongoing refinement and continuous improvement across the enterprise; improvement gains are sustained.
Level 5	Exceptional, well-defined, innovative approach is fully deployed across the extended enterprise (across internal and external value streams); recognized as best practice.

Case 2: Advanced Electronic Systems Incorporated

Advanced Electronic Systems Incorporated (AESI) has four primary business units: radar (commercial and military), data bus design and integration (commercial and military), electronic warfare system integration services, and fire control system development. The company runs each business unit as a separate enterprise serving individual customers. They share common support services such as finance, human resources, business development, and procurement, each of which functions as a cost center for the company. AESI employs 11,000 people at its four facilities in California, New Jersey, Pennsylvania, and Texas. The company has annual revenues of US$1.9 billion and more than 450 suppliers.

AESI has been a member of MIT's Lean Advancement Initiative

(LAI) consortium for two years and has sent its business unit executives to the annual LAI plenary conference, executive board meetings, and some of the LAI lean workshops.

AESI's president, Ray Leblanc, is convinced that the changing landscape of the aerospace industry is creating a need for AESI to find a new source of competitive advantage on the commercial side of its businesses, while making itself more attractive to its military customers in its defense contracts. In Leblanc's opinion, the future of AESI is to create a lean enterprise. He is banking on the fact that transforming to a lean enterprise will reduce overall operating costs, increase profitability, make the company more competitive on government contracts, and provide better returns to their shareholders. While Leblanc wants to transform quickly, he is unsure of the state of leanness of his company. He knows that the business units have some very good managers, but overall he is uncertain about the understanding or application of lean principles within the organization.

About three months ago, Leblanc promoted Allison Hughes to be vice president of lean for AESI. She had been vice president of the radar business unit. Leblanc's goal in this promotion was to orchestrate his lean goals across the enterprise. Working closely with Hughes and the executive committee comprising business unit and cost center leaders, Leblanc has since initiated a strategic planning process, with lean at the core of the operations philosophy for the company. Guided by the Enterprise Transformation Roadmap, Hughes decided that an assessment was necessary to establish a baseline understanding of the strengths and weaknesses of AESI with respect to becoming a lean enterprise. Within days of the strategic planning sessions, Hughes began preparing to use LAI's Lean Enterprise Self-Assessment Tool with the business unit and cost center leaders as a means to understand the current state of leanness in each of these AESI groups.

LESAT Sessions

The first LESAT introductory session was planned and executed within a month's time. Three MIT researchers were present for the first LESAT introduction session. Professor Debbie Nightingale provided an overview of the tool, and then Hughes described how the assessment would be performed. It was her intent that the executives would take the assessment back to their respective business units or support functions and perform the assessment with their senior management committees. She would then collect the results and compile them to get an overall picture of AESI's current state.

Ray Leblanc asked that the executives make this assessment a priority. "Folks, it is my opinion that the move toward a lean enterprise is at the core of our future success. I am considering the work that Allison is doing in this assessment a priority for all of us, as it will establish a better understanding of where we are and where we need to go as a lean enterprise."

The AESI executives left the meeting with their LESAT books in hand and with instructions to get their results to Hughes within two weeks. This goal was met. Using a spreadsheet, Hughes compiled all the results and began preparing for the report-out session. It took some effort to coordinate schedules, but the executives at AESI were able to find a time to meet the following week that accommodated everyone's schedule.

LESAT Results

Hughes began the report-out session by reviewing the purpose of the LESAT with the executives. She then reminded them of the generic definitions associated with the capability maturity model used in the assessment. Hughes presented the general results shown in Table A-6 as her high-level summary. She commented on the fact that their overall assessment of about a level 2 indicated that there was a general aware-ness of lean, with informal approaches deployed in a few areas with varying degrees of effectiveness. (AESI's general maturity capability lev-els may be found at the end of this case study, in Table A-7).

In addition, Hughes pointed out that AESI's enabling infra-structure was averaging below a level 2 in the assessment. [The full current-state LESAT results may be found at the end of this case study (Tables A-8, A-9, and A-10), including the average LESAT practice val-ues based on all eight respondents and the ranges[1] in responses.] Seeing these results provoked several questions from the director of data bus design and integration, Sandra Evans: "How does this com-pare to our competitors in the industry? Are we scoring too low? What does this score mean to us?"

Hughes reminded the executives that the assessment was an in-ternal perception of their maturity, not an industry standard tool for comparing multiple companies. She continued by saying that the meaning of the results is a statement of AESI's current leanness as per the description of the 54 LESAT measures.

Ray Leblanc then said, "I think we have to realize that we are only just starting this transformation process. We are obviously doing

Table A-6

AESI LESAT Averages

Section I: Lean Transformation/Leadership		Average = 2.2
I.A	Enterprise Strategic Planning	2.8
I.B	Adopt Lean Paradigm	2.7
I.C	Focus on the Value Stream	1.7
I.D	Develop Lean Structure and Behavior	2.2
I.E	Create and Refine Transformation Plan	2.3
I.F	Implement Lean Initiatives	1.6
I.G	Focus on Continuing Improvement	1.9
Section II: Lifecycle Processes		*Average = 2.2*
II.A	Business Acquisition and Program Management	2.5
II.B	Requirements Definition	2.4
II.C	Develop Product and Process	2.9
II.D	Manage Supply Chain	1.7
II.E	Produce Product	1.8
II.F	Distribute and Service Product	1.8
Section III: Enabling Infrastructure		*Average = 1.7*
III.A	Lean Organizational Enablers	1.9
III.B	Lean Process Enablers	1.5

better in some areas than others. The areas where we are not doing as well should be an indication of a need we have to address."

The discussion in the meeting then centered on a review of each of the LESAT averages in Table A-6. The executives reviewed each result and then discussed the impact the result would have on AESI's lean transformation plan. Although this seemed to sit well with the busi-

Table A-7

AESI Generic Capability Maturity Level

Capability Maturity Level	*Generic Definition*
Level 1	Some awareness of this practice; sporadic improvement activities may be underway in a few areas.
Level 2	General awareness; informal approach deployed in a few areas with varying degrees of effectiveness and sustainment.
Level 3	A systematic approach/methodology deployed in varying stages across most areas; facilitated with metrics; good sustainment.
Level 4	Ongoing refinement and continuous improvement across the enterprise; improvement gains are sustained.
Level 5	Exceptional, well-defined, innovative approach is fully deployed across the extended enterprise (across internal and external value streams); recognized as best practice.

ness unit leaders, some of the support function executives were finding it difficult to understand their role in the value stream process.

James Devans, the director of finance, spoke up: "I can understand that we have to improve in areas like focusing on the value stream, where we scored a 1.7, or managing the supply chain, where we also scored a 1.7, but I am unclear of how the finance department provides value to the end customer. I would like to figure this out."

This point raised several further questions about how the value stream was defined and from whose perspective. Was it solely the customer's perspective, or did each function deliver a product/service to the business units via a separate value stream? Also, some of the executives were wondering how they would allocate resources to act on some of the transformation plans they were going to develop. How would they prioritize their actions, since the effort required for the number of actions would most likely be greater than the available resources? The

(text continues on page242)

Table A-8

AESI LESAT Results for Section I: Lean Transformation Leadership

Roadmap Link	Lean Practice	State	Mean	Range
I.A Enterprise strategic planning	I.A.1. Integration of lean in strategic planning process	Current	3.5	1
	I.A.2. Focus on customer value	Current	2.0	2
	I.A.3. Leveraging the extended enterprise	Current	3.0	1
I.B Adopt Lean Paradigm	I.B.1. Learning and education in lean for enterprise leaders	Current	2.5	1
	I.B.2. Senior management commitment	Current	3.5	1
	I.B.3 Lean enterprise vision	Current	2.2	1
	I.B.4. A sense of urgency	Current	2.4	1
I.C Focus on the Value Stream	I.C.1. Understanding the current value stream	Current	1.7	2
	I.C.2. Enterprise flow	Current	2.0	1
	I.C.3. Designing the future value stream	Current	1.5	1
	I.C.4. Performance measures	Current	1.6	2

Table A-8 (Continued)

Roadmap Link	Lean Practice	State	Mean	Range
I.D Develop Lean Structure and Behavior	I.D.1. Enterprise organizational orientation	Current	2.0	2
	I.D.2. Relationships based on mutual trust	Current	2.2	1
	I.D.3. Open and timely communications	Current	2.0	1
	I.D.4. Employee empowerment	Current	2.5	1
	I.D.5. Incentive alignment	Current	1.4	2
	I.D.6. Innovation encouragement	Current	2.8	1
	I.D.7. Lean change agents	Current	2.2	1
I.E Create and Refine Implementation Plan	I.E.1. Enterprise-level lean implementation plan	Current	1.9	1
	I.E.2. Commit resources for lean improvements	Current	3.0	1
	I.E.3. Provide education and training	Current	1.9	1
I.F Implement Lean Initiatives	I.F.1. Development of detailed plans based on enterprise plan	Current	1.2	1
	I.F.2. Tracking detailed implementation	Current	2.0	1
I.G Focus on Continuous Improvement	I.G.1. Structured continuous improvement process	Current	1.6	2
	I.G.2. Monitoring lean progress	Current	2.0	2
	I.G.3. Nurturing the process	Current	2.0	1
	I.G.4. Capturing lessons learned	Current	2.0	1
	I.G.5 Impacting enterprise strategic	Current	2.0	3

Table A-9

AESI LESAT Results for Section II: Lifecycle Processes

Roadmap Link	Lean Practice	State	Mean	Range
II.A. Business Acquisition and Program Management	II.A.1. Leverage lean capability for business growth	Current	1.9	1
	II.A.2. Optimize the capability and utilization of assets	Current	2.4	1
	II.A.3. Provide capability to manage risk, cost, schedule, and performance	Current	3.0	1
	II.A.4. Resource and empower program development efforts	Current	2.8	2
II.B. Requirements Definition	II.B.1. Establish a requirements definition process to optimize lifecycle value	Current	2.4	1
	II.B.2. Utilize data from the extended enterprise to optimize future requirement definitions	Current	2.4	1
II.C. Develop Product and Process	II.C.1. Incorporate customer value into design of products and processes	Current	3.0	2
	II.C.2. Incorporate downstream stakeholder values into products and processes	Current	3.2	1
	II.C.3. Integrate product and process development	Current	2.4	1

Table A-9 (Continued)

Roadmap Link	Lean Practice	State	Mean	Range
II.D. Supply Chain Management	II.D.1. Define and develop supplier network	Current	1.4	1
	II.D.2. Optimize network-wide performance	Current	1.8	1
	II.D.3. Foster innovation and knowledge sharing throughout the supplier network	Current	1.9	1
II.E. Produce Product	II.E.1. Utilize production knowledge and capabilities for competitive advantage	Current	2.0	1
	II.E.2. Establish and maintain a lean production system	Current	1.5	2
II.F. Distribute and Service Product	II.F.1. Align sales and marketing to production	Current	2.0	1
	II.F.2. Distribute product in lean fashion	Current	1.5	1
	II.F.3. Enhance value of delivered products and services to customers and the enterprise	Current	2.0	1
	II.F.4. Provide postdelivery service, support, and sustainability	Current	2.3	2

Table A-10

AESI LESAT Results for Section III: Enabling Infrastructure

Roadmap Link	Lean Practice	State	Mean	Range
III.A. Lean Organizational Enablers	III.A.1. Financial system supports lean transformation	Current	1.1	1
	III.A.2. Enterprise stakeholders pull required financial information	Current	2.0	1
	III.A.3. Promulgate the learning organization	Current	1.5	1
	III.A.4. Enable the lean enterprise with information systems and tools	Current	1.8	2
	III.A.5. Integration of environmental protection, heath, and safety into the business	Current	2.9	1
III.B. Lean Process Enablers	III.B.1. Process standardization	Current	1.4	1
	III.B.2. Common tools and systems	Current	1.2	1
	III.B.3. Variation reduction	Current	2.0	2

discussions were enthusiastic, and participants seemed to have a common desire to figure out how they would enable the transformation of the enterprise.

With time running out in the meeting, Ray Leblanc decided to wrap things up with some final comments and actions. "I think we have uncovered some good insights into our current leanness. We should not be worried about our exact score, but rather what the individual LESAT levels are telling us about AESI's current lean maturity. We have already identified some actionable issues, and can incorporate them in our strategic plans—but I think that the findings have highlighted the need for deeper analysis. Allison—can you take the next step and figure out a way for us to build an actionable transformation plan?"

The executive committee applauded Hughes's effort for orchestrating the assessment process and were excited about taking an enterprise perspective.

Tables A-7 presents AESI's generic capability maturity levels.

Tables A-8, A-9, and A-10 present AESI's current-state LESAT results.

A Brief Comparison of Other Approaches to Process Analysis

A S EXPLAINED IN CHAPTER 6, process architecture analysis for enterprise transformation integrates ideas from a number of different approaches that are widely used by businesses. These approaches include value chain analysis, business process reengineering, value stream analysis, and process modeling. Each is best suited for a specific unit of analysis; we draw on their strengths and avoid their weaknesses to create a method for a less narrow, more robust process architecture analysis that allows you to identify opportunities for transforming the way the enterprise creates and delivers value to its key stakeholders.

Because these other approaches are in such widespread use and may be familiar to many readers, it is appropriate to compare and contrast them to show why we have chosen to create an integrated process of our own that is specific to enterprise transformation. Table B-1 provides an overview of these other approaches, along with the approach we detail in Chapter 6.

Value Chain Analysis

When Michael Porter framed his value chain construct in his 1985 book *Competitive Advantage*,[1] it was based on the idea that organizations could position themselves differently than others in their industry to gain competitive advantage.[2] Porter realized, though, that it wasn't enough to talk about positioning without also discussing the functions and activities within the organization. So he introduced a generic

243

Table B-1

Approaches to Process Analysis

Approach	Unit of Analysis	Primary Focus
Value chain analysis	Business unit	Competitive positioning
Business process reengineering	Specific process	Intrafirm integration of improved processes
Value stream analysis	Product, product family, or service	Minimize waste
Business process modeling	Process, workflow	Enhance understanding
Enterprise process analysis	Enterprise	Enhance stakeholder value creation

value chain model consisting of a sequence of activities he found to be common to a wide range of firms.

In Porter's generic value chain, nine activities are grouped in two broad categories: *primary* activities (inbound logistics, operations, outbound logistics, marketing and sales, and services) and *supporting* activities (firm infrastructure, human resource management, technology development, procurement). According to Porter, a firm's products pass through all activities of the value chain in order, and at each activity the product gains some value. The value *chain* gives the products more added value than the sum of added value of all activities.

Value chain analysis centers on what activities the organization *should* perform and *how* it should perform them to enable the organization to have the most value-adding chain possible and thus compete better.

From an enterprise perspective, value chain analysis has several limitations. First, it focuses on the *business unit* as the unit of analysis and emphasizes value as defined solely by the customer. Second, its focus on improving competitive position, while admirable, addresses only one component of enterprise transformation efforts. Competitive positioning may be reflected in an enterprise's strategic objectives, but there is much more to understand about the enterprise if you are to undertake genuine transformation.

Business Process Reengineering

First popularized in the 1990s, business process reengineeing (BPR) is—according to its creators Michael Hammer and James Champy—a way to achieve a "fundamental rethinking and radical redesign of business processes to achieve dramatic improvements in critical contemporary measures of performance, such as cost, quality, service, and speed."[3] BPR's strengths lie in the emphasis on radical change through strong top-down leadership and employee empowerment, once business processes have been analyzed and their redesign has been completed.[4] In these respects, BRP has synergies with our approach to enterprise transformation.

BPR involves the analysis and design of workflows and processes with an organization. It provides a means to gauge whether the steps and procedures an organization uses to create its products and services meet the needs of particular customers or markets. Typically, a BPR analysis involves decomposing a business process into specific activities so that it can be measured and then improved, completely redesigned, or eliminated altogether. The amalgam of processes so analyzed and redesigned forms the backbone of the overall reengineering.

There are rich frameworks for carrying out BPR, along with numerous techniques and tools.[5] However, while BPR has improved some organizational performance, it has never encompassed holistic *enterprise* transformation.[6] Instead, so much of BPR focuses on the lone project associated with a single business process, with only a single stakeholder involved. Usually, that stakeholder is the customer.

Absent the holistic enterprise perspective, BPR runs the risk of taking you down a road of improving processes without integrating your efforts into an overall enterprise transformation.

Value Stream Mapping

Value stream mapping (VSM) comes from the world of lean manufacturing. It originated at Toyota as the mapping of material and information flow and examines the specific parts of the organization that actually add value to the specific product or service under consideration.

Using VSM, you identify the product, product family, or service to be analyzed. Then you draw a map that shows the current-state value stream, that is, the steps, delays, and information flows that are required to deliver the product or service in question. Streams may be shown as design (concept to launch) or as production (raw materials to consumer). The value stream map shows each step in the value stream and allows you to assess whether the step is value added, necessary but non-value added, or purely non-value added. You can look for ways to increase productivity by eliminating waste along the streams, creating an ideal future-state value stream map. Then, improvement projects may be established to work toward achieving the future state.

Value stream maps are a useful tool, but, from an enterprise transformation perspective VSM, it has two serious limitations. One is that not every transformation effort is about productivity improvement through waste elimination. The other limitation is that VSM simply does not support building an effective understanding of the overall enterprise by senior leadership. As value stream maps become more complex and show subsystems and subprocesses, they are difficult to read and even more difficult to analyze. Ideally, enterprise leaders should be able to see key enterprise processes holistically; then, if appropriate as part of specific enterprise improvement processes, more detailed maps can be used.

Business Process Modeling

The fourth common analysis approach is business process modeling. Its origins can be traced back to the many modeling approaches that evolved over the last 120 years or so, from the GANTT charts of the early twentieth century to the PERT diagrams in the 1950s and integrated definition (IDEF) modeling in 1970s software engineering. The term "business process modeling" was coined in a 1967 article in the journal *Automation*, which posited that techniques that had long been used to understand physical control systems could also aid the understanding of business processes.[7]

In BPM, the fairly standard definition of a process is "a lateral or horizontal organizational form that encapsulates the interdependence of tasks, roles, people, departments and functions required to provide a customer with a product or service."[8] BPM typically identifies three types of such processes: management processes that govern the operation of a system; operational processes that constitute the core business and create the primary value stream; and supporting processes that support the core processes. These categories are quite similar to those in the LAI Enterprise Process Architecture we use (see Chapter 6). In BPM, processes are decomposed into subprocesses, and the analysis includes mapping down to the activity level.

A *model* in BPM represents one or more processes, and defines how operations are carried out to accomplish the intended objective. It may describe the integration or workflow among multiple processes.

The problem with BPM is that the workflows capture only the flow of artifacts in a typical box-and-line type of diagram. Such diagrams, though, do not give a view beyond that two-dimensional representation of the process. Models created using BPM fail to identify the underlying reasons that work is done or even to articulate who does the work. Hence, BPM's value as an enterprise transformation tool is limited because the approach fails to provide decision makers with a holistic representation of enterprise-level processes that is simple to understand and yet captures complex information about the enterprise that makes it possible to analyze not only *what* the enterprise does (its processes), but *who, how,* and *why.*

Endnotes

Chapter 1

1. Aristotle (384–322 BCE), Greek philosopher.
2. Kurt Lewin, *Field Theory in Social Science* (New York: Harper & Row, 1951).
3. This approach was originally developed by Motorola, USA, in 1981.
4. W. Edwards Deming, *Out of the Crisis*, Cambridge, Mass.: MIT Center for Advanced Engineering Studies, 1986.
5. Earll W. Murman et al., *Lean Enterprise Value: Insights from MIT's Lean Aerospace Initiative* (New York: Palgrave Macmillan, 2002).
6. Avarind Immaneni et al., "Capital One Banks on Six Sigma for Strategy Execution and Culture Transformation," *Global Business & Organizational Excellence* 26, no. 6 (September 2007): 43–54.
7. Robert S. Kaplan and David P. Norton, "Having Trouble with Your Strategy? Then Map It," *Harvard Business Review* (September–October 2000).
8. Michael Treacy and Fred Wiersema, *The Discipline of Market Leaders* (Reading, Mass.: Addison-Wesley, 1995).

Chapter 2

1. Tsunesaburo Makiguchi (1871–1944), Japanese geographer, educational theorist, and religious reformer.
2. Henri Fayol, *General and Industrial Management*, Constance Storrs, trans. (London: Pitman and Sons, Ltd., 1949), 19. Originally published in 1916 as *Administration Industrielle et Générale*.
3. Y. Sugimori, K. Kusunoki, F. Cho, and S. Uchikawa, "Toyota Production System and Kanban System: Materialization of Just-in-time and Respect-for-human System," *International Journal of Production Research*, no. 15 (November 6, 1977): 553–564. The first widely disseminated academic paper on the Toyota production system.
4. James P. Womack, Daniel T. Jones, and Daniel Roos, *The Machine That Changed the World* (New York: Rawson Associates, 1990).
5. James P. Womack and Daniel T. Jones, *Lean Thinking: How to Banish Waste and Create Wealth in Your Corporation* (New York: Simon & Schuster, 1996).
6. Murman et al. (2002) was one of the first books to advocate the need to understand the enterprise value proposition as a basis for transformation efforts.
7. Rockwell Collins broke into the *Aviation Week & Space Technologies* Top Per-

forming Companies ranking (for companies making between $1 and $5 billion) in 2005, in sixth place, and took the top spot the following two years. In 2009, it held its top spot for avionics companies and was second in its income bracket. In 2010, it ranked third in the same income bracket. See Joseph C. Anselmo, "Top Performing Companies," *Aviation Week & Space Technology* (June 1, 2009): 56, and Joseph C. Anselmo, "Top Performing Companies," *Aviation Week & Space Technology* (May 31, 2010): 53.

8. John Child, "Strategic Choice in the Analysis of Action, Structure, Organizations, and Environment: Retrospect and Prospect," *Organization Studies*, no. 18 (January 1, 1997): 43–76. Provides a detailed review of Strategic Choice theory.

9. George Roth, "Rockwell Collins: Lean Enterprise Change Case Study," *LAI Lean Enterprise Change Research Case Study Series* (September 2006): 5.

10. Comments made by Clayton M. Jones in his keynote address at the 2006 Lean Advancement Initiative Plenary Conference, April 19, 2010.

11. Information on the value proposition for people at Rockwell Collins can be found at the company's Web site (www.rockwellcollins.com/careers/value-proposition-people/index.h tml).

12. The effectiveness/efficiency debate manifests itself in many domains, ranging from technology and operations management to strategy formulation and execution. In the technology management domain, the problem is framed as the productivity dilemma; that is, an organization can be designed to be either highly efficient or highly innovative, but not both [William J. Abernathy, *The Productivity Paradox Roadblock to Innovation in the Automotive Industry* (Baltimore: John Hopkins University Press, 1978)]. In the economics literature, the distinction is framed as static efficiency, that is, as the optimal combination of given inputs subject to the constraints imposed by a fixed production function, or as Benjamin H. Klein puts it [*Prices, Wages, and Business Cycles: A Dynamic Theory* (New York: Pergamon, 1984)], fine-tuning; the objective is to make the best use of existing information. This view is in contrast with the dynamic efficiency or flexibility that is built into the system in the face of unanticipated uncertainty [Pankaj Ghemawat and Joan E. Ricart I Costa, "The Organizational Tension between Static and Dynamic Efficiency," *Strategic Management Journal*, 14 (Winter 1993): 59–73].

13. Nelson P. Repenning and John D. Sterman, "Capability Traps and Self-Confirming Attribution Errors in the Dynamics of Process Improvement," *Administrative Science Quarterly* 47, no. 2 (June 2002): 265–295.

14. The 10X Program began in 2004 to encourage Rockwell Collins employees to submit high-risk ideas that would result in a minimum of one order of magnitude (10 times) improvement in at least one of three parameters: cost, size, or power requirements. Each accepted idea would be funded with $50,000 for proof-of-concept work, and, once proven viable, it would join the traditional R&D pipeline. The proposing engineer is allowed to spend the next year developing the proof of concept. The program has since become an enterprise-wide effort [Jayakanth Srinivasan, "Creating a Lean System of Innovation: The Case of Rockwell Collins," *International Journal of Innovation Management* 14, no. 3 (June 2010): 379–397].

15. David Nadler, Michael Tushman, and Mark B. Miller, *Competing by Design: The Power of Organizational Architecture* (New York–Oxford: Oxford University Press, 1997), 23.

16. Susan Avery, "Lean, but Not Mean, Rockwell Collins Excels," *Purchasing* (September 1, 2005): 26.

17. Jody Hoffer Gittel, *The Southwest Airlines Way: Using the Power of Relationships to Achieve High Performance* (New York: McGraw-Hill, 2002).

18. Cliff Purington, Chris Butler, and Sarah Fister Gale, *Built to Learn: The Inside Story of How Rockwell Collins Became a True Learning Organization* (New York: AMACOM, 2003), 8.

19. "Learning and Networking," *Aviation Week & Space Technology* (August 20, 2007): 92.

Chapter 3

1. William Arthur Ward (1921–1994), American author and educator.

2. Jorge F. Oliveira, Deborah J. Nightingale, and Maria T. Wachendorf, "A Systems-of-Systems Perspective on Healthcare Insights from Two Multi-Method Exploratory Cases of Leading UK and US Hospitals," *4th Annual IEEE Systems Conference* (April 2010): 450–453.

3. Nicola Clark, "Power Struggle Adds to Woes at Airbus Enhanced Coverage Linking Airbus—Resignation of Chief Expected Soon," *International Herald Tribune* (October 9, 2006).

4. Larry Bossidy and Ram Charan, *Execution: The Discipline of Getting Things Done* (New York: Crown Business, 2002).

5. Leonardo Patacchini, Augustine Tibrazawa, and Hrishikesh Ballal, "Final Class Project Report," Massachusetts Institute of Technology, ESD 61J Integrating the Lean Enterprise (December 2008).

6. ames P. Womack and Daniel T. Jones, *Lean Thinking: Banish Waste and Create Wealth in Your Corporation* (New York: Simon & Schuster, 1996).

7. Lean Advancement Initiative, "Lean Enterprise Self Asessment Tool v1.0" (2001) and "LESAT Facilitators Guide v.1.0" (2001), at lean.mit.edu/products/lean-enterprise-self-assessment-tool-lesat.

Chapter 4

1. Mehmet Ildan (b. 1965), Turkish novelist and playwright.

2. The notion of transactional and transformational leaders was first formulated in James MacGregor Burns, *Leadership* (New York: Harper & Row, 1978). It was later defined as complementary constructs by Bernard M. Bass, *Leadership and Performance Beyond Expectations* (New York: The Free Press, 1985).

3. John P. Kotter, *A Sense of Urgency* (Cambridge: Harvard Business School Press, 2008).

4. John P. Kotter, *Leading Change* (Cambridge: Harvard Business School Press, 1996).

5. Rick Reilly, CNN Sports Illustrated (March 14, 2000).

6. Earll W. Murman et al., *Lean Enterprise Value: Insights from MIT's Lean Aerospace Initiative* (New York: Palgrave Macmillan, 2002).

7. Noel Tichy and Warren Bennis, "Wise Judgement: It Takes Character and Courage," *Leadership Excellence* (May 2010): 5.

Chapter 5

1. Confucius (551–479 BCE), Chinese thinker and social philosopher.

2. R. Edward Freeman, *Strategic Management: A Stakeholder Approach* (London: Pitman Publishing, 1984).

3. The term *satisfice* was first introduced a half century ago by economist Herb Simon. The notion here is of an outcome that is good enough for all stakeholders, as opposed to maximizing the value for a given stakeholder. See Herbert A. Simon, *Models of Man* (New York: Wiley, 1957).

4. Brandon Chu et al., "Final Class Project Report," Massachusetts Institute of Technology, ESD 38J Enterprise Architecting (May 2007).

5. For an interesting example of generating a usable (albeit nearly exhaustive) list of stakeholders involved in the unmanned aerial vehicle flight certification domain, see Luke C.G. Cropsey, "Integrating Military Unmanned Aircraft into the National Airspace System: An Application of Value-Focused Thinking and Enterprise Architecting," Unpublished Master's Thesis, Massachusetts Institute of Technology (2008): 321–336.

6. R. K. Mitchell, B. R. Agle, and D. J. Wood, "Toward a Theory of Stakeholder Identification and Salience: Defining the Principle of Who and What Really Counts," *Academy of Management Review* 22, no. 4 (1997): 853–886.

7. Ignacio Grossi, "Stakeholder Analysis in the Context of Lean Enterprises," Unpublished Master's Thesis, Massachusetts Institute of Technology (2003).

8. The inclusion of the "nonstakeholder" category in Table 5-2 highlights that an organization or group related to the entity but without power, legitimacy, or urgency as defined above is *not* a stakeholder, although it may become one at some point in the future. See R.K. Mitchell, B.R. Agle, and D. J. Wood, *op. cit.*

9. Ibid.

10. M. J. Polonsky, D. S. W. Schuppisser, and S. Beldona, "A Stakeholder Perspective for Analyzing Marketing Relationships," *Journal of Market-Focused Management* 5, no. 2 (June 2002): 109–126.

11. Earll W. Murman et al., *Lean Enterprise Value: Insights from MIT's Lean Aerospace Initiative* (New York: Palgrave Macmillan, 2002).

12. R. Edward Freeman, "The Politics of Stakeholder Theory: Some Future Directions," *Business Ethics Quarterly* 4, no. 4 (October 1994): 409–421.

Chapter 6

1. W. Edwards Deming (1900–1993), American statistician, professor, and author.

2. Deborah J. Nightingale and Joe H. Mize, "Development of a Lean Enterprise Transformation Maturity Model," *Journal of Information Knowledge Systems Management* 3, no. 1 (December 2002).

3. These questions are an adaptation of Michael Porter's notion of how an activity system fits with strategy. See Michael E. Porter, "What is Strategy?" *Harvard Business Review* 74, no. 6 (November–December 1996): 61–77.

4. For an example, see Elizabeth Keating et al., "Overcoming the Improvement Paradox," *European Management Journal* 17, no. 2 (1999).

5. Paul Milgrom and John Roberts, "Complementarities and Fit: Strategy, Struc-

ture, and Organizational Change in Manufacturing," *Journal of Accounting and Economics* 19, no. 2–3 (March–May 1995): 179–208.

Chapter 7

1. William Dean Howells (1837–1920), American realist author and literary critic.
2. Doug Henschen, "Smarter Execs Focus on Goals, Not Just Metrics," *Intelligent Enterprise* (November 13, 2009).
3. Robert G. Eccles, "The Performance Measurement Manifesto," *Harvard Business Review* 61, no. 1 (January–February 1991): 131–137.
4. Robert S. Kaplan. and David P. Norton, "The Balanced Scorecard: Measures That Drive Performance," *Harvard Business Review* 62, no. 1 (January–February 1992): 71–79.
5. Robert S. Kaplan and David P. Norton, "Transforming the Balanced Scorecard from Performance Measurement to Strategic Management," *Accounting Horizons* 15, no. 1 (March 2001): 71–79.
6. These critiques are found in, respectively, Malcolm Smith, "Measuring Organizational Effectiveness," *Management Accounting: Magazine for Chartered Accountants* 76, no. 9 (1998): 34–37; Anthony A. Atkinson, John H. Waterhouse, and Robert B. Wells, "A Stakeholder Approach to Strategic Performance Measurement," *Sloan Management Review* 38, no. 3 (Spring 1997): 25–37; and Alan C. Maltz, Aaron J. Shenhar, and Richard R. Reilly, "Beyond the Balanced Scorecard: Refining the Search for Organizational Success Measures," *Long Range Planning* 36, no. 2 (2003): 187–204.
7. John R. Hauser and Gerald Katz, "Metrics: You Are What You Measure!" *European Management Journal* 16, no. 5 (October 1998): 517–528.
8. Roger W. Schmenner and Thomas E. Vollmann, "Performance Measures: Gaps, False Alarms and the 'Usual Suspects,'," *International Journal of Operations and Production Management* 14, no. 12 (1994): 58–69.
9. See Vikram Mahidhar, "Designing a Lean Enterprise Performance Measurement System," Unpublished Master's Thesis, Massachusetts Institute of Technology (2005): 120–121.
10. Michael Hammer, Carole J. Haney, Anders Wester, Rick Ciccone, and Paul Gaffney, "The 7 Deadly Sins of Performance Measurement and How to Avoid Them," *Sloan Management Review* 48, no. 3 (Spring 2007): 19–28.
11. Steve Kakouros, Brian Cargille, and Marcos Esterman, "Reinventing Warranty at HP: An Engineering Approach to Warranty," *Quality and Reliability Engineering International* 19, no. 1 (2003): 21–30.
12. Roxana A. Ion, Valia T. Petkova, Bas H. J. Peeters, and Peter C. Sander, "Field Reliability Prediction in Consumer Electronics Using Warranty Data," *Quality and Reliability Engineering International* 23, no.4 (2007): 401–414.
13. In the 1960s, the U.S. Department of Defense developed earned value management as a means of gathering coherent and meaningful information on program cost and schedule performance. It is now an American National Standards Institute and Electronic Industries Alliance (ANSI/EIA) standard developed in 1998 (ANSI/EIA-748-A) and updated in 2007 (ANSI/EIA-748-B).
14. U.S. Government Accountability Office, "GAO-08–756 Air Traffic Control: FAA Uses Earned Value Techniques to Help Manage Information Technology

Acquisitions, but Needs to Clarify Policy and Strengthen Oversight" (July 2008).

15. Andy Neely, Richard Huw, John Mills, Ken Platts, and Mike Bourne, "Designing Performance Measures: A Structured Approach," *International Journal of Operations and Production Management* 17, no. 11 (1997): 1131–1152.

16. Clemens Lohman, Leonard Fortuin, and Marc Wouters, "Designing a Performance Measurement System: A Case Study," *European Journal of Operational Research* 156, no. 2 (July 2004): 267–286.

17. Steven A. Melnyk, Douglas M. Stewart, and Morgan Swink, "Metrics and Performance Measurement in Operations Management: Dealing with the Metrics Maze," *Journal of Operations Management* 22, no. 3 (June 2004): 209–218. Melnyk and colleagues use the individual metric, metric set, and measurement system typology as a means of addressing abstraction levels.

18. Laurie Bassi and Daniel McMurrer, "Maximizing Your Return on People," *Harvard Business Review* 85, no. 3 (March 2007): 115–123. Human capital metrics have historically been difficult to connect directly to organizational performance. Bassi and McMurrer provide an empirically validated starting point that enterprises can use to tailor their measurement for people. They include a fifth metric set called "leadership practices."

19. Rita G. McGrath, "Business Models: A Discovery Driven Approach," *Long Range Planning* 43, no. 2–3 (April 2010): 247–261. McGrath uses the idea of key metrics capturing operational activities, but the idea scales to performance management systems in enterprises as well.

20. Marc Wouters, "A Developmental Approach to Performance Measures—Results from a Longitudinal Case Study," *European Management Journal* 27, no. 1 (February 2009): 64–78.

21. The Raytheon story comes from several graduate theses at MIT. See Craig D. Blackburn, "Metrics for Enterprise Transformation," Unpublished Master's Thesis, Massachusetts Institute of Technology (2009); Padmaja S. Vanka, "Line Coordination in a Rapid Change, High Volume Environment," Unpublished Master's Thesis, Massachusetts Institute of Technology (2004); Neville G. McCaghren, "Enabling Process Improvements Through Visual Performance Indicators," Unpublished Master's Thesis, Massachusetts Institute of Technology (2005); Daniel J. Wolbert, "Utilization of Visual Metrics to Drive Intended Performance," Unpublished Master's Thesis, Massachusetts Institute of Technology (2007); Charalambos J. Antoniou, "Using Visual Analytics to Drive Lean Behavior in the Program Management Office," Unpublished Master's Thesis, Massachusetts Institute of Technology (2008); and Purdy P. Ho, "Using Virtual Business Systems to Drive Lean Behavior in Engineering Design and Support," Unpublished Master's Thesis, Massachusetts Institute of Technology (2008).

22. David J. Ballard, "Indicators to Improve Clinical Quality Across an Integrated Health Care System," *International Journal for Quality in Health Care* 15 (suppl. 1) (2003): 13–23.

23. Elizabeth Gardner, "Turning Talk into Action: Clinical Performance—and Transparency with the Data—Help Earn Baylor the Annual National Quality Healthcare Award Modern Healthcare," *Healthcare Business News* (May 12, 2008).

24. David J. Ballard, Barbara Spreadbury, and Robert S. Hopkins III, "Health Care Quality Improvement Across the Baylor Health Care System: The First Cen-

tury," *Proceedings (Baylor University Medical Center)* 17, no. 3 (July 2004): 277–288.

Chapter 8

1. Ralph Waldo Emerson (1803–1882), American poet, essayist, and lecturer.
2. Cynthia R. Cook and John C. Graser, *Military Airframe Acquisition Costs: The Effects of Lean Manufacturing* (Santa Monica, CA: RAND, 2001).
3. R. E. Freidman and J. S. Pollack, *Standard and Poor's Industry Survey: Aerospace and Defense* (New York: McGraw-Hill, 2002).
4. Bryan Bergsma, "Lean Beyond Manufacturing, Leveraging Principles into Innovation and Design, " Presentation at the LAI Annual Conference (March 2010).
5. Barry W. Boehm and P. N. Papaccio, "Understanding and Controlling Software Costs," *IEEE Transactions on Software Engineering* 14, no. 10 (October 1988).
6. Deborah J. Nightingale and Joe H. Mize, "Development of a Lean Enterprise Transformation Maturity Model," *International Journal of Information Knowledge Systems Management* 3, no. 1 (January 2002): 15–30.
7. Cory R. A. Hallam, "Lean Enterprise Self-Assessment as a Leading Indicator for Accelerating Transformation in the Aerospace Industry," Unpublished Doctoral Dissertation, Massachusetts Institute of Technology (2003).
8. Ibid.
9. Hugh McManus, "Identifying the Product Development Value Stream," Presentation at the Lean Aerospace Initiative Plenary Workshop (October 14, 1998).
10. Binoy Cherian et al. "Final Class Project Report," *ESD 61J Integrating the Lean Enterprise* (December 2005).

Chapter 9

1. Epictetus (55–135 CE), Greek Stoic philosopher.
2. "System of Systems (SoS) Systems Engineering Implementation Plan, Predecisional Working Papers, SOS SE Implementation Plan—as of 23 Sept 2009."
3. James C. Collins and Jerry I. Porras, "Building Your Company's Vision," *Harvard Business Review* 74, no. 5 (September–October 1996): 65–77. The authors also used this concept in a book. See James C. Collins and Jerry I. Porras, *Built to Last: Successful Habits of Visionary Companies* (New York: HarperCollins, 1994).
4. Nancy Moulton, "Material Enterprise Transformation Overview," Presentation at Lean Advancement Initiative Annual Meeting (March 24, 2010).
5. MIT Center for Biomedical Innovation, "NEWDIGS: Catalyzing the Transformation of Healthcare Innovations," at web.mit.edu/cbi/research/newdigs/resources.html.

Chapter 10

1. David Lloyd-George (1863–1945), prime minister of the United Kingdom.

Chapter 11

1. Johann Wolfgang von Goethe (1749–1832), German writer and polymath.
2. James Allen, Nerina L. Jimmieson, Prashant Bordia, and Bernd E. Irmer,

"Uncertainty During Organizational Change: Managing Perceptions Through Communication," *Journal of Change Management* 7, no. 2 (June 2007): 187–210.

3. Travis L. Russ, "Communicating Change: A Review and Critical Analysis of Programmatic and Participatory Implementation Approaches," *Journal of Change Management* 8, no. 3–4 (September 2008): 199–211.

4. Wim L. J. Elving, "The Role of Communication in Organisational Change," *Corporate Communications: An International Journal* 10, no. 2 (2005): 129–138.

5. Peter Richardson and D. Keith Denton, "Communicating Change," *Human Resource Management* 35, no. 2 (Summer 1996): 203–216

6. National Quality Forum, "NQF 2010 Award Program" (2010).

7. Tom Emswiler and Len M. Nichols, "Baylor Health Care System: High-Performance Integrated Health Care," *The Commonweath Fund* 10 (March 2009).

8. Ziad Haydar et al., "Accelerating Best Care at Baylor Dallas," *Proceedings (Baylor University Medical Center)* 22, no. 4 (2009): 311–315.

9. Clayton M. Jones, "Lean Electronics is essential to our role in modernizing air transportation," *Horizons* 15, no. 3 (2010).

10. "Using Lean Electronics in an Office Environment," *Horizons* 14, no. 2 (2009).

11. Ibid.

12. Charles W. L. Hill and Gareth R. Jones, *Strategic Management* (Boston: Houghton Mifflin, 2001).

13. Earll W. Murman et al., *Lean Enterprise Value: Insights from MIT's Lean Aerospace Initiative* (New York: Palgrave Macmillan, 2002), 151–152.

14. Jayakanth Srinivasan and Kristina Lundqvist, "Organizational Enablers for Agile Adoption: Learning from GameDevCo," *Proceedings of XP 2009* 31, no. 2 (May 2009): 63–72.

15. Jayakanth Srinivasan, "Architecting a Lean Software Organization: The IndiaCo Experience," *Strategic Management Society India Special Conference* (2009).

16. This was one of the reasons that Rockwell Collins' income bracket dropped to third in the *Aviation Week & Space Technology* Top Performing Companies.

17. Rockwell Collins, "Staying on Course: Lean Electronics Helps Rockwell Collins Remain Competitive," *Horizons* 15, no. 1 (2010): 19.

Chapter 12

1. John Dewey (1859–1952), American philosopher, psychologist, and educational reformer.

2. In system dynamics, this is referred to as creating and exploiting a reinforcing loop.

Appendix A

1. The range is a measure of the variability in responses and is calculated as the highest maturity level versus the lowest maturity level for the set of responses to a given LESAT practice.

Appendix B

1. Michael E. Porter, *Competitive Advantage: Creating and Sustaining Superior Performance* (New York: The Free Press, 1985).

2. Michael Porter, Nicolas Argyres, and Anita M McGahan, "An Interview with Michael Porter," *The Academy of Management Executive* 16, no. 2 (2002): 43–52.

3. Michael Hammer and James Champy. *Reengineering the Corporation: A Manifesto for Business Revolution* (New York: Harper Paperbacks, 1993).

4. Michael Hammer, "Reengineering Work: Don't Automate, Obliterate," *Harvard Business Review* 68, no. 4 (July–August 1990): 104–112.

5. The Stage-Activity framework by Kettinger, Teng, and Guha integrates 70 techniques and 102 tools into a framework to better guide project implementation [William J. Kettinger, James T. C. Teng, and Subhashish Guha, "Business Process Change: A Study of Methodologies, Techniques and Tools," *MIS Quarterly* 21, no. 1 (March 1997): 55–78].

6. Thomas H. Davenport, "Business Process Reengineering: Where It's Been, Where It's Going," in *Business Process Change: Concepts, Methods and Technologies,* V. Grover and W. J. Kettinger (eds.) (Harrisburg: Idea Publishing, 1995), 1–13). See also Thomas H. Davenport and Donna B. Stoddard, "Reengineering: Business Change of Mythic Proportions?" *MIS Quarterly* 18, no. 2 (June 1994): 121–127.

7. S. Williams, "Business Process Modeling Improves Administrative Control," *Automation* (December 1967): 44–50.

8. Michael J. Earl, "The New and Old of Business Process Redesign," *Journal of Strategic Information Systems* 3, no. 1 (March 1994): 5–22.

Key Terms

effectiveness   doing the right job

efficiency   doing the job right

engaged leadership team   understands the context in which enterprise transformation must take place and that is committed to making it happen

enterprise   a complex, integrated, and interdependent system of people, processes, and technology that creates value as determined by its key stakeholders

enterprise alignment   consistency among an enterprise's strategic objectives, performance measures, stakeholder values, and enterprise processes

enterprise maturity   the extent to which an enterprise employs a variety of practices that are key to enterprise transformation

enterprise process   a process the enterprise uses to create value for its stakeholders

enterprise process architecture   the structure of all enterprise processes together and how they interconnect and interact

enterprise project   a project that affects the enterprise as a whole and enables the enterprise to transition from its current state to its desired future state

enterprise transformation   the taking of an enterprise from its current state to an envisioned future state, a process that requires a significant change in mindset, the adoption of a holistic view, and execution to achieve the intended transformational goals and objectives

enterprise value proposition   description of the unique mix of products and service attributes, stakeholder relationships, and other intangibles that an enterprise offers to its key stakeholders

Execution Cycle   the section of the Enterprise Transformation Roadmap during which the transformation plan is put into practice

focus area   an area in which an enterprise must concentrate its transformation efforts *lean*   a philosophy centered on minimizing resources and eliminating waste to create value

metric   the objective, quantified data or information an enterprise collects to support decision making

performance measurement system   a system of metrics used to gather the performance data and information from throughout the enterprise that are needed to assess overall enterprise performance

Planning Cycle   the section of the Enterprise Roadmap that involves analyzing and defining both the current and future states of the enterprise, and then articulating a transformation plan to achieve the future vision

stakeholder   any group or individual that can affect or that is affected by the achievement of the enterprise's objectives

stakeholder salience   the degree to which the enterprise gives priority to different stakeholder needs

Strategic Cycle   the section of the Enterprise Transformation Roadmap in which the business case for transformation is made as the organization's leadership becomes engaged

value   the particular worth, utility, benefit, or reward that stakeholders expect in exchange for their respective contributions to the enterprise

waste   an action, process, or activity that does not directly add value for a stakeholder but that still consumes resources

Index

Rockwell Collins (*continued*)
    information flows at, 24
    innovation at, 22
    key messages in annual reports of, 13,
        15–16
    leadership at, 18
    lean thinking at, 17–18
    organizational learning at, 26
    stakeholders at, 20–21
    success of, 175, 180

satisficing, of stakeholder groups, 61, 76
SBIR, *see* Small Business Innovation
    Research
A Sense of Urgency (Kotter), 50
services industry, 45
shareholders, 19, 60, 65, 76
short-term efforts, 46
short-term goals, 51
Sierra Club, 63, 65
silos, 2, 38, 52–53, 176
Six Sigma, 5
Small Business Innovation Research
    (SBIR), 186, 187, 190, 196–201, 203,
    219
SMART (strategic, measurable,
    actionable, relevant, timely) metrics,
    102, 103, 105, 110
society, as stakeholder, 65, 66
Southwest Airlines, 24–25
stability, 24–25, 88
staff meetings, 169
stakeholder analysis, 60–79
    and defining stakeholders, 60
    determining value elicitation in,
        72–74
    as essential step in transformation, 19,
        20
    and flow of value, 60–61
    function of, 61
    in Planning Cycle, 41
    stakeholder identification in, 61–66
    stakeholder prioritization in, 66–72,
        76
    stakeholder relationships in, 70–72
    stakeholder salience in, 67–69
    in StayCool case study, 218
    of value exchange, 73–78

stakeholder(s)
    as change agents, 146
    definition of, 2, 60
    delivering value to, 42
    downstream, 123
    in enterprise thinking, 7
    in enterprise value proposition, 9–10
    in holistic approach, 14
    identification of, 19–21, 61–66, 218
    identifying value propositions of,
        19–21
    and interactions, 92, 130
    involvement of, 170, 171
    needs of, 50
    prioritization of, 66–72, 76
    relationships of, 9, 70–72
    satisfaction of, 91
    in StayCool case study, 191–196
    and transformation leadership, 47
    and transformation progress, 173
stakeholder salience, 67–69
stakeholder value(s), 19–21
    delivery of, 150
    and leadership commitment, 18
    linking processes to, 114, 117
    and maturity lens, 122, 123
    recognizing, 6
    in StayCool case study, 201, 203
StayCool case study, 183–220
    alignment lens in, 201–203
    focus areas in, 210–216
    future-state vision in, 209–210
    maturity lens in, 204–208
    performance measurement lens in,
        200–201
    process architecture lens in, 196–200
    resource lens in, 203–204
    stakeholder lens in, 191–196
    strategic issues in, 186–189
    strategic objectives in, 189–191
    transformation principles in, 213–219
    waste lens in, 208–209
    workforce in, 184–185
Steelcase, 57–58
Stonegarth, David, 222–223, 225–226
strategic, measurable, actionable,
    relevant, timely metrics, *see* SMART
    metrics